MEXICO AT THE BAR OF PUBLIC OPINION

MEXICO AT THE BAR OF PUBLIC OPINION

*A Survey of Editorial Opinion
in Newspapers of
The Western Hemisphere*

By BURT M. McCONNELL
Member of The Literary Digest
Editorial Staff, 1919-1929

MAIL AND EXPRESS PUBLISHING COMPANY
160 Varick Street   New York, N. Y.
1939

Newspaper editorials not only reflect public opinion; they mould it.

> —CARL W. ACKERMAN, *Dean of the Columbia University Graduate School of Journalism.*

The taking of property without compensation is not expropriation. It is confiscation.

> —SECRETARY OF STATE CORDELL HULL, *in a Note to the Mexican Government.*

PREFACE

The author was a member of the editorial staff of *The Literary Digest* between 1919 and 1929, when that publication still quoted freely from newspaper editorials and dispatches and gave both sides of political and economic questions. In that decade *The Digest* prided itself on its impartial surveys of editorial opinon. Millions of readers, including business, professional, and public leaders and more than three hundred thousand school children depended upon the magazine for the reaction of American newspapers to important events, both foreign and domestic.

In looking over the field of troublesome public questions which might be treated in the old *Literary Digest* manner, none seemed of greater import to the America of tomorrow than Mexico's treatment of United States citizens. The author approached the Standard Oil Company (N. J.) with the proposal that he prepare for the company an editorial digest of American newspaper opinion concerning Mexico's confiscation of American-owned property. That company financed the undertaking. The copy herein is the work of the author. The work of preparing and presenting the quotations from newspaper editorials from all over the nation has been a fascinating one. It has been an inspiring one, too, for it is uniquely American. In no other nation could one find such a variety of able, independent, clearly-written editorials on any public question.

These editorials must be accepted at their face value. They are independent, unbiased observations of trained writers. They truly represent national opinion, for they are taken from newspapers published all over the nation. The text thus presents a national, rather than a partisan, sectional, or group viewpoint. It thereby serves the best interests of the nation. If the record of the past is borne out, these editorial comments unerringly have marked the course our Government yet will take in solving its Mexican problems.

Naturally, no editorial writer attempts to cover the entire problem created by Mexican confiscation of American-owned properties, because the problem is so involved. Included in it are principles of international law, protection of nationals, the silver policy, and the "good neighbor" policy. Included also are hundreds of thousands of United States citizens who are stockholders of 1,750 corporations which have direct investments in foreign countries. These corporations have invested approximately five billion dollars in Latin America. The rights of their stockholders were entirely ignored by President Cardenas when he confiscated American-owned properties in Mexico. Of even greater import to our national economy than the loss or jeopardy of such investments caused by President Cardenas's action is the loss in foreign trade which directly followed. This directly affects American labor. Eventually, if unchecked, it will cause the loss of millions of man-days' work by American workmen.

The editors of American newspapers have written on all phases of these subjects, some on one phase and some on another. Regardless of the extent of the newspaper's circulation or of the section of the country in which it is located, one finds almost unanimous editorial objection to the fundamental principles advanced by Mexico in support of her program of confiscation.

The author is grateful to the newspapers of the Western Hemisphere for permission to print portions of their editorials and dispatches, without which this book could not have been written and to the special writers, magazines, and press associations.

Their treatment of the Mexican case is presented herein.

BURT M. MCCONNELL.

33 Riverside Drive,
New York, N. Y.,
April 4, 1939.

TABLE OF CONTENTS

▼

ILLUSTRATIONS

I

EFFECT OF EXPROPRIATION ON FOREIGN CAPITAL

Our "Good Neighbor" Policy—American Investment in Latin America—History of Oil Development—Mexico's Expropriation of Foreign Oil Property—How Expropriation Affects Foreign Trade—Mexican Economy—Stockholders and Investors—Mexico's Promise to Pay.

For several years the United States has maintained a "good neighbor" policy toward Mexico. The foundations of this policy were laid by Ambassador Morrow, back in the Coolidge era, and since then efforts have been made by Presidents Hoover and Roosevelt to keep the political and economic relations of the two countries on a cordial basis, and to deal with problems that might arise in a way that would be mutually helpful.

In its relations with Latin American countries, the United States pursues two general principles—that we must not interfere in the domestic affairs of any country in the Western Hemisphere; and that we must not use force to collect debts from any of these republics. The "good neighbor" policy is just that; it was embodied in a resolution adopted at the Buenos Aires Conference in December, 1936. Taken in conjunction with the Monroe Doctrine, the policy virtually precludes the direct intervention of any other nation in the domestic affairs of any country in Latin America.

The Roosevelt Administration's ardent pursuit of the "good neighbor" policy received a sudden check on March 18, 1938, when President Lazaro Cardenas of Mexico signed an executive decree confiscating the properties of seventeen British, Dutch, and American oil companies. This somewhat rash—and entirely unexpected—act raised questions which involve the economic well-being and political responsibility of the American people.

With approximately $1,000,000,000 of American money invested in Mexico, and another $3,500,000,000 of investments in Central and South America, everyone in the United States who

1

owns a single share of stock in an American corporation has a financial interest in the expropriation program of the Mexican Government. The outcome of the legal actions instigated by the expropriated oil companies has profound significance for the future of American investments, not only south of the Rio Grande, but throughout the world. As David Lawrence puts it in one of his Washington dispatches: "If American oil properties can be seized with impunity in Mexico, and no payment made for them, then American property of all kinds in all parts of the world suddenly becomes insecure. And this involves many billions of dollars." "If the United States allows a Communistic government in Mexico to seize foreign property, a direct incentive will be provided for radicals in other republics to prey upon American investments," believes the Indianapolis *News*.

A generation ago the decree expropriating foreign-owned oil properties in Mexico would have been an open invitation to war. Such was the temper of the world at that time that if the United States had been disinclined to intervene, British pressure would have been so strong that we would have been compelled to act in support of the Monroe Doctrine. "But the Roosevelt Administration, judging by its domestic policies in recent years, apparently is not disposed in this instance to risk serious trouble," thinks the South Bend (Ind.) *Tribune*. Yet, maintains the Rochester (N. Y.) *Democrat and Chronicle:*

> "The affected oil companies cannot be expected to stand by and see their property go by the stroke of a pen. President Cardenas has agreed to indemnify the owners within ten years, as provided by Mexican law, but the indemnification terms will of course be Mexico's own terms, and in the meantime the companies will take heavy losses through idle plants and frozen investments. . . .
>
> "Our oil investments were legitimately made. They were welcomed by the Mexican people. The Mexican Government has a number of times invited such investments. The companies have a strong case."

More than the interests of a few ranch-owners and oil company stockholders are involved in the expropriation of American-owned property in Mexico, point out a number of our newspapers.

2

It is far more serious than that. *The peace and prosperity of all Latin America is concerned. The United States must maintain the integrity of American capital invested in Latin America.**

The Stockton *Independent,* in California, insists that the United States has a tremendous interest in the situation: "First, the protection of the rights of its own citizens; second, the sanctity of the traditional principles of the Monroe Doctrine; third, the upholding of international agreements which are the basis of peace in this hemisphere."

Mexico's present policy of antagonizing foreign investors is quite at variance with her previous attitude of encouragement. Incidentally, it is completely at variance with the attitudes of many other Latin American countries. One also recalls that not so very long ago our own Government was urging American capitalists to invest their money in development abroad. According to the Magdelena (N. M.) *News:*

> "The policies of our Government toward oil development in foreign lands were established in the years when Woodrow Wilson was having troubles with Mexico; when Calvin Coolidge was urging American interests to go abroad with the support and encouragement of their Government to develop new oil fields; when the Geological Survey was urging the pioneer spirit to lead American capital and engineering to seek new petroleum supplies for the 'America of tomorrow'; when the Federal Trade Commission and the Fuel Administration were emphasizing the importance of protecting American capital and workers in foreign oil fields; when all responsible parts of the United States Government were encouraging plans to insure the oil supplies of the future through operations exactly like those in Mexico."

Earlier Administrations in Washington, in the words of the New York *Journal of Commerce,* "repeatedly encouraged American oil companies to acquire and develop petroleum reserves abroad, and it was in response to such encouragement that American companies made large investments in other parts of the globe, particularly in Latin America." The New York *Herald Tribune* recalls that the Democratic platform upon which Woodrow Wilson

---

* The author has italicized this paragraph and a number of others throughout the book.

3

was elected President called for the full protection of American citizens having property abroad. Immediately after the World War, foreign Powers began their search for oil, and the head of the fuel division of the United States Fuel Administration said: "In the national interest, American petroleum companies will be encouraged by the Government to acquire foreign sources of oil supply wherever they can be found." A joint report to this effect, signed by the State Department, the Bureau of Mines, the United States Geological Survey, and the Fuel Administration in 1919 said, according to *The Herald Tribune:*

"The United States departments should exert every effort to encourage and protect its citizens in securing petroleum wells and concessions for petroleum developments in foreign countries, and in working these properties and concessions."

Our consular officers were instructed to aid American interests that were seeking concessions. As late as 1926, the Federal Oil Conservation Board reported:

"The oil fields of Mexico and South America are of large yield, and much promising geological structure is yet to be drilled. That our companies should vigorously acquire and explore such fields is of first importance, not only as a source of future supply, but as a supply under control of our own citizens."

Thus, in response to such official encouragement, concludes *The Herald Tribune,* "the American ownership of all foreign oil production rose from 1.37 per cent in 1920, to 24.89 per cent in 1937."

Turning now to consider Mexican policy, we note in General Hugh S. Johnson's *United Feature Syndicate* column the statement that half a century ago, President Porfirio Diaz invited foreign investment in Mexico. As the Santa Rosa (Calif.) *Republican* puts it:

"Lacking capital and skill in such matters, Mexico invited industrialists from the United States to go down there and develop the mining and oil resources of that country. Mexico also invited railroad men from the United States to come in and take charge of the long-haul freight and passenger business between Mexico and the United States."

4

American capitalists went to Mexico because they were invited, insist a number of our papers. As late as New Year's Day, 1938, reports the Birmingham *News,* President Cardenas affirmed that his Administration welcomed the coming of foreign capital into Mexico, and said his "original program for the development of Mexico counted on capital's co-operation." Most of the investments made by Americans in Mexico were made, not only with the approval of the Mexican Government, declares the Bridgeport (Conn.) *Telegram,* "but under specific treaties guaranteeing fair treatment." A summary of the whole story of oil operation in Mexico and the expropriation proceedings has been prepared by four of the companies involved,—the Huasteca Petroleum Company, the Standard Oil Company of California, the Mexican Sinclair Petroleum Corporation, and the Penn Mex Fuel Company. E. C. Krauss calls attention to it in his column in the Los Angeles *Times,* and says:

> "In this summary we learn that foreign capital investment in the Mexican oil fields resulted in a development which added greatly to Mexico's national wealth, improved the Mexican standard of living, raised wages for many Mexicans, and brought sanitation, modern improvements, better schooling and housing, and many other advantages to areas which would otherwise have been without them.
> "The development took place in about eighteen years. Before 1900, Mexico produced no petroleum; by 1918, it was the world's second largest producer."

But such a change of attitude is not a rare thing, philosophizes the Saginaw (Mich.) *News;* it is not uncommon for "the developer of lands and treasures" to become in the course of time "a rapacious bandit and despoiler." This, we are told, is how it happens:

> "Undeveloped countries,when they have reached the stage of desiring greater prosperity, uniformly want the assistance of outside capital and skill. They have land, but it is largely undeveloped and inaccessible. They have minerals, perhaps, but they are locked in the ground where they do nobody any good. They may have water power sites, but these are useless without dams and power plants. They are delighted to

5

see the foreign capitalists and engineers who make all these things available to the people. True, the foreigners make a profit for their efforts, else they would not take the large risks involved. But they also build roads and railways, mines, dams; and open up territories to settlement that were useless before. They pay millions in wages and more millions in taxes. They take away some wealth, but an enormous amount remains in the country.

"But after the pioneer stage has passed, men forget how eager they were to have their resources made available. They forget how useless these things were before the developers came. They forget the risks involved and the number of capitalists who went broke. Then comes the feeling that the developers were a bunch of robbers and despoilers of the people's wealth.

"Mexico is now suffering from an aggravated case of this ailment. It has benefited by the development of foreigners, and now thinks it is able to get along without them. So they are to be thrown out without any regard for the value of their services. It may be true that in some instances these men have been greedy and unscrupulous. But if Mexico were back where it was before they came, if it had no mines or railroads or oil wells, if all its natural wealth remained locked in the ground, would the Mexican people be any better off?"

In spite of much thought, J. C. Rovensky, Vice President of the Chase National Bank of New York City, confesses that he has not been able to draw the line between "exploitation, in the sinister sense of the word, and development, as we should like to interpret it." And he goes on to explain, in the New York *Commercial and Financial Chronicle:*

"A new and untried undertaking always represents an unusual risk, and when that undertaking is in a foreign land, the dangers and risks are multiplied. Naturally, profits have sometimes been made by many foreign entrepreneurs. Naturally, too, profits were high in the case of a new undertaking, for who can determine in advance in a highly risky enterprise what is an exorbitant profit and what is a reasonable one? What assurances could one have that his entire capital investment would not be lost?

"I believe that fair-minded citizens of Latin American countries are entirely aware, on their part, of the advantages which have accrued to them from our collaboration in their

6

development. Greater opportunities for work have been created, and their standard of living has improved. Homes are being lighted and factory wheels are being turned by electricity generated in plants which foreign capital has constructed. Messages speed over telephone wires, undersea cables, and now through the air because of the investments of our own nationals and those of other foreign countries. Water and sanitary works have been installed. From the investments in electricity have resulted cheaper production costs for local manufacturers; and from water and sanitation, better living conditions. All these investments were, of course, made with the thought of profit, but clearly there was no intent or desire to hold the people in financial or commercial bondage.

"In short, the economic resources of Latin America have been developed constructively to the lasting benefit of Latin Americans."

To many of us who live in the United States, the Mexican policy of expropriating properties of American investors in Mexico seems sheer ingratitude. There is no question of the benefits Mexico has derived from American initiative in building up its oil-producing areas. As the Syracuse (N. Y.) *Post-Standard* observes:

"It may be true that many of the rights enjoyed in Mexico by Americans were purchased cheaply—but they were not held and enjoyed cheaply. As soon as production began, taxes began. As soon as production began, employment of Mexican labor began. The revenue and purchasing power of the country increased because of developments of these rights. If those who enjoyed the rights benefited, so also did Mexico benefit."

Something that should not be forgotten, in the opinion of the Ardmore (Pa.) *Main Line Times,* is that "for scores of years the only contribution to progress in Mexico was made through foreign—mostly American—investment. Here is what seems so strange about it all to the El Paso (Texas) *Times:*

"The very elements which have made Mexico, which have created payrolls and supported schools and hospitals, developed the country's resources and paid taxes—these are the

7

Doing Business at the Same Old Stand

—Reprinted from the Providence Bulletin.

8

very elements that are being penalized. They are being deprived of what they have built up and accumulated.

"The most constructive elements in Mexico are being treated as if they were stumbling blocks in the path of social progress.

"The investors, the developers, the builders, the employers —are they the enemies of social welfare?

"That seems to be the idea. And yet Mexico's idealists seem puzzled and annoyed that the country is in an economic tailspin."

Hundreds of millions of dollars, J. H. Carmical reminds us in the New York *Times,* have been spent in Mexico by citizens of the United States in the construction of railroads, roads, bridges, the development of the light and power industry, the mines, and the petroleum industry. To build the highway from Laredo, Texas, to Mexico City, the Mexican Government, this writer recalls, obtained a loan of $7,000,000 from the British and American oil companies operating in Mexico; and, "despite the fact that a substantial portion of this loan is unpaid, their oil properties were expropriated and they were expelled from the country."

South of Mexico, the Panama City *Star and Herald* calls attention to the fact that:

"Mexican labor in the oil fields enjoyed special school facilities, supplied at the expense of the oil companies; recreation facilities, medical and surgical care for the entire family, long vacations with pay, pensions, and other advantages."

Mexico's oil industry took its place in the sun after the discovery of the Golden Lane field south of Tampico, so the story is retold in *The Shell News* (New York City), and "the peak production—194,000,000 barrels in 1918—made Mexico the world's second largest producer, for this was one-fourth of the entire world output in that year." All this development was warmly welcomed by the Mexican Government because it brought prosperity in its wake. Continues *The Shell News:*

"Much-needed foreign capital, totaling over $500,000,000, was expended between 1900 and 1926. During the period 1916-1926 the Mexican Government was paid taxes averaging $25,000,000 annually. Fifty thousand workers then were

9

given employment, where before only the jungle prevailed. Their wages averaged $37,500,000 annually. The most of them were indigenous to the country, and enjoyed earnings and living standards far beyond anything previously known. The companies built camps, introduced modern housing, sanitation, and medicine; and encouraged education. Local suppliers of raw materials and local freight carriers received their share of expenditures, as did also the land and royalty owners. From 1926 to 1938, a further sum of $340,000,000 was similarly distributed."

Nor have the oil companies been the only benefactors of Mexico. There are concerns like the sugar firm taken by the El Paso (Texas) *Times* as a case in point:

"United Sugar Company went into Sinaloa, Mexico, and built up the country. It created a new industry for that region. It developed farms, gave employment to labor, was responsible for the building of at least one town, built a sugar mill, caused a shortline railroad to be constructed, and by reason of all this new development and investment was in no small measure responsible for the building of the Southern Pacific of Mexico from the United States boundary down the West Coast to Tepic, and eventually to Guadalajara—a $25,000,000 investment at the very outset, and the major force in the upbuilding of the entire Pacific Coast region of Mexico.
"By investing capital and labor, by developing industries, by creating commerce, by giving employment, by creating new properties and tax values, by encouraging other investors and developers and builders to follow where they had pioneered, the United Sugar Company has been a great constructive and helpful influence in the State of Sinaloa."

Nor has Mexico been the only scene of such happenings. The Indianapolis *Star* speaks of the resentment stirred up by demagogues in some of the smaller Central American Republics by pointing to the evidence of wealth along the coasts, mostly in the hands of the fruit companies. But, it continues, "they do not call attention to the primitive conditions and poverty in the hills where there are no foreign investments." The coast people, argues *The Star,* owe their measure of prosperity and affluence to the aid of outside capital.

The question: "Where has a single investment of foreign capital ever contributed to the political, social, and economic well-being of any country in Latin America?" has been put by a correspondent to Frank L. Perrin of *The Christian Science Monitor* (Boston). Mr. Perrin thinks he has a convincing answer in a recent annual report of the United Fruit Company:

"In a single year, says the report, the sum of $26,000,000 was paid out in wages and for purchased fruit to the nationals of the nine countries in which the company maintains plantations, and to one with whom trade relations exist. These expenditures reached a total of $34,500,000 in the period covered by the report issued in 1937. Employment is given regularly to some 50,000 nationals in the countries where plantations and canefields are established. The company owns or holds under lease more than 3,000,000 acres of land, nearly a half million acres having been brought by it under cultivation.

"And it is self-evident that the regular employment, the better housing and nourishing of a people, to say nothing of the enjoyment of improved conveniences of travel, communication, and amusement, have in some degree elevated social standards and contributed to the happiness of the people concerned and of the communities in which they reside."

The Mexican oil fields, confined to some 10,000 square miles largely on the eastern coast, were first exploited in 1900 by foreign companies, for the most part American and British, who came at the special invitation of the Mexican Government. In the face of tremendous difficulties and at a cost of more than $500,000,000, we are informed by the St. Louis *Globe-Democrat,* these companies developed a producing area where native workers received higher wages than were paid in any other Mexican industry.

At the time the British, Dutch, and American oil properties were taken over by the Mexican Government in March, 1938, the oil industry still was paying the highest wages in Mexico. According to the New York *Times,* this was about double the legal minimum for Mexican industry. Moreover, says *The Times,* ten per cent more was paid into the workers' protection fund. Work-

11

ers in the oil fields had a 40-hour week—with 56 hours' pay, three weeks' vacation with pay, and pay for 16 additional festive days.

Two weeks before the Cardenas decree went into effect, the various oil companies announced that they were making housing allowances, providing free medical treatment for workers and their families, full pay for 18 months if hurt at work, full pay for 460 days if permanently injured, retirement with 70 per cent of pay at 55 after 25 years of service, and numerous other benefits. These were said to be the most liberal anywhere in the industry. The workers received double pay for overtime, and triple pay for work on holidays. In fact, says the Grand Rapids (Mich.) *Press*, "the standard of living among the oil workers was far above that of the rest of the country. But under government pressure the labor syndicate kept asking for more and more until it had reached the point of demanding the right to take over the management of the companies themselves." The Houston (Texas) *Chronicle* is authority for the statement that "the unions demanded annual wage increases representing an amount double the companies' net earnings." It was then that the oil concerns announced that these demands could not be complied with—unless they were to go into bankruptcy. To quote one of David Lawrence's Washington dispatches:

> "All sorts of trumped-up excuses are being proclaimed by those defending the Mexican action, one to the effect that the oil industry has paid low wages, when, as a matter of fact, the data from the Mexican Department of Labor for 1936 show that the average daily wage in the oil industry was more than double that which was being paid in other Mexican industries. Likewise, the items furnished free to workers by the oil companies—including housing, light, education, transportation, medical and hospital facilities for the family of the worker—amounted to the equivalent of about 36 per cent over and above the basic wages actually paid by the oil companies."

In the opinion of the Chicago *Tribune*, "it was the very improvements brought about by the British, Dutch, and American oil companies which led the ambitious politicians of Mexico

12

and the unintelligent workers to insist upon the policy of robbery." Yet, maintained the New York *Herald Tribune:*

"Save for foreign capital, Mexico would have no oil wells, no pipe lines, no refineries. The American and British investors and engineers who developed the Mexican fields gave Mexico new wealth that the Mexicans never could have gained for themselves. The Mexicans who worked for the oil companies were better paid than they otherwise would have been, lived in more wholesome surroundings, and received many of the benefits of civilization which they could not have enjoyed except for the presence of foreign capital. The foreign companies did all this, and in addition paid substantial taxes and royalties to the Mexican Government. The benefits which Mexico has received are incalculably greater than the benefits which accrued to the foreigners who put up the money, assumed all the risks, and provided the skill for the developing of the oil fields."

Mexico's expropriation of British, Dutch, and American oil properties is quite contrary to every legal and moral principle of right and justice, in the opinion of many American newspapers. For example, says the Cincinnati *Times-Star:*

"Three things are obvious: (1) No government has the right to take, from its own citizens or those of a neighbor, what it is unable to pay for.

"(2) If it finds itself unable to make payment, it should restore these properties to their owners.

"(3) If it does neither, it is an outlaw in the eyes of the world, and a country dependent, as Mexico is, on outside markets and capital, cannot have this status and escape eventual smash-up."

Mexico purports to observe the requirements of law by promising "future" payments, but the slightest scrutiny of its finances shows its inability to make any worth-while compensation. Since 1914, it has been in default on practically all its foreign obligations. In January, 1938, the foreign default was approximately $1,000,000,000 and the internal default $400,000,000. Thus, promises of "future" payments have already proved worthless. Secretary Hull, in his note of July 21, 1938, in regard to Mexico's expropriation of agricultural lands, stated a principle that applies with equal force to oil properties. He wrote:

"If it were permissible for a government to take the private property of the citizens of other countries and pay for it as and when, in the judgment of that government, its economic circumstances and its local legislation may perhaps permit, the safeguards which the constitutions of most countries and established international law have sought to provide would be illusory.

"Governments would be free to take property far beyond their ability or willingness to pay, and the owners thereof would be without recourse. We cannot question the right of a foreign government to treat its own nationals in this fashion if it so desires. This is a matter of domestic concern. But we cannot admit that a foreign government may take the property of American nationals in disregard of the rule of compensation under international law."

Americans who maintain that the Government should have taken a stronger line with Mexico over the oil land seizures point out that a real duty is owed to our nationals engaged in business in foreign lands. It is not a question of using the Government to pull chestnuts out of the fire for foreign and domestic oil companies. Issues are involved, they insist, which are vitally important to all of us. Our citizens working abroad have every right to protection, because on them depends the foreign trade which is essential to the prosperity of us all. As a matter of fact, declares David Lawrence in one of his syndicated dispatches from the nation's capital:

"Foreign trade is considered one of the essential parts of any sound recovery program in America, but there can hardly be any tendency on the part of American citizens to invest abroad if their own Government refuses to protect such investments with the ordinary safeguards of international law."

"If the peoples of the world expect to have business relations," declares the San Francisco *News*, "they must have and observe a code of fair dealing. Otherwise the whole structure of international economics will break down. If that happens—if world trade collapses—then international relations generally will become impossible and, along with them, efforts for world peace."

14

H. V. Kaltenborn, writing in the Brooklyn *Eagle*, describes in more detail the issues involved:

"When a country depends on foreign trade, its citizens must go abroad to protect and further the trade. American business men resident in China, Spain, and Mexico are largely responsible for our export and import trade with those countries. Without their presence overseas our business opportunities would be very much reduced. It would be impossible for the United States to succeed in foreign trade competition without the co-operation of those Americans who serve as the ambassadors of American business.

"They are entitled to a reasonable measure of protection. If every American business man had left China when the State Department told them it was dangerous to remain, our exports to that country would have soon been taken over by our competitors.

"The Standard Oil Company, for example, has labored faithfully for nearly half a century to build up its business in China against foreign competition. It has invested millions in plants, warehouses, piers, storage facilities, tankers, and fuel stations to facilitate the sale of American products in China. It has done an excellent job in building up a special trained personnel that knows how to deal with the Chinese people.

"When the writer traveled through the interior of China during the height of Chiang Kai-shek's Nationalist Revolution in 1927, he obtained much more practical aid from Standard Oil representatives than from American diplomatic officers. The Standard Oil men stuck to their posts at interior points through war and revolution. Thanks to them and men like them, American business has been able to carry on in Spain and China and Mexico, in the face of death, danger, and discouragement.

"Let us not, therefore, be too casual about what happens to Americans and their investments in foreign lands. Most of our business abroad is now done on a legitimate basis. If we do not protect it against confiscation, it will be lost. Because the United States Government has taken no effective steps to protect American oil property in Mexico, Mexican labor unions are now taking over American mines. Neither the American nor the Mexican Government is doing anything to stop the process of expropriation. Within a few months 15 mining properties, five of them American, have been taken

15

away from their owners. Stealing becomes a habit when it is not punished."

Mr. Kaltenborn speaks in behalf of our nationals abroad. The Kansas City *Star* applies the same set of facts to the United States as an exporting nation:

"We shipped out into a troubled world merchandise valued at nearly $3,500,000,000, despite the continuance of many trade barriers and the disruption of at least two important foreign markets by war. Both agriculture and industry share heavily in this business.

"Ten per cent of our total production of motor cars went out of the country; 12 per cent of our radios, 23 per cent of our office equipment, and 35 per cent of our aircraft. But so did 18 per cent of our lard, 36 per cent of our tobacco and dried fruits, and 44 per cent of our cotton. It is essential to bear these figures in mind in any discussion of our future foreign policy.

"It is absurd to say that in demanding that nations deal fairly with foreign interests the American Government is simply protecting large corporations. In fact, it is defending the welfare of American farmers and the jobs of American industrial workers. Economic isolation is impossible for the world's greatest exporter."

Business cannot enjoy prosperity unless the rights of business men are respected, we read in essence in many an editorial. The Boston *Post* recalls the days when American interests were protected by force or show of force. That method is out of favor now, but the Boston paper observes that we have developed no better way of protection.

As the St. Paul *Pioneer Press* reminds us:

"Private capital is a part of national wealth, as much when it is invested abroad as when it is put to work at home. If Mexico is encouraged to play fast and loose with American oil investments, other similarly inclined governments will not be long in finding high-sounding names under which to loot American wealth wherever they can get their hands on it.

"Mutually beneficial international economic relations cannot exist unless there is respect for foreign property rights.

"The United States will cease to be a trading nation on the day when its Government adopts the policy of acquiescing in the trampling of the rights of its citizens abroad."

President Cardenas's expropriation policy had the laudable purpose of increasing Mexico's commerce and prosperity. To date, however, the results have been just the opposite. Expropriation has halted commercial expansion, and there is no prospect of any change for the better. Last January the Secretary of National Economy reported that Mexican oil exports dropped from 23,972,483 barrels in 1937, to 14,800,000 barrels in 1938, when the Government expropriated the properties of seventeen American, Dutch, and British firms.

The Wichita (Kan.) *Eagle* lists some of the specific effects:

"The country's economy was dealt a heavy blow; business confidence received a disquieting shock; the value of the peso dropped from 20 to 25 per cent; the oil workers suffered at least temporary losses in wages and welfare benefits; the Government incurred a serious cut in revenue, resulting specifically from the decline in oil taxes, and generally from the deepened depression."

The Bristol (Conn.) *Press* supplies further information of similar nature, while *Fortune* (New York City), in an issue devoted to Mexican affairs, surveys certain specific fields:

"Some small firms have failed. The shoe industry is reported to be operating at 30 per cent of capacity. With the Mexico City silk and rayon mills on a three or four-day week, and the nearly bankrupt big cotton mills in Puebla and Vera Cruz threatening to shut down unless the Labor Board authorizes a three-day week, the textile industry is badly off.

"The importation of agricultural machinery has been cut to 25 per cent of its 1937 volume. Frightened away by the bad news from Mexico, the inflow of tourist dollars has fallen to a trickle."

The drop in agricultural production is explained by the San Francisco *Chronicle:*

17

"A serious fall in agricultural production followed the expropriation of the big ranches. Naturally the drop did not come as fast as it has in oil; and the reason for the decrease in production was different. The reason in this case was that the peon, given a plot of land, was not much interested in raising more than enough corn, garbanzas, and chili for his family to eat. So in the case of well-managed large ranches, cut up and handed over to the peons, production fell sharply."

Economically, the Baltimore *Sun* warns, "Mexico cuts off a large proportion of her income with no immediate prospect of replacing it." "No country," the Dallas (Texas) *News* adds, "can guarantee its future when it must seek in the loan market for dollars that are skeptical of security." The Houston (Texas) *Chronicle*, speaking of the oil business, tells us that "the whole Mexican people will have to make up the deficit through taxation."

Taking a broad view of Mexico's expropriation policies, the San Jose (Calif.) *Mercury-Herald* says: "Widespread repudiation of government obligations to foreign governments and citizens, and revolutionary Socialistic movements designed to destroy the institution of private property, make the question raised one of vital importance." "The exploiters of Mexico have sown the wind, and all investors there, it appears, must reap the whirlwind," remarks the Youngstown (O.) *Vindicator*. Now, observes the McComb (Miss.) *Enterprise*, "the Mexican Government is trying to exploit and rob American investors more shamelessly than Americans ever robbed Mexico."

But we must insist upon the integrity of American capital, declare the New York *Herald Tribune*, Augusta (Ga.) *Chronicle*, Detroit *News*, and *The Texas Weekly*, of Dallas. Men like President Cardenas "ignore entirely the interests of stockholders and investors," the Fort Worth *Star-Telegram* points out, and another Texas daily, the Greenville *Herald*, is mindful that in the case of both Great Britain and the United States, "the oil properties in Mexico do not represent the money invested by two or three individuals, but the money placed by thousands of small investors, who put their savings into Mexican oil enterprises because they

18

believed in the promise of the Mexican Government that foreign investments would be secure."

Other editors seem to consider the Mexican expropriation program as a warning against indulging in foreign trade generally. The Council Bluffs (Ia.) *Nonpareil* thinks it all ought to be "a final warning to investors and business men who think they see greener pastures in other lands." Conditions are too unsettled in all the countries to the south of us to warrant any development of their resources by outside capital, believes this Iowa paper.

Other papers point to the widespread benefits that result from international trade. Mexico needs foreign capital, agree three such representative dailies as the New York *Times,* Mobile (Ala.) *Register,* and Los Angeles *Times.* Mexicans, thinks the Phoenix *Arizona Republic,* "fail to realize that none of the industries now engaged in turning the natural resources of the country into wealth would have been possible except for the entrance of foreign capital." The New Orleans *Times-Picayune,* looking ahead, opines that the "future progress and well-being of Mexico is likely to depend on large capital investment, technical development, and venturesome enterprise." These, it adds, must come from the more highly developed nations. And in Mexico City, *Excelsior* sums it all up like this:

> "Without the advent of foreign capital, Mexico would have retained its condition of a country of small industry, limited production, high prices, and low wages. Foreign capital has brought large-scale industry, abundant production, low prices, and high wages.
> "How, then, can we reject an element that contributes in such a decisive manner to the prosperity of the class it is desired to protect?"

The good name of the American countries, insists *El Universal,* also of Mexico City, demands the repudiation of the policy of confiscating properties of foreign investors.

"Such a sensitive thing as capital, ever seeking the safest refuge, might well be expected to give the country below the Rio Grande a wide berth in the future," agree the Atlantic City (N.J.) *Press,* Milwaukee *Journal,* Philadelphia *Inquirer,* and Topeka

19

(Kan.) *Capital.* And this is the way it appears to the El Paso *Times,* on the Mexican border:

"There was a time when men spent their time, labor, and money developing Mexico's resources; making employment, paying taxes and wages; building industries and towns and railroads, and improving the country. There was a time when they were appreciated.

"Now, it seems, they are 'exploiters' who should be divested of their property and discouraged in every manner possible.

"Query: *When private initiative has been thoroughly discouraged in Mexico; when men of ability and energy and money have had their backs completely broken, who is going to develop Mexico's resources?*

"Who is going to create new industries and new wealth? Who is going to cut away the brush and put the plow to soil that has lain for a million years waiting for someone to grow grain and fruit and vegetables on it? Who is going to build towns and create payrolls to be spent with the merchants?"

The problem in Mexico is not unique, the Savannah (Ga.) *News* is moved to remark. In fact:

"All over the world in recent years the politicians of debtor countries have been yielding to the temptation to rob the foreign investor. It seems such a simple way of obtaining assets for nothing. But it has two disadvantages: It can't go an forever. Some day the reservoir of foreign investments must be exhausted. And, secondly, it is destroying the confidence upon which the whole structure of international spending is based."

But most of the Latin American republics would like to see Mexico make a settlement satisfactory to foreign interests, reports the Newark (N. J.) *News.* For "they fear stopping investment flow." And in the capital of Brazil, the Rio de Janeiro *O Jornal,* while sympathizing with the motives of the Mexican Government, cannot see how, in the case of foreign owners, it can take their property "without providing compensation, as universally established in international law." And the Brazilian daily concludes:

Poor Way to Pick Apples

—*Reprinted from the Newark, N. J., Ledger.*

"The right of ownership is the basis of the social and political organization of the civilized nations. Such rights cannot be granted to the nationals and denied to foreigners, under penalty of creating a situation capable of destroying the principles on which the relationship between nations is based."

And, looking at the matter from the British angle, a writer in the New York *Times* points out: "Great Britain has in mind more than collecting indemnity for the seized oil properties." According to this writer:

"The seizure of the oil properties was a great blow to the foreign business of Great Britain, as well as to British investors. If British commerce is permitted to be disjointed by such a seizure, then it is reasonable to believe that in time the entire principle of British foreign trade may be violated. Thus it is not a question of cash payment to Great Britain, but a matter of keeping inviolate the principle of international commerce, which is so necessary to its national economy."

And what foreign trade means to the United States is thus broadly and briefly stated by J. H. Carmical, in the New York *Times:*

"With the development of our western frontiers, United States capital around the turn of the century began to flow into other lands. Thus, by extending the country's economic frontier beyond its territorial boundaries, it has paved the way for the continuance of national prosperity which the full development of these frontiers had threatened. In other words, it has established the foothold so necessary to open the foreign markets for American goods."

In the opinion of Mr. Carmical, it is our trade with Latin America that will suffer most from the consequences of the trouble with Mexico, and it is in Latin America that almost 50 per cent of the total direct foreign investments of United States citizens have been made. So, for our better understanding of the situation, this writer presents a picture of those investments, as follows:

22

"In accordance with the latest Brookings Institute study, the United States investments in Latin America amount to $4,551,000,000, of which a total of $3,261,200,000 is in direct investments in industry. They follow by subdivisions and classifications:

	Direct	Portfolio*	Total
Mexico	$ 651,700,000	$ 261,200,000	$ 912,900,000
Central Amer.	160,000,000	32,000,000	192,000,000
South America	1,718,200,000	856,200,000	2,574,400,000
West Indies	731,300,000	140,400,000	871,700,000
	$3,261,200,000	$1,289,800,000	$4,551,000,000

Portfolio investments cover private or individual investments in foreign securities, foreign currency, loans, etc.

"That the direct investments of United States citizens in Latin America have not been confined to one industry, but are well scattered in every major group, is shown by the following classification:

Trading companies and sales agencies.......	$ 119,200,000
Oil distribution	86,000,000
Mining and Smelting	771,200,000
Oil production	687,500,000
Agriculture	475,600,000
Manufacturing	258,000,000
Railroads	186,300,000
Public Utilities	592,900,000
Miscellaneous	84,500,000
Total	$3,261,200,000

"Largely as a result of these investments, the United States in 1937 had exports to these countries of $640,000,000 and imports of $705,000,000. Literally thousands of items are traded, but exports consist almost entirely of manufactured goods, such as machinery, automobiles, chemicals, textiles, electrical equipment, radios, and paper. On the other hand, imports consist mostly of raw materials and commodities which we are not able to produce here, and they are limited mainly to coffee, cane sugar, fruits, petroleum, oil seeds, wood, and tobacco."

Whether foreign capital, which in the past has played a major part in Mexican development, can continue its role, in view of the drastic policies of the Cardenas régime, is now an important factor in the international situation. Frank L. Kluckhohn states the fundamental problem in a Mexico City dispatch to the New York *Times:* "The future status of foreign capital in Mexico, and the question whether Mexico can continue its present policies, are the two major issues" in the legal controversy between the Mexican Government and British, Dutch, and American oil companies, with investments in the country of $450,000,000. According to the San Francisco *Chronicle:*

"Ever since the inauguration of Lazaro Cardenas as President on November 30, 1934, the position of foreign capital in Mexico has been increasingly endangered by a social-economic program threefold in scope: The gradual extension of State Socialism in the industrial life of the country; widespread seizure of lands which were turned over to the peons; and an ever-increasing program of labor legislation.

"In June, 1937, the Government took over the railroads. It moved more slowly against the mining industry; but the oil companies soon found themselves in the middle of a pincer movement. Increasing regulation, official intervention, and government competition faced them on the one side; on the other, there was the threat to profits by the demands of the labor unions, reinforced by government support.

"Finally, the oil companies said they could go no further in meeting these demands; and on March 18, 1938, President Cardenas signed a decree taking over the oil companies in the name of the Government."

Foreign capital, as we have shown, went into Mexico at the urging of its own particular government. It was necessary, of course, for companies to incorporate under Mexican law. And now the New York *Journal of Commerce* reports an attempt by Mexico to remove the right of foreigners to appeal to their own home governments when they feel that they have a grievance! "Mexico, if it persists in its present attitude, probably will find it difficult to induce foreign capital to aid in the development of natural resources or invest in business enterprises," warns the Scranton (Pa.) *Times.*

At present there are four major developments in Mexico as a result of the expropriation policy, and any one of them may have a decisive influence on Mexican history:

1. Seizure of foreign-owned farm land, oil land, etc.
2. The move against the mining industry.
3. The break with Great Britain.
4. The problem of how to market the products of the seized properties and how to pay those from whom they were seized.

It seems to David Lawrence, widely syndicated commentator, that:

"What the Mexican Government has overlooked is that the theory of confiscation without proper payment simply restores jungle law—the might-makes-right concept which diplomacy throughout the last few generations has been struggling to erase."

Mexico has frequently declared her intention to pay for the confiscated oil properties. However, such representative papers as the Boston *Transcript*, the El Paso (Texas) *Herald Post*, the Manchester (N. H.) *Union*, and the Atwater (Calif.) *Signal* do not place much faith in Mexico's intentions. In the case of the farm lands, $10,000,000—payable in ten annual installments— was settled on by arbitration as a fair valuation. But, the Manchester paper explains:

"The joker in the whole transaction is the source from which the Mexican payments are to come. This is not in the agreement, but it is well understood that *the indemnities are to be taken from revenue obtained from new taxes on American mining properties in Mexico,* against which the American Government has raised no word of protest. In fact, the Mexican press is chuckling over the prospect of these taxes netting a neat profit of $5,000,000 after the $1,000,000 promised [each year] under the land-claims agreement is paid."

In the case of the oil lands, the Mexican President has offered to permit the British, Dutch, and American oil companies to take a percentage of the oil output in the next ten years to pay for the expropriated holdings. But to accept such an indemnity payment, the oil companies argue, would set a precedent that might lose them their holdings in other Latin American countries.

Mexico's action, declares the Anderson (S. C.) *Independent Tribune,* is aimed at filling the Mexican Government's coffers at the expense of the foreigners who had put their capital in Mexican farm lands, and oil and railroad and mining properties; men who helped build up Mexico's industry and agriculture. In the same vein, the Elizabeth (N. J.) *Journal* remarks: "It is a dangerous policy—for Mexico—that President Cardenas has adopted." Continues this paper:

> "There may have been exploitation in Mexico and other Latin American countries by foreign capitalists. But the fact remains that all of these nations needed foreign money in large amounts to develop their natural resources. Without such aid from abroad they would not have attained to the places they now hold in the economic world."

In explanation of what has happened in Mexico, the Columbus *Ohio State Journal* writes:

> "The Government there either sided with labor or was too weak to protest. The result is, foreign capital will no longer aid in the development, and Mexico will lose the experienced, aggressive leadership which was helping her to assume a place of importance."

And the New York *Times* adds a warning note:

> "President Cardenas may, in a sense, be on a spot and the prisoner of his own policies, but he will do well to consider whether such a price may not be too high either for his own position or for the future of his country."

The National Railways of Mexico, and other roads which were expropriated without indemnification of their French, British, German, American, and Canadian bond-holders, have been taken over—and are being run—by the workers. No quarrel, says *The Christian Science Monitor*, "has been made with their management or their technical skill. But a grave problem is presented in the outworn equipment of the railways and the deteriorated condition of the roadbeds." These, it adds, can be restored only through a huge added investment—and capital is not available in Mexico to purchase the machinery required.

Universal Grafico, a Mexico City paper, quotes a report on the railroads, published by the National Chamber of Commerce and Industry, in effect as follows:

"The railroads are sustaining themselves out of the capital inherited from past governments, without any amortization. The tracks are in poor condition. Rails are worn, cross-ties are rotten, locomotives are getting old and cannot be used much longer in spite of repairs being made in a vain effort to rejuvenate them; there are not enough freight cars, and the bridges built for operation under conditions prevailing twenty years ago cannot stand the weight of fast trains with more powerful and heavier modern locomotives.

"The outlook cannot be darker. Under these conditions, within ten years the railroads will practically be out of existence."

In June, 1938, the employe-controlled railways issued an ultimatum: Shippers must pay freight-rate increases ranging up to 100 per cent, or the roads must have a loan of 50,000,000 pesos (about $10,650,000) at once!

Now, asks the Washington *Post:* "If qualified railway workers cannot operate the railroads successfully, how can a country which lacks the technicians and organizing genius so essential in the oil business run the properties taken over from their British, Dutch, and American owners?"

American prosperity in many lines outside of the oil business is being hit by the slump in our sales to Mexico which has followed the expropriation of the oil properties. In the first place, Mexico has lost its former revenue from the oil companies and has thus had less money for the purchase of our goods. In the second place, it has been trading oil for German goods formerly bought here. According to Mexican bank figures, the public income there dropped 50 per cent in 1938, and United States trade with Mexico fell to less than 33 per cent of its former level. In the same period Germany gained in her trade with Mexico through barter deals.

A report by the Department of Commerce at Washington, issued in November, 1938, showed that in the first nine months of last year our sales to Mexico were only 55 per cent of those for the same period of 1937, falling from $83,021,000 to $46,480,000. The Mexican Government's revenues also fell 20 per cent as income from the oil business dwindled to a thin trickle under government operation.

All sorts of manufactures made up the great tide of exports formerly flowing into Mexico from American factories, and the slump has, therefore, hit thousands of homes of the workers who made those products. Makers of automobiles, farm machinery, cash registers, shoes, hats and a hundred other products have felt the pinch. As the Dayton (O.) *Journal* puts it:

> "In certain quarters at Washington there has been a theory that Mexico's recent acts of expropriation were aimed at big corporations. In practice, however, expropriation of American-owned property is being followed by the loss of markets for American manufactured goods. Some American corporations operating in Mexico have suffered a severe falling off in business as a result of what has happened to the oil companies.
>
> "When the United States loses its outlet for manufactured goods—which it previously sent to Mexico—the whole country suffers. The inconvenience is not limited to the corporation stockholder, but includes the employe, who suddenly finds his factory without orders and himself temporarily out of work."

"Señor Cardenas, in fact," observes the New Haven (Conn.) *Journal-Courier*, "takes our money for silver we can't use; seizes our property; trades the property with Germany, our Number One economic enemy, and uses the proceeds to increase American unemployment."

Writing in the Washington *Post*, Fred Moore explores this phase of the situation only to reach the conclusion that New Deal policies at home and a lack of understanding by the American public of foreign affairs are responsible for the Mexican mess. He says:

> "Our people seem to know little of our foreign trade. Yet, under our present economic system, it means a difference between good times and bad times. We cannot hope to absorb all the manufactured goods we ordinarily produce."

One of the most distressing features of the Mexican expropriation program is the resulting dislocation of normal international

Another "Gusher" Gone Dry?

—*Reprinted from the Chattanooga, Tenn., Times.*

trade. And this is true whether the matter is considered from the United States or the Mexican standpoint. Both countries are losing business which they normally would enjoy. Mexico was in 1937, the fifth best customer the United States had in the entire world, and the best customer in Latin America, recalls the Des Moines *Register.* But now, continues this mid-western daily, "Mexico's purchases here have dropped 60 per cent." The New York *Times* points to similar statistics of the decline of commercial relations between the two countries.

With the oil properties taken over by the Mexican Government under the definite promise by President Cardenas that they will be paid for, the question that interests the practical-minded man in the street is: How can Mexico pay for them? As the San Francisco *Chronicle* puts it:

"Suppose the former owners of the oil properties spoke by the book when they said the money was not in the business to pay those wages. How is the Mexican Government going to find more money in the business? It is not likely to operate more economically than the former owners. It cannot raise the price of its product, because oil has to be sold on the world market at world prices.

"If the Mexican Government does not find the money in the business, how is it going to pay off the former owners? And, still more important for it politically, how will it pay that wage scale?"

At the outset Ambassador Daniels asked Mexican officials how they proposed to compensate the owners of the expropriated oil properties. One plan contemplated a domestic bond issue of 100,000,000 pesos. But such a bond issue, explains *The Christian Science Monitor,* "at best would produce less than ten per cent of the value set on the oil properties. Moreover, the pesos would have to be converted into dollars and pounds."

At a time when the existing Mexican external debt is in default, as well as most of the internal debt, "the promises to pay have a very hollow sound" to the St. Paul *Pioneer Press.* For—

"If Mexico cannot pay even interest on its present foreign debt of $315,000,000, how it is going to pay $450,000,000 for the oil properties is a mystery, especially now that the oil taxes and royalties are lost.

"The Mexican Government took over some railroads last year. That debt plus its previous railroad loan, is in default. It took over a packing industry many years ago, and that debt is in default. The agrarian debt is in default, and the recently expropriated foreign land-owners have yet to see the color of Mexican money. Six years ago Mexico borrowed $7,000,000 from the foreign oil companies, and needless to say that debt is in default. The bonds of Mexico are selling at about two cents on the dollar."

It does not matter much whether we accept at full value Mexico's assertions of willingness to pay, she simply cannot pay, assert newspapers all over the United States, emphatic statements to this effect being found, for instance, in the editorial columns of the New York *Journal of Commerce*, Washington *News*, Cincinnati *Enquirer*, Grand Rapids (Mich.) *Press*, Miami Beach (Fla.) *Times*, and San Bernardino (Calif.) *Sun*. The Foreign Policy Association published a report by Charles A. Thomson, until recently its Latin American expert, arriving at the same conclusion.

From Mexico itself comes a despairing statement on this point. The Mexico Institute of Economics and Social Studies estimates Mexico's debt at 8,584,873,000 pesos, while the Government's total annual revenue is about 350,000,000 pesos. "It is easily seen," remarks the Institute, "that we are in bankruptcy and are incapable of complying with our commitments."

Whether the new Mexican taxes on products of mines will be sufficient to help materially in making payments for the oil properties is something which cannot be estimated as yet. No one knows what the yield will be, or whether any part of these revenues will be used for this purpose.

As for the suggestion by the Mexican Government that the expropriated companies can be paid off with government-produced oil from the very fields under discussion, the position of the companies on this point was stated very definitely in their petition: *"This is equivalent to no payment, and clearly violates the*

31

terms of the Constitution; an uncertain expectation of payment cannot be considered real indemnization." Moreover, there are two difficulties advanced by oil men which render this plan almost impossible of achievement, observes the New York *Herald Tribune:*

"In the first place, there is the underlying principle involved. By accepting oil revenues as payment for their properties, the companies would be contributing largely to their own ruination.

"Such a procedure would set a bad precedent that might well harm American interests elsewhere in Latin America. Once foreign capital accepted this policy, there would be nothing to stop Mexico from seizing the properties of American Smelting and Refining Company, for example, and then paying for them with silver from the company's own mines. The same may be said for Venezuelan oil, Chilean copper, and all other foreign-owned properties.

"In addition to this, oil circles here believe that it is a physical impossibility for Mexico to produce sufficient oil to compensate the owners for their properties. It is thought that unless additional capital is made available, present Mexican oil fields, with the possible exception of the rich Poza Rica area, cannot produce sufficient oil to pay for the properties."

President Cardenas's uncomfortable position is thus crisply described by the Cincinnati *Enquirer:*

"He cannot compensate the companies, because he simply hasn't the money. He cannot pay out of oil receipts, because he cannot market the oil."

Mexico's record of keeping financial pledges is far from clean, we are reminded by more than one American newspaper, and the Mexican Government's assertion that the oil companies will be compensated does not mean much, when we recall that American citizens hold some $200,000,000 in unsettled claims against Mexico. The oil companies would not be likely to accept dubious Mexican bonds in payment for their tangible and profitable properties, points out *The Herald Tribune,* and "additional capital will hardly be attracted to Mexico in view of the past treatment of foreign savings invested in that country." Moreover:

32

"Since the 'adequate, prompt, and effective payment' for the properties mentioned by Secretary Hull appears impossible of realization, the only practicable and, in this case, just, solution is a return of the properties to the rightful owners—the American, Dutch, and British oil companies."

Across the continent, a similar view is taken by the San Francisco *Chronicle*, which predicts:

"It may be that Mr. Cardenas or his successors will find out, before they are through, that the best way to profit by American and British-owned oil is to let the owners operate it and provide employment for Mexican workers, and royalties and taxes for Mexico."

II

"MEXICO FOR THE MEXICANS!"

The History of Mexico—The Diaz Régime—The Rise of Cardenas—How Mexico Controls Her Supreme Court—Mexico's Agricultural Economy—Mexico's Need of Foreign Capital—The Mexican Constitution of 1917—Workers' Syndicates—Mexico's Labor Board.

Mexican history, in the light of the present situation, falls into three main periods: Events up to 1910; 1910 to 1917; 1917 to the present. At the moment the review may well end with 1928, when Plutarco Elias Calles went out of office and the interregnum of Gil, Rubio, and Rodriguez began. During most of these years conditions were chaotic, and the present state of affairs may be regarded as fruit of the past. The nation has had forty-five Presidents and dictators in one hundred and fourteen years, according to the New York *Mirror*. The Lexington (Ky.) *Herald*, reviewing recent events, tells us that:

"During the past twenty-seven years Mexico has had seventeen rulers, only two of whom were able to serve out the full terms for which they were elected.

"Madero, Carranza, and Obregon were assassinated. Three rulers resigned, one was deposed, and six have been exiled. Only Portes Gil and Rodriguez managed to serve out terms, theirs being for two-year periods.

"There have been eleven revolutions or major insurrections in Mexico in twenty-seven years—revolutions at the rate of about one every two and a half years."

The Paducah (Ky.) *Sun-Democrat* agrees that the basis for Mexico's present difficulties is historic:

"When Cortez conquered it for Spain, he found an Indian civilization that was primarily Socialistic. Practically all farm land was the property of communities, not of individuals. When a family stopped tilling the soil, its plot reverted to the village, which disposed of it anew. During the three hundred years of Spanish rule, the Spaniards progressively broke this native system down, dividing up the

34

Indian property among themselves and making slaves of the natives.
"In 1810, Mexicans revolted against this heartless practice, and won complete independence in 1821."

Mexico, by 1876, we read in the Chattanooga (Tenn.) *Times,* had changed governments seventy-four times. "She had had two regencies, two Emperors, and several dictatorships." In 1876, the account continues:

"Porfirio Diaz rode into power on the crest of a bloody revolution. He ruled for more than thirty years.
"This was Mexico's golden era. Almost devoid of civil strife, the country prospered amazingly. Foreign capital, poured into the development of Mexico's resources, took huge profits from the soil and subsoil. These investments opened new mines, uncovered oil deposits which made the country a leading world producer, developed industries, and encouraged agriculture."

But in 1910 the peasants revolted. Their cry was: "Land and Liberty!"

This was the period which began with Francisco Leon de la Barra as Provisional President, and Francisco I. Madero.

In 1917, revolution came again to Mexico, and the principles of the change which had begun in 1910 were written into the Constitution. According to the New York *Sun:*

"Mexico by 1918 had become the second largest oil producer in the world, and in 1921 her production reached a peak of 193,000,000 barrels. Taxes going into government coffers averaged around $25,000,000 annually from 1916 to 1926 inclusive.
"In that eleven-year period, wages averaged $37,500,000 annually. Higher living standards were encouraged. Further distribution of new money was made through freight, local purchases, rents and royalties. In the past twelve years alone $340,000,000 has been pumped into Mexico in this way.
"During the World War, local politicians began to see possibilities of profit in the petroleum industry. Not satisfied with its contribution to the national welfare, they set about systematically to take it away from those who had built it up."

35

The racial makeup of Mexico is important in considering the present crisis. There are approximately 18,000,000 people in Mexico. In the Cleveland *Plain Dealer*, Arthur J. Culler tells us about the situation created by the racial mixture there:

"There are fifty-four recognized dialects and thirteen major language groups.

"Above all this great body of Indians and deep-dyed meztizos is a small crust of white folk with untainted blood, and more white folk with a trace of Indian blood who live in the cities, own property, top the professional and business life, penetrate into political circles, and move somewhat freely about the world. *But they do not rule Mexico; the Indian rules Mexico.*"

The story of President Cardenas and his rise is that of an obscure Army man who became the most radical of the forty-five Presidents whom Mexico has had in one hundred and fourteen years.

The result was a considerable surprise to the sponsors who elevated him to the Presidency—particularly Plutarco Elias Calles, former President of Mexico. What actually happened is described by Betty Kirk in *The Christian Science Monitor:*

"Cardenas came into office as an obscure General, slated to carry out the commands of Mexico's political 'boss', General Calles. For almost fourteen years General Calles had ruled Mexico with a strong hand, both as President and as a maker of Presidents. Yet a year after Cardenas became President he exiled General Calles from Mexico, seizing the political reins with which General Calles had ruled."

The chief score on which United States editors criticize the President of Mexico is lack of wisdom. According to the Kansas City *Star:*

"The President's dilemma is evident. He has based his domestic program largely on Socialistic doctrine. He has consistently sought the friendship of organized labor and promised the gradual nationalization of land and industry.

36

But he either miscalculated the consequences or was driven into what may prove for Mexico a disastrous experiment."

The Chicago *Daily News* believes that it sees a close relationship in both principal and operation between the Cardenas program in Mexico and the New Deal program in the United States. In its appraisal of this aspect of the two programs it adds:

"President Cardenas likes to compare himself to Mr. Roosevelt. His labor policies, he boasts, have the approval of John L. Lewis. Like the New Deal, he has an unbalanced budget. Like the New Deal, he has brought on a serious depression. Under his leadership, food prices have risen and the currency is depreciating."

Cardenas *"dominates the courts completely,"* maintains the Council Bluffs (Ia.) *Nonpareil. "They decide cases the way he instructs them to decide."* "It is obvious that he has a dual personality," according to a detailed analysis by Clifton E. Hooper, of the firm of Anderson and Hooper, from which a few excerpts are quoted:

"He has strength of character without a deep cultural background; and a keen mind with a shrewdness which reflects strongly of his racial Indian characteristics. He affects a knowledge of social and political economy, which fails of convincing the student of these matters because of his rather confused utterances on various subjects, and also by his endorsement of programs of doubtful feasibility."

The great majority of Mexican people favor a change, says the Houston (Texas) *Post,* examining Cardenas's domestic standing:

"They want a government that will give them an opportunity to work. They want to get away from the Communistic experiment which the Cardenas Administration has launched and under which private property is drifting more and more into government ownership."

Is Cardenas a Communist in any strict sense of the word? If he is, he practices Communism of a peculiarly indigenous sort, according to the San Francisco *Chronicle,* which explains itself thus:

"Though Cardenas has been called a Communist, he owes his social ideas to no foreign schooling. Save for a few excursions across the Rio Grande, he has never visited a foreign country. He is a revolutionist of a purely indigenous brand.

"It is this impulse to bring most of Mexico under his governmental wing which is threatening Cardenas's main objective today. Government receipts have dropped 50 per cent. Oil workers are unemployed. Government salaries are partly unpaid. Prices are going up, and money and credit are becoming scarce."

In much the same vein the Cleveland *News* adds:

"Lazaro Cardenas runs this nondescript Government in his own way. As near as his philosophy can be pegged, it is State Socialism. He is devoted to the lower classes, and, with great skill he keeps them in tow. In his book, they fall into three classes—workers, peasants, and the Army rank and file.

"Among the peasants, he divides the land taken from both Mexican and foreign owners. He has raised his soldiers' pay. He encourages unionization of workers, and he lets these unions run the industries he takes in the name of the state.

"Mexico's President has had four busy years. He has worked hard at settling peasants on land, at building schools and highways, and at nationalizing key industries to squeeze out foreign capital.

"If the United States goes on supporting Cardenas, our prestige will suffer and other countries will feel free to rob our citizens."

President Cardenas has thrown overboard his original plan to develop Mexico with the co-operation of capital, according to William H. Lander, *United Press* correspondent at Mexico City. The essence of his new program for the economic rehabilitation of the republic, it seems, counts upon the aid of neither foreign nor domestic capital. Salvation is to be secured by a three-point program, reports Mr. Lander:

"Labor has been urged to achieve the development of Mexico into a great and rich country by itself, under its own management, principally in three ways:

"1. Pooling its savings to form labor co-operatives, which will stimulate the construction of railways, irrigation works,

Cornucopia

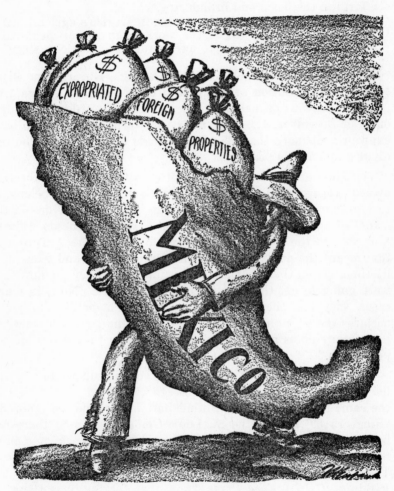

—*Reprinted from the Chattanooga, Tenn., News.*

development of mining, build hydro-electric plants, textile mills, and utilize natural gas.

"2. Besides the capital obtained from savings, this industrializing program is to go forward by creating capital out of extra work, or, as Cardenas put it, through 'doubling our efforts in the fields and in industry.'

"3. Besides increasing production in Mexico's agricultural fields, Cardenas has urged the workers in the oil fields to dedicate their spare time to agriculture and cattle-raising."

One of the principal policies of the Cardenas Government seems to be a redistribution of the wealth of Mexico, with organized labor taking the lion's share. Since President Cardenas assumed office in December, 1934, for a six-year term, he is said to have expropriated more than 35,000,000 acres of land, which he has divided among the peasants.

The Mexican Government has not questioned titles to foreign-owned property; it has simply seized the big haciendas belonging to Mexicans, Britishers, Americans, or Spaniards. Nor did the owner of a small tract escape; we learn from the Tucson *Arizona Star* that in the case of many Mexican landowners, "expropriation meant the actual confiscation of the savings and work of a lifetime. Even the agrarians are grumbling. They thought they were going to get the land in their own names. Now, in many cases, they find they have just exchanged bosses." Moreover, declares the Clinton (Ill.) *Journal-Public* "no agrarian bonds or promissory notes of any kind were given to the owners of the properties."

"From Mexico's point of view, it is not difficult to understand her attitude," observes the San Diego (Calif.) *Tribune*, "but at the same time, the rights of other nationals cannot be ignored." "Since 1915," asserts the St. Louis *Globe-Democrat*, "there has been accumulating in the State Department a stack of claims, filed by Americans who have been despoiled of their properties." The majority probably were claims for large estates, but, says the Redding (Calif.) *Free Press*, "now that the Supreme Court of Mexico has handed down a decision, nullifying that part of the Agrarian Law which permitted owners to retain about 150 acres of their holdings, even the small farms owned by Americans may be taken from them."

We read in the Rome (Ga.) *News-Tribune* that "these land seizures are made by the reigning political group to make themselves 'solid' with the unthinking." A Mexican paper, *El Mundo* of Tampico, goes into greater detail when it says:

"Mexico is faced with the paradox of a Government whose policies are inspired by the vehement desire of President Cardenas to attain the welfare of the proletarian classes, while in reality the result has been to increase the hunger of the people to the point of despair.

"This is what has actually happened. From the time it came into office up to the present, the Administration of General Cardenas has sustained a policy, definitely inclined to favor the proletarian classes. The laws, the acts, the decisions—everything that is done by the President and his collaborators and by the Governors of all the states, who feel compelled to follow the President's policies, tends to improve the living conditions of industrial laborers and peasants. *No quarter has been given industrialists, land owners, capitalists, or merchants. And when they have complained of weariness, the President of the Republic advises them that if they do not want to continue the struggle, they should withdraw and turn over their factories or their commercial establishments to the workers.*"

Betty Kirk, in a *Christian Science Monitor* article, tells us that:

"During the period between 1915 and 1934, 20,000,000 acres of land were divided and given to 760,000 heads of families, or a little over an average of 1,000,000 acres annually. When President Cardenas took office this gradual process was suddenly speeded up, with the result that from December, 1934, to August, 1937, more than 24,000,000 acres of land were give to 565,000 heads of families, and the process has continued uninterrupted since. He has then been averaging the donation of 8,000,000 acres of land annually, and already has exceeded the total of his predecessors.

"It is estimated the entire area in the country suitable for cultivation is 56,810,000 acres. Since the 44,250,000 acres given to peons must comprise the bulk of the arable land, it becomes apparent that the impact the division has had upon the agricultural economy of the nation has been tremendous."

The joker in the whole Cardenas agrarian program, it seems, has been discovered by the New York *Mirror*. It is this:

"The Cardenas political party promised to give approximately 25 acres of land to some 1,800,000 Mexican families. *"But the Mexican doesn't 'own' his land. He cannot rent, mortgage, or sell his farm. It is only his while he works it. If he fails to work it for two years, he loses it.*

"The real owner is the Government, whose Land Bank stakes the farmer to seed, tools, and other equipment; they are charged against the farmer on the books.

"The Government markets the farmer's crops, balances the books at the end of the year, subtracts the peso and a half a day advanced to him, then pays him the profits from the crops—if there are any.

"To date, production has decreased under this plan, necessitating the importation of basic agricultural products, leaving the farmer in debt to the Government."

The Rome (Ga.) *News-Tribune* take the stand that "the whole Cardenas agrarian program is based upon a false philosophy, and will accomplish no permanent good." And John Thompson, in the San Diego (Calif.) *Sun*, tells why. Says this expert on foreign affairs:

"Unlike the United States, Mexico was conquered, not colonized. Peons became used to working for someone else instead of for themselves, so that when Cardenas surprised everyone by actually giving the land back to the peons, they didn't know what to do with it.

"The same situation arose when Cardenas expropriated the oil properties. Mexico didn't know what to do with the new wealth. It will take twenty or thirty years for the Mexican to understand the implications of owning his own land."

From its advantageous position near the Mexican border, the Houston (Texas) *Chronicle* admits that:

"No one would deny that agrarian reform in Mexico is desirable. To put poverty-stricken agricultural workers on farms of their own is a splendid thing—so long as this is done without wrecking the nation's economy, and without taking property from owners without compensation.

"But the agrarian and other policies of the Cardenas régime are wrecking Mexico economically. Aside from the violation of morals and of international law involved, the conduct of the land reform program has been extremely unwise.

"Mexico has vast areas of undeveloped land. The logical thing to do is place the workers on acreage hitherto uncultivated, and thus increase the nation's total production. Instead of that, the Mexican Government has divided up land already being worked; and production on most of these acres has decreased, due to the change from expert to ignorant and frequently shiftless management."

"The redistribution of land may have been politically justified," agrees the Chicago *Tribune*, "but not economically. The Mexican peons have lacked initiative, experience, equipment. And the money and land-credit associations have not met the problem." Besides, the land bought by Americans in Mexico, points out the *Christian Union Herald*, of Pittsburgh, "is real property. It was bought and paid for. Its seizure by the Government is an outrage."

"Back of the debate over the seized farm lands and ranches," in the opinion of the Memphis *Commercial Appeal*, "is the far larger proposition of the expropriated oil properties, valued at many millions." With both the landowners and oil companies in mind, the Tucson *Arizona Star*, near the Mexican border, wants us to realize that:

"Americans went into what was once a barren desert, and with their capital and technique installed irrigation works to make the desert bloom like a Garden of Eden. Today they stand robbed of the work they have done. Their land has been taken from them. Much of it is reverting to a desert waste.

"Oil prospectors went into the torrid jungles near Tampico, and out of that jungle made a world-famous oil field. They installed modern sanitary devices, and paid the highest wages of any industry in Mexico. The taxes they paid contributed heavily to the support of the Mexican Government. And now the fruits of their work—fruits which added to the well-being of all Mexico—have been taken from them."

In the shadow of the nation's Capitol, the Washington *Star* gives us an inkling as to how the Cardenas agrarian program came into being. Says *The Star*:

"The entire Mexican revolutionary program of the past five years has been basically a reflection of the New Deal in Washington. Sympathetic treatment of American industrial strikes had its exaggerated counterpart in President Cardenas's open advocacy of strikes in some cases as the most effective means for labor to win its just due; the rise of the CIO here was followed by the ascendancy of the similarly inclined Confederacion de Trabajadores de Mexico (CTM). The effort to provide the American farmer with security by price control, rural credit, and resettlement has had its shadow in the new stimulation of land distribution and creation of the communal 'ejidos' among the Indian population of Mexico.

"Encouragement which Washington has lent to the Mexican reforms by careful refusal to intervene in the oil-labor controversy until it reached the critical stage, found outspoken expression through Ambassador Josephus Daniels."

Unsupported charges have been made by irresponsible Mexican leaders and radical writers that title to foreign-owned property in Mexico was obtained by questionable means. The records show, however, that most of the property President Cardenas of Mexico has taken over, in the name of the Government, is owned by British and American citizens, and was obtained by them from a legally constituted Mexican Government, for value received.

The results of the Cardenas land distribution program are typical of the dangers encountered when a political leader tries to make progress too rapidly in carrying out his reforms.

According to Raymond Moley, Editor of Newsweek (New York):

"Lazaro Cardenas took office in November, 1934, for a six-year term. He was the creature of the National Revolutionary Party which, even in 1934 was slipping away from the strong, intelligent guidance of Plutarco Calles, former President. Cardenas was devoid of the statesmanship which characterized Calles. Ambitious, but vastly uninformed, he proved to be an easy prey for the radical group which had been used, but controlled, by Calles.

"Cardenas appointed a puppet Cabinet. Through his Autonomous Department of Press and Publicity, generally referred to in Mexico as the 'Dapp,' Cardenas spread propa-

44

ganda concerning his integrity and honesty of purpose. Everyone in Mexico knows, however, that the 'Dapp' is as strict a system of censorship as those of Russia, Germany, and Italy. Only that which will glorify Cardenas and his Six-Year Plan is permitted publication. "In 1935, Cardenas went on record for the 'Mexicanization of Industry.' That spelled the doom of private property. In 1936, the so-called 'Law of Expropriation' was enacted. That meant that wholesale confiscation would soon be in order. He then proceeded to a ruinous program of agrarian confiscation."

We are assured by the Rochester (N. Y.) *Times-Union* that:

"The Cardenas land distribution program is not directed against Americans. It is simply part of a vast and costly socialization scheme for which the Government now admits it cannot afford to pay.
"Although legally admissable, such a procedure is morally indefensible. Even more important, from Mexico's viewpoint, it may end by alienating the friendship of the American Government."

The breaking up of huge Mexican estates resulted from Mexico's revolutionary Constitution of 1917. But until the present régime, comparatively little was done in carrying out the redistribution policy. The difference between President Cardenas and his predecessors is summed up in these words by the Savannah (Ga.) *News:*

"Until 1933, only 25,000,000 acres had been expropriated and divided among 942,000 peasants, both Obregon and Calles having become convinced that rapid wholesale distribution of large landed estates would destroy the national credit, reduce taxes, and frighten foreign capital. Their successor, Cardenas, had no such fears.
"When President Cardenas took over the reins of government in 1934, business was booming. Federal revenues were rising sharply, no serious labor troubles existed, farms were producing a surplus, and the people generally were contented. Then came his land program. A vast program of building dams, highways, and railroads was launched without regard to cost or ability to finance.
"The much-heralded agrarian program, with which it was hoped to better the condition of the small farmer, has not

45

You're My Sweetie Now!

—Reprinted from the Washington Post.

worked. There is no escaping the conclusion that the Mexican New Deal is now floundering in unmarked jungles, where any new day may bring an unseen precipice."

Some of the steps in the Cardenas program are thus summarized by the Norfolk *Virginian-Pilot:*

"One of these steps was the distribution of land and the organization of a bank to help the peasants finance the purchase of tools and equipment. Another was the expropriation of 1,000,000 acres of cotton-growing land. A third was a similar expropriation of land in Yucatan, where henequin is grown. A fourth step was the encouragement given to organized labor in virtually all industries, particularly those owned largely by foreign interests. A fifth was the expropriation of the National Railways, the largest transportation system in Mexico. It is now held by the Government, but the plan is that railroad workers will manage it for the benefit of the entire nation. Still another was the organization of a bank to supply credit to workers who set up co-operative factories."

Old Mexico—land of revolution—is undergoing what its leaders call modernization, declares a *United Press* dispatch from Mexico City. Some of the changes are listed by the correspondent:

"The new highways, the tourist cabins, the travel posters are the surface signs. But the fundamental change affects the United States business man in Mexico, splits up the vast land concentrations, determines the pay of the oil field workers, the return a small farmer can dig from his land, and the price the housewife pays for beans."

Critics of the Mexican President have declared that he has gone blindly ahead in his "Mexico for the Mexicans" program. He has distributed land to the landless peons when he was unable to provide them with a seed, asserts the Louisville *Courier-Journal,* and the Bridgeton (N. J.) *News* offers the following amplification of this charge:

"After grabbing farms from American owners, they were given to the peons, and it now turns out that these ne'er-do-wells have allowed the land to go into disuse so that there are

47

not enough farm products raised to meet the needs of the consumers, thus compelling importation of basic foods."

Returning to *The Courier-Journal*, we learn that President Cardenas "has embarked on public works projects when there was no material for those projects and no money with which to buy it; that he has driven capital from the country, when capital is the one thing the country needs." In fact:

"Backed by the radical element of the country and the Communistic labor unions, he follows the Bolshevik example of sweeping expropriation without any kind of compensation, and he exhorts other Latin American nations to follow his example."

The Butte *Montana Standard* continues the itemization of Mexico's many troubles:

"A system of land banks set up by President Cardenas has exhausted the resources at its disposal, loaning out more than 12,000,000 pesos of fiat money. The Mexican peso, worth 28 cents last spring, has crashed, and the silver and gold resources of the Bank of Mexico have been exhausted. As the peso went down the cost of living has risen.
"Still another phase of the six-year program in Mexico has come to grief as a result of the strained financial condition of the Government. A series of irrigation dams, sadly needed in Mexico, and supplementary public works stand today half completed and neglected."

Despite Cardenas's grandiose scheme of "Mexico for the Mexicans," declares the St. Louis *Globe-Democrat*, "his country has added progressively to long-standing economic chaos."

In commenting on Mexico's expropriation policy, the Fairhaven (Vt.) *Era* explains:

"There are, of course, two sides. The American side is that a lot of people in this country, in all good faith, invested about $1,000,000,000 in Mexico under assurances of good Mexican laws. They bought farm machinery, and paid for improvements; they bought oil leases, they drilled wells, they laid pipe lines, they built refineries. Then the Mexican Government simply came along and took these things away from them.

48

"The Mexican side of the story is just as plain and simple. The Cardenas Government sets out to give the Mexicans good government. But Mexico's resources of land, mines, and oil fields, have been owned by foreigners. She cannot buy this property, so Cardenas chooses to expropriate it."

The seizure of the American-owned oil properties was a part of President Cardenas's program of "Mexico for the Mexicans." He would raise the underprivileged Mexican peons to higher industrial, educational, and economic levels; he would elevate their moral and physical standards, improve working conditions, foster the acquisition of property. But he would finance all this by seizing the property owned by British or American citizens in Mexico. The uplift program is sketched by Margaret Gould in the Toronto (Canada) *Star:*

"Thousands of Mexicans have for generations been living in poverty, filth, and ignorance. Off the beaten tourist track are millions living in huts, caves, and dugouts. Only 24 per cent live in houses of any description. About 60 per cent of the population were until this year illiterate.
"Yet Mexico is called the 'treasure-house of the world.' An observer writes: 'Mexico possesses wealth and diversity of resources capable of giving her people a standard of living second to none.'
"The present Government is making the first real attempt to make an equitable distribution of that wealth. President Cardenas is attempting to turn back the pages of Mexico's history—back to the days when there was collective ownership of the land, before the land was taken away from the Indians.
"It is this background which explains the present drive to recover 'Mexico for the Mexicans.' The Cardenas Government is pledged to a six-year plan, by which to rectify the economic and social abuses of several hundred years."

It is reported that Cardenas spends little time in Mexico City, but travels around talking to his people. As we read in the Council Bluffs (Ia.) *Nonpareil:*

"The peasants and common folk of Mexico look upon Cardenas as a sort of god. But the Church opposes him, for he adheres to the anti-Church policy of his predecessors. The

49

business men do not like his Communistic tendencies. And the tribal chiefs in isolated sections of the country would like to turn him out."

Nor are the people affronted by ethical irregularities, says the San Francisco *Chronicle:*

"The voters on whom Cardenas depends for support have not our conceptions of property and of law, and they do know exactly what they want. They want land, without paying for it; they want high wages in the oil fields, regardless of whether the output, at the world price of oil, can pay those wages plus the cost of keeping the plants going. And, of course, they care not at all whether those who supplied the capital for these developments receive any return on their investments."

Yet it seems that things have not been going well under this program. As was said in France after the Revolution: "The King is dead, but the poor are still poor." In Mexico the properties of the foreigners have been seized, but the peons are no richer. In fact, foreign money has been frightened away, and economic conditions are worse than ever before. As Frank L. Kluckhohn explains in a Mexico City dispatch to the New York *Times:*

"Those who knew Mexico intimately five years ago would not recognize it today. State control has grown and spread in all directions. Even those who knew it a year ago would see a major change, for a year ago Mexico was a beehive of construction, land division, and social activities. Today it feels the paralyzing effect of lack of funds; it feels foreign opposition, both diplomatic and financial. Activity has been almost stilled, but the buzzing about events is louder than ever. A government-conducted publicity campaign grows in proportion to the faltering of constructive activity.

"The public is being told by the press, the radio, and even the movies that Mexico must be freed of foreign domination; that Mexicans are the most progressive people in the world today and must march forward amid present difficulties to a new and fuller life. The people are told that they are leading all Latin America 'out from under the yoke of the Colossus of the North.' Something approaching a holy crusade has taken the place of material achievement.

50

"Mexico is a third as large as the United States, but it has only one-seventh as large a population. Its people are dispersed among vast mountain ranges, great deserts, remote valleys. To understand the effect of the propaganda and to see the stoppage of activity, one must leave the paved arterial highways.

"Off the beaten track one sees the huge, half-finished dams which were to make dry valleys blossom and which now stand like gaunt and silent monuments to great hopes."

What Mexico might have learned from the early history of the United States is that foreign capital brings wealth and creates wealth. Mexico has raw materials that need development. "Such development does not occur automatically," observes the New Haven (Conn.) *Journal-Courier;* "there is no brand of oratorical magic, no legislative miracle, that will work oil wells, or silver mines, or the manifold enterprises making modern industrialism." Capital is needed, and capital must be allowed to make a profit, or it will not come. Continues the Connecticut paper:

"Some countries, like the United States, are quite ready to receive capital on that basis. They are thus enabled to build themselves toward a measure of such economic independence that they may begin to export capital on their own account. Then they look in the new countries for the qualities they themselves displayed.

"What will result in Mexico is likely to be a dearth of foreign capital. That that will rest heavily on the Mexican rank and file goes without saying. It is possible, of course, to build up an industrial economy practically from scratch; that is essentially what Russia has been trying to do since her Revolution. But it takes a lot of suffering, a lot of hardship; millions of peasants have starved to death in Russia, and death by starvation is a rather substantial price to pay for the seizure of other people's property.

"Señor Cardenas may some time have cause to reflect on some of these questions."

"What the Mexican Government has overlooked, in its seizure of British, Dutch, and American oil properties," notes the Boston *Transcript,* "is that confiscation without proper payment simply restores jungle law." To quote the *Southwest American,* of Ft. Smith, Arkansas:

"The Mexican Constitution, adopted in 1917, provides for expropriation on behalf of the Government of properties owned by foreign nationals or by Mexicans. It provides for compensation by the Government for such properties, before or at the time of expropriation. The Mexican Government has the right under its Constitution to take over American farm lands or American oil properties or American-owned railroads or any other property it desires. *But it has the obligation, inseparable from the right, to pay for the properties before or at the time of the expropriation.*"

The Mexican Constitution of 1917 proclaims that all subsoil minerals, including petroleum, are the property of the Government. It provides for expropriation, on behalf of the Government, of properties owned by foreigners or Mexicans. But, points out the New York *Times*, "it also stipulates that private property shall not be expropriated except for reasons of public utility." The requirement as to indemnity, we are told, has been repeatedly and consistently interpreted by the Supreme Court of Mexico to mean that the indemnity must be definite, and that it must be made at the same time as the expropriation.

While the Constitution was adopted in 1917, that part dealing with the subsoil rights, explains the Milwaukee *Journal*, "was not enforced by the Mexican rulers who followed Carranza, probably because the foreign-owned companies were a juicy source of taxes." George Creel, writing in *Collier's* after a visit to Mexico, thinks there are other explanations:

"Carranza, President of Mexico, had no money for indemnification and lacked the daring to confiscate on any large scale. Obregon went farther, expropriating estates here and there to satisfy importunate Generals, but for the most part took pains to keep within the bounds of international law. Calles, after three years of enmity and aggression, calmed down and negotiated a peace pact with Dwight Morrow in 1928, that safeguarded American investments against actual confiscation, although restrictive laws continued to be passed. Ortiz Rubio and Abelardo Rodriguez, both Callistes, respected the agreement.

"Not so with Lazaro Cardenas. A soldier throughout his adult life, and unembarrassed by the doubts and fears that come from intimate contact with the complexities of finance and economics, he had gone about endorsing every article of Mexico's Constitution with all of the simple directness of a range bull."

According to the Baltimore *Sun:*

"Secretary of State Hughes, now Chief Justice of the United States Supreme Court, refused to recognize the Obregon Government in 1921, until the Mexican President would declare that Article 27 of the 1917 Constitution did not mean confiscation. The Obregon Government refused, and friction continued throughout the Harding Administration and well into the Coolidge Administration. Dwight Morrow's mission in that era resulted in a decision by the Mexican Supreme Court that Article 27 did not contemplate confiscation in a retroactive sense; in other words, that it did not apply to companies which had acquired land before the adoption of the Constitution of 1917. Recognition quickly followed in late August, 1923."

According to spokesmen for the oil companies:

"Article 27 of the Constitution authorizes only the expropriation of lands and waters, and has for its purpose the distribution of real property. This article has been violated by extending the faculty of expropriation to personal property, such as tools, plants, and equipment.

"Article 27 also provides that expropriation may be made only by means of indemnification. This also has been violated.

"Article 28 of the Constitution is violated by establishing a government monopoly of the petroleum industry. Article 14 of the Constitution is controverted, since the companies were deprived of their properties, possessions, and rights without due legal procedure before the courts."

Mexico's controversy with the oil companies is of long standing, and on one occasion brought Mexico and the United States close to war. The situation was tense when President Coolidge appointed Dwight Morrow as Ambassador to Mexico. During the Morrow régime, a new era of good feeling was inaugurated between the two countries. As the Philadelphia *Inquirer* put it: "Ambassador Morrow was able, through the exercise of exceptional diplomatic abilities, to convince the Mexican authorities

Mexican Version of Bronx Cheer

—Reprinted from the Miami, Fla., Herald.

that it would be bad business for the Government and the workers to expropriate the foreign-owned oil properties."

But the ferment of revolution continued, and Cordell Hull, as Secretary of State, inherited the problem that other Secretaries had struggled with since the turn of the century, when Porfirio Diaz ruled Mexico. When the Diaz régime was overthrown in 1911, and industrial and agrarian reform got under way in Mexico, American holdings were caught in the onward sweep of readjustment and redistribution of land holdings. As J. H. Carmical explains in a New York *Times* article:

"Francisco I. Madero, successor to Diaz, wished to see a redistribution of the great estates that had grown up under Diaz.

"Much of the land concentration—large haciendas, mines, and oil fields—was in the hands of foreign firms and individuals. More was owned by native Mexicans of Spanish blood. The predominant Indian strain in the Mexican population, suppressed and mute for generations, was fanned by revolutionary fervor to a flame of hatred against the landholders. Under leaders like Emiliano Zapata in the south, and Pancho Villa in the north, the agrarian question soon became one of major importance.

"Madero was ousted and slain by a conservative revolt led by Victoriano Huerta, but the latter, actively opposed in the United States by the Wilson Administration, resigned in 1914, and Venustiano Carranza obtained a more or less precarious predominance. He had promised the return of as much of the peasants' land as could be proved to be illegally taken, and the expropriation of enough more to supply other small holders. His constituent assembly, which met at Queretaro in 1917, also adopted a clause calling for restrictions on the acquisition of agricultural land by foreigners—and asserting the national ownership of all subsoil deposits.

"This last was an immediate threat to all owners of mineral lands. The Mexican contention was that Diaz had reversed the traditional mining laws of the state, which had vested ownership of subsoil deposits in the sovereign—first the King of Spain, then the republic. The Diaz laws had given mineral rights to the owners of the surface land, and had attracted foreign capital in large amounts.

55

"The mine operators, faced with the loss of tremendous sums invested in good faith, protested vigorously. The petroleum industry, rapidly growing in importance, was one of the strongest dissidents, and by a threat to cease production, it was able to force Carranza to abandon his policy temporarily.

"But the problem still remained. Carranza was ousted and assassinated, and in 1920 Alvaro Obregon became President. Negotiations for recognition of the new régime by the United States dragged. In 1923, an agreement was reached as to the agricultural land owned by Americans and expropriated by the Mexicans, the latter promising payment in bonds. The mineral land question was not settled, but it was further refined. By definition and by decision of the Mexican Supreme Court, Obregon and his successor, Calles, eliminated from discussion all those lands which has been leased or owned prior to 1917, on which some positive act, such as drilling, had been performed. This left untouched reserves open to expropriation, but the United States, through Ambassador Morrow, accepted in 1928.

"Mexico moved cautiously within the sphere of the Morrow-Calles agreement for some years. Then, in 1934, Lazaro Cardenas became President.

"Cardenas represented the radical wing of the Mexican revolution. He declared that his term of office would be devoted to working out a six-year plan of Mexicanization. This comprised nationalization of the subsoil, agrarian reform, and protection of the workers. Under Cardenas, the influence of the labor unions was strengthened and the expropriation of agricultural land was greatly speeded up. Provision was made by law for payment for all land taken over by the Government, but in actual practice this did not work out too well for the former owners. Agrarian bonds on the market fell to a fraction of their face value.

"Though the seizure of the agricultural lands evoked individual protests, it was not made the subject of official diplomatic action. However, the oil situation soon became openly precarious, and with all its politico-economic significance, developed into a serious threat. But this was not because of any further efforts to apply the provisions of the Constitution; instead, it came through the efforts of the Cardenas régime in applying the third plank of its program—protection of its workers.

"This elastic phrase may have been used as a cloak and a weapon to further nationalization of the petroleum industry. Labor troubles began in the oil fields early in Cardenas's Administration and (so the companies assert) resulted in workers for foreign concerns receiving a much higher scale of wages than obtained in Mexico generally. Moreover, a year ago Cardenas formed the General Administration of National Petroleum to work the state fields, compete with private concerns and, presumably, to take over any of the latters' leases which should not be renewed or which should be forcibly seized.

"The crisis was brought on by a general strike in the oil fields which began in May, 1937, involving fifteen companies and 18,000 workers. It was ended after twelve days by submission of the issues to the Federal Labor Board. A commission of experts, studying the situation reported on August 3rd that the oil companies could pay increases totaling some $7,000,000 a year.

"The Labor Board's award was deferred until December, and then was made substantially in accordance with the experts' opinion. The companies protested that the actual rises involved would total 41,000,000 pesos, or $11,400,000. In addition, the administration clauses of the award providing for worker co-operation in management would, they claimed, make the difficulty of maintaining discipline, already serious, quite insurmountable. Consequently, they appealed to the Mexican Supreme Court.

"While the case was before the Court, President Cardenas openly accused the oil companies of attempting to coerce the Government, chiefly through the withdrawal of company funds from Mexican banks. The atmosphere was becoming dangerously heated. On March 1st, the Supreme Court unanimously refused to enjoin the Government against proceedings to put the Labor Board's award into effect. The companies still maintained the impossibility of complying with the award. On March 14th, Cardenas sent what was virtually an ultimatum, which was refused the next day. Meanwhile, high-pressure propaganda directed against the companies was in progress. The companies offered to meet the wage increases if the administrative clauses were altered in their favor. This was refused, and on March 18, 1938, expropriation was decreed."

According to Edwin C. Krauss, writing in the Los Angeles *Times,* the pressure applied to the oil companies by the successive

Mexican Governments and labor organizations gradually squeezed the operating concerns into a position where compliance with further demands became impossible. This, they say, was made the excuse for expropriation. Continues Mr. Krauss:

"The first step in this process was the nationalization of subsoil rights in 1917. Prior to that time, by Mexican law, the owner of the surface owned all under it; but the new Constitution of that year claimed for the nation all oil and other wealth below ground. At first it was declared the rule would not be applied retroactively; but in 1918, decrees by Carranza indicated a retroactive policy. These virtually stopped all new development. There was a period of uncertainty until 1925, when statutes were enacted requiring oil companies to exchange their land titles for fifty-year government concessions.

"There followed much litigation and negotiation, and a compromise was at last worked out in which the Mexican Government agreed to recognize the rights of oil companies as they existed in 1917, by means of confirmatory concessions. According to the companies, such concessions were delayed months and years, and applications covering some 6,000,000 acres never were acted upon. Meanwhile, the companies declare, their failure to make development expenditures on the disputed lands, which they were naturally reluctant to make in view of the uncertainty as to title, was construed against them and declared cause for forfeiture.

"Meanwhile, the Mexican Government entered into direct competition in 1923, not by developing new areas of its own, but by seizing lands in proved fields. The companies also declare that the Government discriminated in various ways against the private companies, and in favor of its own agencies.

"One of these ways was through the labor unions, or workers' syndicates, which were encouraged in increasing demands through a labor law in many ways parallel to the American Wagner Act. This was culminated in 1934, by insertion of the exclusion clause in labor contracts, which gave syndicate leaders power to expel any worker from membership and forbade any company to employ a non-member. This put the workers completely under the thumb of the labor leaders.

"But, it is charged, the government petroleum agency was under no such restriction. Its workers were federalized and denied rights under the labor law, hence worked for much lower wages and under harder conditions than those in private employ. This gave the government agency an overwhelming competitive advantage.

"In 1935, the Government took another step by reducing and fixing the price of gasoline sold domestically, thus cutting the companies' income. At the end of 1935, wage scales in the oil industry were as much as four times the average scale for similar work in other industries."

The Labor Board, notes the St. Louis *Globe-Democrat,* was ordered to make a survey of the situation, and render a report. "This it did, after only thirty days of inquiry. Its findings were unanimously upheld by the Supreme Court, which President Cardenas controlled. The decision of the Labor Board was so unfair to the oil companies, and so impossible in its demands, that the companies were forced to quit their properties and turn them over to the Government."

Roscoe B. Gaither, a member of the New York bar and a recognized authority on Latin American law, writing in the *United States Law Review,* says the first attempt to get control—by constitutional means—of the British, Dutch, and American oil properties was made in 1917. As the Beaumont (Texas) *Enterprise* interprets the Gaither article:

"Article 27 of the Mexican Constitution declared all oil in Mexico belonged to the Mexican people. But the Mexican Supreme Court held that the act was not retroactive, so the rights acquired by Americans and other outside interests were entitled to recognition. The Mexican Government tried to ignore the decisions of its own highest court. During the Harding Administration a commission headed by Messrs. Warren and Payne went to Mexico to take the matter up with the Mexican Government.

"The Warren-Payne or Bucareli Agreement was based on recognition of the Obregon régime by the United States, and the oil companies enjoyed comparative freedom from governmental interference until the Calles Government tried to repudiate the Warren-Payne Agreement. Again representations were made by foreign governments. This time, however, the Mexican Government, instead of agreeing to recognize foreign rights in perpetuity, limited its recognition to fifty years. Again the Supreme Court of Mexico ruled that such limitation of rights was unconstitutional. As a result, the law was amended to confirm rights in perpetuity or to recognize leasehold rights for the duration of the lease. The expropriation law was signed by President Cardenas on November 23, 1936.

"Mr. Gaither says: 'This seizure of property in Mexico presents a new and novel political philosophy hitherto unknown to democratic nations. *It is the greatest blanket seizure of foreign properties since the Russian Revolution.* The Russian seizure, which took all property, whether Russian or foreign, was accompanied by a complete change in the theory of government of the country. Mexico, on the other hand, pretends to be a democratic nation, working under a constitution with a balanced government, in which the executive and legislative branches are kept in line by a theoretically neutral court whose decisions are supposed to limit the inevitable tendency of administrations toward excessive liberality.'

"Mexico is supposed to be a democracy functioning like that of the United States. As a matter of fact, under President Cardenas, Mexico is more Socialistic than democratic. One of the first symptoms of the development of a Socialistic State is disregard of the property rights of individuals, whether nationals or foreigners. Another symptom, which may appear at the same time or a little later, is disregard of the political rights of the individual."

"How Mexico goes about her problems of social reform is not our business. It *is* our business, however, to see that our nationals are not robbed of the property which they have acquired by legal methods," maintains the Salt Lake City *Deseret News*. Since there is no money with which to pay for expropriated properties, points out the Louisville *Courier-Journal*, "there is nothing to do but return the properties to their rightful owners."

III

MEXICO'S FINANCIAL AND ECONOMIC DIFFICULTIES

Mexico's Expropriation Program—Statement of the Oil Companies—Text of the Cardenas Decree—State Department Negotiations—The Legal Battle of the Oil Companies—Mexico's Idea of "Justice and Equity"—Mexico's Foreign Debt—Effect of Expropriation on American Tourist Trade—Effect of Expropriation on Mexico's Revenues—On Trade—On Wages—On Employment.

As early as March 1, 1938, it was apparent to Frank L. Kluckhohn, then Mexico City correspondent of the New York *Times*, that the dispute between the British, Dutch, and American oil companies, on the one hand, and the Government of Mexico, on the other, had reached an acute stage. On that day the Supreme Court of Mexico ruled against the seventeen oil concerns in their wage controversy. The producers promptly announced that they were unable to accept the decision—and remain solvent. Expropriation followed.

According to Mr. Kluckhohn, Mexico tested the reaction in the United States by nationalizing 350,000 acres of the Standard Oil Company of California concessions several months before the expropriations of March, 1938. Briefly, observes the New York *Sun*, the principal events preceding the Cardenas decree of last March were:

"The Petroleum Workers Union, in November, 1936, presented new demands for a standard collective contract.

"After fruitless negotiations extending over several months, the unions called a strike in May, 1937. Subsequently, the strike was abandoned, and the union began an 'economic suit' before the Labor Board. An investigating commission was appointed to determine whether the companies could grant the union demands. The report of the commission recommended increases in wages, and so forth, which would have entailed an additional yearly cost to the companies of approximately 41,000,000 pesos, and made further recommendations which, in effect, would have removed control of the companies from their owners.

61

would be unable to do. *There was no defiance of the Court, since the Court had issued no order.*

"Virtually at the same moment the banana companies operating in the States of Tabasco and Chiapas were experiencing a similar situation. In the face of exorbitant demands from their workmen, and with their properties tied up by a strike, these companies had no other course open to them than to agree to submit their case to the private arbitration of the Chief of the Labor Department. So soon as he rendered his award, the banana companies notified him that they were unable to comply, and that they would accordingly be forced to suspend operations in Mexico.

"Upon receipt of this statement, negotiations were reopened by the Labor Department and the original award substantially modified to a degree which, in the opinion of the banana companies, allowed them to continue operating in the country. The workmen at first rejected the proposed compromise; whereupon the Labor Department, acting throughout under the full authorization of the President, exerted extreme pressure upon them to accept the arrangement on the ground that if they did not do so, the Government could not extend any further aid to them, and the banana companies would withdraw from Mexico.

"It is evident that the two cases are identical in the fundamental principle involved—a labor decision with which in both cases the respective companies alleged their inability to comply. Yet, in the banana case the Labor Department, under authority from the President, urged the workers to accept a substantial reduction from the original wage and social benefits granted in the award; while in the case of the oil companies, which granted even greater benefits, they were forthwith accused of a rebellious attitude and the extreme step was taken of expropriating all their properties on the plea that it was essential to assert the sovereignty and to maintain the dignity of the nation.

"The natural inference is that this discriminatory treatment was due to the fact that, in the one case there were no realizable assets to seize; in the other, valuable properties and assets were immediately available."

However, remarks the Beaumont (Texas) *Enterprise,* "this was not the first time that Mexico attempted to seize foreign-owned oil wells." It is merely another chapter in the long controversy with various Mexican Governments that began when the

62

Metropolitan Sketches

By Medina De La Vega

. . . But what do we care, if the country floats serenely? . . .

—*Reprinted from Ultimas Noticias of Mexico City.*

1917 Constitution was adopted, explains the Milwaukee *Journal*. In fact, T. W. Woodlock, writing in *The Wall Street Journal* (New York) declares:

"For twenty-five years, beginning with the accession to the Presidency of Woodrow Wilson, Mexico has been a thorn in the side of the United States. Her dealings with us have at all times been predicated on the certainty that, whatever happened, she could count upon our abstention from the use of force and upon a degree of patience under provocation approaching that of Job himself. Her statesmen, since the advent of Carranza, have with uncanny accuracy appraised the nature and measured the influence of American public opinion, and have played upon it with considerable skill. Up to the end of the Calles régime they handled us with perfect ease."

Henry J. Allen, former Governor of Kansas, writing in the New York *Herald Tribune*, is even more specific. According to Mr. Allen:

"Mexico has always abused foreign investors. For twenty-five years she has pursued a ragged but not extreme policy of seizing the property of investors, as she has been tempted in individual cases. There are probably a thousand notes of protest from our State Department. The first startling example of confiscation had to do with the Mexican railways, which were taken over by Cardenas even without pretense of law, and their operation turned over to the workers. The direct confiscation of the railways, the oil companies, American ranches, and some of the mines, does not tell the whole story. The indirect seizures under what is known as the 'labor squeeze' and which now threaten public utilities, manufacturing industries, and large mining interests, arrive at exactly the same result as direct confiscation."

Since 1915 the Mexican Government has been expropriating farm lands owned by American citizens. So the issue raised by the seizure of foreign-owned oil properties was not a new one, but an old one suddenly rendered acute.

In another summary of the events leading up to the dramatic decree of March 18, 1938, the Manchester (N. H.) *Union* says:

"In return for its 'good neighbor' attitude, the United States has been met by a series of high-handed moves in Mexico City in which its interests have been rudely ignored. First, Mexico defaulted on its bonds outstanding to the United States. Then it adopted agrarian reforms under which foreign-owned agricultural properties were taken over by the Government. Later it made discriminatory tariff increases on goods that came chiefly from the United States. Finally, the American oil companies had their property confiscated by executive decree.

"This last action constitutes a violation of the most elementary property rights of citizens of friendly countries. Without consulting the United States Government and without any announcement regarding indemnities, the properties were confiscated by the state."

B. C. Forbes, in his syndicated column on business and finance, declares that in signing the expropriation decree against the oil companies, "President Cardenas was sure he was acting in accordance with the anti-business policies of President Roosevelt." This astounding information was obtained by Mr. Forbes "from two sources close to the Mexican Administration." Continues this financial authority:

"For the first time in Mexico's history, her Administration includes a number of youngish men educated in America's highest institutions of learning.

"These and other advisers convinced President Cardenas that he would make a tremendous hit with President Roosevelt by doing things which, they explained to him, the latter would love to do but was handicapped in the doing of them by Congress. They convinced Mexico's President that expropriation of the oil properties of towering American (and British) companies was exactly in harmony with Franklin D. Roosevelt's attitude toward 'economic royalists'. "

After the Supreme Court upheld the Labor Board's decision of December, 1937, the oil companies, including subsidiaries of Royal Dutch-Shell and the Standard Oil Company (N. J.) issued the following statement:

"The undersigned petroleum companies have heard that the Supreme Court at a public session denied the appeal for

65

an injunction against the judgment recently handed down by the Federal Labor Board in connection with the economic conflict between the companies and the Petroleum Syndicate.

"The companies have made it abundantly clear during the past months to their employes and to the general public that the conditions recommended by the commission of experts that served as the basis of the Labor Board decision are of such a nature that it would be impossible to comply with them. Their inability to comply remains unaltered by today's verdict.

"Accordingly, they regret deeply the decision of the Supreme Court on their appeal for a permanent injunction, which cannot but have serious consequences for the companies, for their employes, and for those dependent on the industry."

The statement was signed by Royal Dutch-Shell's Mexican Eagle Company, the Standard Oil Company (N. J.) subsidiary, Huasteca, the Sinclair-Pierce Oil Company, the Mexican Sinclair Petroleum Corporation of California, the California Standard Oil Company of Mexico, and its producing subsidiary, the Richmond Petroleum Company. The companies' labor contracts were cancelled by the Labor Board on the ground that the British, Dutch, and American concerns had not complied with the Supreme Court's wage-scale decision, under which the companies were instructed to put into effect increases amounting to 40,000,000 pesos in compensation and wages.

According to a *United Press* dispatch from Mexico City, dated March 19, 1938:

"The executive decree expropriating American and other foreign oil companies' properties in Mexico became effective today with its publication in the official daily.

"After two long whereases describing the long-standing oil conflict and the Government's reasons for the seizures, the text of the decree was as follows:

"Article 1. Expropriation on account of public usefulness and in benefit of the nation is declared of the machinery, installations, edifices, pipe lines, refineries, storage tanks, means of communication, tank cars, distribution stations, vessels and all other furniture and real estate belonging to (here follows a list of the companies concerned) which may be con-

"The companies thereupon presented evidence to the Board to show that the report was not only biased, but contained glaring errors of omission and commission. But the Board handed down a decision following the recommendations.

"The companies appealed to the Supreme Court, which upheld the Labor Board. On March 14, 1938, the Board gave the companies twenty-four hours within which to put into effect the disputed award. This, the companies protested, they sidered necessary, in the judgment of the Department of National Economy, for exploration, extraction, conduction, storage, refinery, and distribution of products of the petroleum industry.

"Article 2. The Department of National Economy, with the intervention of the Department of Finance as administrator of the nation's possessions, will proceed with immediate occupation of the things affected by this expropriation.

"Article 3. *The Department of Finance will pay the indemnity due the expropriated companies in accordance with the Constitution and the law of expropriation in cash and within a time limit of ten years.* The Department of Finance will take funds to make the payments from so much per cent, which will later be determined, of the production of petroleum, its derivatives. . . .

"Article 4. The representatives of the companies will be notified personally. The decree is effective from the moment of its publication in the official daily."

Thus at one fell swoop the oil concerns were faced with the loss of investments and concessions valued at $450,000,000. For the first time in many years a foreign industry of great magnitude admitted that it had reached the limit of what it could pay, and that it was unable to make further concessions to the Mexican Government. The New York *Times* correspondent declared that the oil industry knew from official statements that it was merely the focal point of "a government-backed labor drive to keep a lion's share of the profits of all foreign industries within Mexico." If the Government wins the struggle, Mr. Kluckhohn believes, "its power over foreign corporations is almost certain to be uncontestable."

Oil company officials conferred with the Secretary of State about the critical situation, and asked the support of the Government. Although the Government disclaimed any attempt to exert economic pressure on Mexico, the Treasury Department announced that for the time being it would discontinue the direct purchase of silver produced in Mexico.

Meanwhile, in Mexico men in the oil fields were laid off. Double pay, usual for work under certain conditions, was discontinued by the Government. Economic and social benefits, formerly enjoyed, were sharply curtailed. The workers, in short, soon learned that they were not so well off under the Government. The newspapers of Mexico, operating under a strict censorship, were unable to communicate to the Mexican people the full facts concerning the oil controversy. It was therefore possible for the political leaders to give the Mexican people the impression that the oil seizures were carried out with the knowledge—and even the blessing—of the Roosevelt Administration!

Mexican revenues were sharply cut as a result of the loss of the oil companies' taxes and the curtailment of import duties due to the upheaval. Retail stores suspended credit, and demanded cash for all goods. Some even insisted that they be paid in dollars. The Central Bank of Mexico suspended dealings in foreign currency, and the President indicated that devaluation of the peso was under official consideration. Finally, President Cardenas summoned an "urgent" session of the Mexican Congress to discuss the problems arising out of the expropriation decree.

On March 30th, the Washington correspondent of the New York *Times* reported that the United States had demanded effective compensation from Mexico for her expropriation of American-owned agrarian properties; and that Great Britain also had submitted a note of protest to Mexico in behalf of the British oil companies affected. Said Secretary of State Hull in the press conference at which he stated he had sent a note to Mexico:

"During the past few years the Mexican Government, in pursuance of its national policy, has expropriated and is continuing to expropriate the properties of citizens of other countries in Mexico and of its own citizens. Among these have been many hundreds of farms and other properties of American citizens. Many of our nationals have invested their savings in these properties, have undertaken improvements therein of various kinds, and have been dependent upon them for their own livelihood.

"This Government has not undertaken and does not undertake to question the right of the Government of Mexico in the exercise of its sovereign power to expropriate properties within its jurisdiction. This Government has, however, on numerous occasions and in the most friendly manner pointed out to the Government of Mexico that in accordance with every principle of international law, of comity between nations, and of equity, the properties of its nationals so expropriated are required to be paid for by compensation representing fair, assured and effective value to the nationals from whom these properties were taken.

"The recent expropriation by the Mexican Government of oil properties belonging to American citizens is therefore but one incident in a long series of incidents of this character, and accordingly raises no new question. The subject now under consideration between the Government of the United States and the Government of Mexico is the matter of compensation for various properties of American citizens expropriated in the past few years."

The reply of the Mexican Government, in part, was as follows:

"The attitude adopted by the Government of the United States in the matter of the expropriation of the petroleum companies reaffirms once more the sovereignty of the peoples of this continent. . . .
"You may be sure that Mexico will know how to honor its obligations of today and its obligations of yesterday."

The Houston *Post*, however, from its vantage point near the Mexican border, was only slightly impressed by Mexico's promise to discharge its obligations; it recalled the contemptuous attitude of the Mexican Government toward those pioneers who had accepted Mexico's invitation to help develop the country's natural resources. Moreover, the Texas paper declared this attitude "is encouraged by condonement, if not support, in Washington." In fact:

"It frequently has been said that Cardenas would not have ventured to take the drastic step of confiscating those prop-

69

erties if he had not had some assurance of indulgence from the United States.

"This conclusion is supported by developments, such as the reported pigeon-holing by Ambassador Daniels of a strong note of protest, forwarded to him by the State Department shortly after the expropriation act, for delivery to the Mexican Government.

"Coincident with this was a statement from Warm Springs, in which sympathy was expressed for the despoiled small land owner, while owners of large estates were said to have acquired their holdings by illegal and immoral means, and oil companies were said to be entitled to be paid only the cost of their investment less depreciation."

The editorial reaction of American newspapers to the situation in Mexico was quick and decisive. And, since newspapers reflect public opinion, what they say in their editorial pages is important. Declared the Washington *Post*, in its blunt fashion: "There is no getting around the facts in the case. *Seizure of property, without immediate and just compensation, is confiscation. It is a violation of the fundamental principles of international law and international morality.*" "Seizure of the oil properties without legal procedure and without compensation is clearly against Mexico's Constitution," pointed out the Rochester (N. Y.) *Democrat and Chronicle*. "Empty promises of future indemnity mean nothing to the British and American owners," declared the Salt Lake City *Deseret News*. To the Boise *Idaho Statesman*, the seizure "savored of Communism, and will not help convince the world that President Cardenas is sincere in his declaration that he desires to protect foreign investments in Mexico—investments designed to develop the country's resources." And the New York *Times* maintained:

"It is necessary to recognize frankly that the situation created by this disagreement between the two countries threatens to have highly disturbing consequences for both of them in a number of different ways. This is a development which may readily lead to international complications; for other countries as well as the United States are heavily involved in the seizure of foreign property in Mexico."

Generous Neighbor

—*Reprinted from the Austin, Texas, Statesman.*

Of the intentions of Mexico's President to pay for the expropriated oil properties, J. H. Carmical, special writer for the New York *Times,* has this to say:

"President Cardenas has made known a plan whereby payment would be made with a percentage of the oil derived from the wells over a ten-year period. Such a plan is said not to be in accordance with fundamental principles of compensation for property taken in eminent domain.

"As the plan outlined by President Cardenas contemplates many speculative conditions which might never be realized, the oil companies of this country say it is not acceptable to them. They assert that the plan presupposes the efficiency and capacity of Mexico's administrators to manage and exploit the properties; and presumes further that a margin will be left over after payment of production costs. In addition, they maintain that payment would depend entirely upon the will of the administration in power in Mexico."

In the opinion of the Springfield (Mass.) *Republican,* "President Cardenas acted indiscreetly, if not rashly. His chief motive, perhaps, was to arouse the patriotism of his people in order to strengthen his Government at home." His accusation that the oil companies caused a business depression in Mexico by withdrawing their funds from Mexican banks "strikes a naive note," according to the San Diego *Tribune.* For, remarks this California daily, "with their activities suddenly stopped; with their commitments for overhead expenditures and payrolls no longer required, it was quite natural that the companies should withdraw their funds." Particularly, it might be added, since the Mexican Government, a few weeks before the oil properties were seized, placed an embargo on the bank accounts of the seventeen concerns sufficient to cover 75 per cent of the wages due for the duration of the strike in the oil fields in May, 1937.

As the Philadelphia *Evening Public Ledger* sees it, "the Mexican idea is that the country's programs for social and economic betterment take precedence over the property rights of foreign investors." The Government, we are told, is striving to raise the living standards of Mexican workers. But the method President Cardenas is employing, complains the Bristol (Conn.) *Press,* "is that of the highwayman." "Suppose," reflects the Charlotte (N. C.) *Observer*, "the shoe were on the other foot! *Suppose the United States Government had expropriated hundreds of millions of dollars' worth of property in this country owned by Mexicans!*"

The arbitrary methods Mexico has pursued in the oil-expropriation matter "are rather disturbing" to the Mobile (Ala.) *Register.* "She has committed a blunder, both from the political and economic standpoint," believes the Denver *Post.* Certainly, maintains the Muncie (Ind.) *Press,* "the 'good neighbor' policy of the Roosevelt Administration has received a severe jolt." So, it might be added, have the oil concerns.

"Some recourse remains in the Mexican courts," remarked the Milwaukee *Journal,* last year. But in the same breath it admitted that "when a case involves foreign interests, it may be assumed that the courts will be 'patriotic'—that is, nationalistic." Continues *The Journal:*

"The government of a country can exercise sovereignty down to the point of confiscation, if it so wills. It can violate agreements, even treaties, take the property of its own citizens and of foreigners. And there is no power to forbid, for there is no super-government to compel performances of obligations."

Referring specifically to our neighbor to the south, Duncan Aikman wrote in a Philadelphia *Record* article:

"The President of Mexico controls the courts through political appointments.

"He controls Congress by controlling elections. That is, except in a few negligible districts, no candidate for Congress can be elected against the Presidential opposition.

"He controls the state governments through his powers to remove state governors on virtually any grounds, from treasury shortages to seditious political activity.

"Finally, he controls mass political activity, as much as any one man can in a turbulent republic, by his ability to suspend civil rights, and impose censorships, either in local areas or for the whole nation.

73

"In other words, the Mexican President has a combination of constitutional and political-machine power in his hands which makes it possible for him to impose his personal will in practically every process of government, and at the same time to prevent all serious political opposition to himself from even functioning."

It did not surprise the El Paso *Times,* therefore, when the Supreme Court of Mexico upheld the expropriation of oil properties. As this Texas daily reminds us:

"In so doing the Court sustained the verdict of a District Court denying an application by the oil companies for an injunction to restrain the Government from the expropriation.

"The Supreme Court upheld the constitutionality both of the expropriation decree and the act itself. The Court also declared the creation of the Federal Oil Administration to be constitutional. In short, it gave the stamp of highest judicial approval to everything relating to the expropriation.

"In the exercise of the right of eminent domain, recognized and practiced in nearly all countries, the Mexican Government could justify the expropriation of these foreign-owned properties.

"The process, as usually applied, is that a government attempts to purchase the privately-owned property it desires to acquire. If the owner declines to sell at the price offered, even at a figure arrived at by a disinterested board of appraisal, the government files a condemnation suit in court, acquires the property by court order, and pays the ex-owner the appraised price.

"This has not been the procedure followed by the Mexican Government. It made no effort to buy the property. It merely seized it. The matter of payment—how much and when—remains exceedingly hazy and indefinite."

In carrying their legal battle up through the lower courts of Mexico to the Supreme Court, therefore, the oil companies were fighting not only their own battle, but the battle of all corporations throughout the world which happened to have investments in Mexico. Some of the obstacles which the American concerns faced in Mexico were revealed in the 1938 annual report of the

74

Standard Oil Company (N. J.). According to a resumé by the Boston *Transcript:*

"Since 1934 the Mexican Government has set the price at which gasoline shall be sold throughout the republic. At the same time the Labor Board has directed periodically that wages be raised still further. In one instance it ordered an increase which cost the firms more than their entire net earnings of the preceding year."

If the oil companies had agreed to the Labor Board's award which brought about confiscation, declares the President of the above company, workers in the oil fields would have been paid approximately three times the prevailing wage scale elsewhere in Mexico. And the head of the Sinclair oil interests in Mexico is quoted in the New York *Herald Tribune* as saying:

"We never had any labor difficulties in Mexico until the control of the workers became centered in a group of labor politicians who, with the backing of the Government, showed a determined purpose, not merely to secure better wages and working conditions, but to seize control of the oil properties, from production to refining and sale.

"We were not therefore faced with a mere question of bargaining as to terms of employment, but with a demand that we pay vastly more than the industry in Mexico earns, and with the certainty that at the same time all effective control of operations would pass from the hands of the owners and managers of the industry to irresponsible persons having no knowledge of any business, much less any specialized knowledge of the oil business.

"*Plans and instructions for taking over the oil properties were prepared by labor syndicate leaders and secretly circulated before the Supreme Court rendered its decision upholding the syndicate demands.*"

There is no doubt in the mind of the Louisville *Courier-Journal* that "the action of the Labor Board and the Supreme Court is arbitrary and illegal. The wage increases put an intolerable burden on the foreign concerns, and allowed no profit on their huge investments." Apparently the Labor Board award put a similar burden on the Government, for, reports Betty Kirk, in a Mexico City dispatch to *The Christian Science Monitor:*

"Labor, which waged the aggressive battle against the companies for increased wages and social benefits, has been the chief loser in the transfer of employers. Not only were wages not increased, as demanded, but many temporary workers have been laid off, overtime pay cancelled, and social benefits such as pension funds, medical service, and so forth, have been suspended."

In 1918, says a comprehensive article in *The Shell News* (New York), Mexico produced one-quarter of the total world output of oil; by 1937, it produced one-fortieth of the world output. We read on:

"During this period the Mexican Government entered the oil business, exempting itself from taxation and commandeering some of the very subsoil rights that it was so reluctant to confirm. Other actions nearly as direct were the encouragement of strikes and endless demands by syndicate or union leaders, many of which were absurd. Unjust awards of arbitration hamstrung the operations and added to the confusion. A total of 787 strikes were recorded during 1935 and 1936, of which 21 were decided by the Labor Department in favor of the companies.

"Arbitration had required the oil industry to pay 56 hours' wages for a 45-hour week. Working conditions were generally superior to those prevailing elsewhere in the country. Nevertheless, a list of nearly 600 demands were presented by the syndicates for wage advances and impractical and restrictive social benefit increases.

"On March 18, 1938, ignoring other procedure that should have followed according to law, the Mexican Government seized all properties and facilities of seventeen companies.

"Although President Cardenas announced by decree that the properties were 'expropriated,' the entire procedure was unreasonable and unjust to the extent that outright confiscation, rather than expropriation, was indicated. The requirements of international law that immediate payment in cash be made for full, fair value for the properties as a going concern, have not been met.

"This ill-considered action has brought dire consequences to those concerned. Field and refinery operations have been greatly curtailed, due to the inadequacy of technical direction in the syndicate-government combination devised to carry on the management. Many of the workers who blindly

76

supported the leaders of the movement have been laid off. Available work hours of others was reduced. Double pay for certain overtime and many social benefits formerly enjoyed were discontinued for those who remained. Paralysis of taxes, royalties, local business, and foreign trade has followed."

American oil executives charge President Cardenas with putting matters in a false light, too, in some of his other excuses for the seizure. As reported in a Washington dispatch of the *International News Service*:

"They accused Cardenas of misrepresentation, moreover, in declaring he took over the properties in accordance with the Mexican Constitution and to avoid a paralysis of the industry, threatened by the companies' asserted defiance of a Mexican Labor Board award.

"They contend no production stoppage was contemplated. They assert the companies had agreed to shoulder 26,000,000 pesos additional wages and services decreed, resisted only a demand that the management be surrendered to the unions, and contemplated supplying Mexican consumption by imports in event of a strike.

"The Mexican Constitution, they say, makes expropriation a judicial, not an executive process. This issue, they contend, the Mexican Supreme Court evaded by declining to pass upon the constitutionality of the seizures until the ministry of economy has acted finally thereon.

"As further evidence of the futility of discussing compensation, the oil interests cite Cardenas's declaration to the Mexican Congress that he will pay nothing for petroleum under the companies' lands. They declare the subsoil deposits comprise up to 90 per cent of the properties' value."

We are told in an article by Hartley W. Barclay, Editor of *Mill and Factory* (New York), that the Mexican Expropriation Law "hangs over the head of every business man in Mexico like the sword of Damocles." He continues:

"It is a constant threat to every classification of business, and may be put into effect in any case at any time as a big-stick to force companies to negotiate with CTM unions for new contracts, to force the payment of new and confiscatory taxes, and to force out employer opposition to 'liberalism.'

"The Mexican Expropriation Law provides that in instances in which industries are considered to involve grounds of public utility, and upon declaration by President Cardenas, the expropriation, the total or partial temporary occupations, or the mere curtailment of property rights in the interest of the state or the community shall proceed. Under this law, at the present time, almost half of the Mexican assets of American companies have been transferred to either the Mexican Government or to 'workers' co-operatives' sponsored by the Government and the CTM, the Confederation of Workers of Mexico.

"Back of the actions for promotion of class struggle is a new national conception of the status of property, according to government officials. Mexico's doctrine is officially enunciated in the following statement: 'Property constitutes no private or individual right at all, but is wholly a social function, and the office and duty of government is to regulate that function so as to favor the interests of at least the majority of the people.' *No one is absolute master of his property in Mexico today.*

"In describing their struggle against the employing class, the CTM uses the following characterization: 'The employing class of Mexico is divided into two groups—the national capitalist class, made up of Mexicans and foreigners settled in the country, and the aggregate of the emissaries of the great foreign trusts which have money invested in the republic. Imperialist capitalism controls the principal sources of the national wealth—mining, metallurgical plants, oil, the electrical industry, telephonic communications, a part of the railroads, and the most important branches of tropical agriculture'. The benefits these companies bring to the country reduce themselves, according to CTM doctrine, to the wages of their workers and the taxes paid the Government. No consideration is given to the social and economic contributions made by these companies in building better homes, railroads, paving streets, providing hospitalization, educating workers, supplying refined commodities for use in foreign trade, and other equally obvious and important benefits."

On numerous occasions, President Cardenas has stated his intention of paying for the confiscated oil properties. So far, however, remarks the Austin (Texas) *American*, "Mexico has failed to offer a definite formula of settlement." It is true that the Mexican President has made some suggestions. According to the

78

—*Reprinted from the Milwaukee Journal.*

New York *Daily News,* he has said that the only methods of payment he can consider are:

"Payment in oil from the expropriated properties.
"Payment in Mexican bonds—which (editor's note) are next to no good."

"That is Cardenas's story," continues *The Daily News.* "As we get it from other sources (including American oil company sources, for which fact we don't apologize), the Mexican situation is a good deal worse than that."

This New York daily, which feels that losses have occurred in the oil situation for which nothing can compensate, continues:

"We do not see how our State Department can agree to either kind of payment—or to any payment. Mexican pesos are bum currency; Mexican bonds are even worse. But payment in gold would not compensate for this attempt to seize petroleum properties developed by English and American capital, and resell the product to other countries.
"Some of those countries might be actual or potential enemies of the United States or Great Britain. Money is something you use to buy power; but oil *is* power in today's world —power to drive airplanes, power to drive battleships, power to keep the people of a whole nation enjoying standards of living far above those prevailing in countries which lack access to oil."

In the New York *Journal of Commerce,* President Cardenas is quoted as saying, in connection with the expropriation of American oil properties: "I will settle the question in justice and equity." In the opinion of the New York financial daily:

"This is an admirable statement of principle. However, its significance necessarily depends upon what constitutes justice and equity in the view of President Cardenas.
"From various statements of the Mexican President on the subject of the confiscated oil properties, we learn that the following are the elements he considers a necessary part of any just and equitable settlement:
"1. The oil companies must abandon all efforts to obtain diplomatic intervention by their own governments to safeguard their rights, and must place themselves under the exclusive protection of Mexican law.

80

"2. The Mexican Supreme Court, on various pretexts, has hitherto refused to rule upon the constitutionality of the expropriation decree. The record of the Mexican courts further shows that they consistently uphold the viewpoint of the Government.

"3. The oil companies must accept in return for their expropriated properties a valuation to be based upon actual investment, without any allowance whatever for the subsoil petroleum. It so happens that this petroleum represents about 90 per cent of the value of the confiscated properties, so that at one fell swoop the bulk of the property would be completely confiscated without payment, despite Mexican court decisions and international agreements to the contrary.

"4. There is no time limit within which any payment for these properties is to be made.

"5. The oil companies are to be given whatever compensation is finally allotted to them *only if they will themselves help Mexico export the oil taken from their confiscated properties.*

"On the basis of these conditions, it will be difficult indeed for the ordinary observer to grasp what President Cardenas really means when he proposes to settle the issue 'in justice and equity'. Clearly he does not use these terms in their ordinary or legalistic significance. To insist that foreigners in Mexico must waive the protection of their government, abandon the bulk of the value of their properties as established under past Mexican court decisions, wait indefinitely for payment, and then obtain whatever compensation they can only by helping to sell the oil that has been taken from them is, to say the least, to present a new standard of justice."

President Cardenas told the foreign newspaper correspondents in Mexico City in July, 1938, that Mexico was pledged to pay within ten years—in oil—for foreign oil properties expropriated on March 18th. The Mexican Government, he added, would fix the valuation. This promise, even if it were carried out, "would set a precedent of which other Latin American governments would immediately take advantage," oil company executives believe; also that it "would lead to a general program of expropriation of all American investments in the Western Hemisphere." Past experience with Mexico "is not of a sort to justify any hope for

81

adequate compensation," remarks the Cincinnati *Enquirer*, and the Dallas *News* is equally dubious. According to the Texas paper:

"The best argument that can be made for Mexico is the actual condition that confronts the Government of that country—its millions of illiterate, desperately poor citizens, whose social and economic status has remained practically unchanged for 400 years. Their salvation justifies revolutionary methods, but the revolution should be conducted honestly."

Another Texas daily, the Houston *Post*, asks us to remember that:

"Secretary Hull's note to Mexico, saying the taking of private property without provision for prompt and adequate payment is confiscation, raised a clear-cut issue. It was an implied acknowledgment of our Government's duty to demand immediate restitution of the properties, as the British and The Netherlands Governments have done.

"And if our Government's failure to take such action is due to the excuse offered by some in the State Department —that such a demand would mean the downfall of the Cardenas Administration and our Government's reluctance to make itself responsible for that—then the Government would seem to be more interested in sustaining Cardenas in power than in the protection of American citizens, and in the principles of international law upon which our civilization rests."

The impression has been spread in Mexico and elsewhere that the United States Government recognizes Mexico's right to expropriate the oil properties. It is true that the United States, has recognized a sovereign right to expropriate. *To expropriate means to take property for public use, upon prompt payment of fair, assured, and effective compensation.* But we have the word of Secretary of State Hull that *"the taking of property without compensation is not expropriation; it is confiscation."*

In the case of the oil properties, Mexico was not in a position legally to expropriate the oil properties. What it did, therefore, amounted to confiscation, although "expropriation" has been generally used to describe the promulgation of the Cardenas decree of March 18, 1938. "Expropriation—without payment" would be a better description. As J. H. Carmical points out in a New York *Times* article:

"The British Government already is on record to the effect that it will not resume diplomatic relations with Mexico until the oil properties of its citizens have been returned, plus recompense for any damage that might have been done since seizure. Such compensation would amount to a rather large sum, since several million barrels of crude oil have been taken from the properties in the last eleven months. In addition, refineries and other facilities have been operated by the Mexican Government, for which no compensation so far has been made.

"One of the reasons believed to be responsible for the delay in the settlement of the oil dispute has been the impression in Mexico that the United States had recognized the right of Mexico to take over the oil properties. It is true that the United States Government and the governments of other countries have recognized the sovereign right of a nation to expropriate any property within its borders for public purposes, but this right requires the payment of fair, assured, and effective compensation."

As a result of the expropriation of oil properties in Mexico, the "good neighbor" policy, remarks Bertram D. Hulen in the New York *Times*, "stands at the crossroads." President Cardenas, in the opinion of the Brooklyn *Eagle*, "will now have to make clear his real attitude toward the United States." In the present crisis, the *Eagle* is convinced, "the Roosevelt Administration has been patient almost to a fault." This lenient spirit, believes the Panama City *Star and Herald*, has been interpreted by Mexico as an indication of weakness. "It is unfortunate," remarks the Meriden (Conn.) *Record*, "that Mexico is unable to see how Canada and the United States have benefited mutually through friendly co-operation." The Mexican people and their Government may not realize it, observes the Houston (Texas) *Chronicle*, "but the 'good neighbor' policy has been of great advantage to them." This policy, explains the Duluth (Minn.) *Herald*, "is based on the principle that decency pays in international relations." But Mexico "is a black sheep in the international flock," asserts the *North Side News*, of New York. "She does not have an enviable record as a neighbor," agrees *The Christian Science Monitor*, of Boston. For, continues this widely read paper, "Mexico has accepted much and given little. Her financial dealings with her northern neighbors will hardly bear close examination. Her credit, when critically analyzed, is not of the best."

In these circumstances, "there are good reasons why Mexico should want to remain on good terms with the United States," concludes the Joplin (Mo.) *Globe*. In the opinion of the Hartford (Conn.) *Times*, "American co-operation is little short of an utter necessity." The Dayton (O.) *Journal* goes even further when it says: "It is almost axiomatic that any Mexican administration must have the support of the United States." Maintenance of mutual good feeling and understanding is important to the United States, admits the New Orleans *Times-Picayune*. But, it maintains, "it is more important to Mexico." Particularly, as Ernest K. Lindley remarks in one of his Washington dispatches, "during the present, when economic and ideological thrusts into Latin America are being made by non-American dictator nations." In fact, believes the San Diego (Calif.) *Tribune, if the "good neighbor" policy and the Monroe Doctrine did not exist, "Great Britain almost certainly would, long before now, have taken punitive action to protect her oil interests in Mexico."*

From its advantageous position at the nation's capital, the Washington *Star* advises Mexico to remember that "the 'good neighbor' policy is not a hollow rhetorical expression." To a South American paper, *La Esfera*, of Caracas, Venezuela, "the 'good neighbor' policy demands equal rights for Americans in our countries in the same degree that the United States concedes them to our nationals." Mexico is rich in resources, admits Frank L. Perrin, in another *Christian Science Monitor* article, "but these are not especially valuable until they are shared with those who need or enjoy them enough to pay for them."

The United States needs the friendship of Central and South American republics, reiterates the St. Louis *Star-Times*, "but we can maintain that friendship only on the basis of mutual respect." "If the 'good neighbor' policy is to be a success, the nations that make up the Western Hemisphere must deal honestly and fairly with each other," declares the Bristol (Va.) *Herald Courier*. "The whole structure of friendly intercourse between nations rests upon a foundation of respect for the rights of others," maintains the Boston *Globe*. "Neither the 'good neighbor' policy nor international law would have a leg to stand on if all nations followed the example of Mexico in seizing property belonging to the nationals of other countries," points out the Philadelphia *Inquirer*.

Recent Department of Commerce figures showing a large drop in the value of United States investments in Mexico over a period of ten years were accompanied by the observation that "economic and political influences" were partly responsible. This leads a Massachusetts daily, the Southbridge *News,* to cite these facts:

"The production of United States auto-plants in Mexico has fallen fast toward zero, the remaining foreign-managed railroads are finding extreme difficulties even in meeting their payrolls, and the Pan American Airways subsidiary, operating throughout Mexico, is unable to meet replacement costs so important to the aviation business."

It seems evident to the Jersey City *Journal* that Mexico is determined to purge the country of American ownership of oil, farm land, and industrial holdings. "Where will it end?" asks the New Jersey paper. "Only the Mexican Government knows." The Nashville *Tennessean* is willing to hazard the guess that "henceforth Mexico is out of the picture, so far as foreign investors are concerned." Naturally, papers in states on the Mexican border are keenly interested. In the opinion of the Silver City *Press*, in southern New Mexico:

"The question is wider than the present diplomatic controversy, and has application to all Latin America. Indeed, its implications are world-wide. *A country that cannot export its capital is as badly off as a country that cannot export its other surplus commodities.* The result is stagnation of industry and unemployment."

A similar broad view is taken by the Long Beach *Sun,* in California, which observes that the situation "not only is threatening the 'good neighbor' policy and the friendly relations between the United States and Mexico, but it looms as an obstacle to this

85

country's economic program for enlarging the Latin American markets." In the same city *The Press-Telegram*, after commenting on the broad international phases of the problem, remarks that the lesser activities revolving about the expropriation of the once-famous Agua Caliente properties are equally baffling:

"First, the Mexican Government seized the palatial Agua Caliente property and announced that it would be turned into a Mexican training school. The race track, however, was leased to an American, who operated it for two seasons. Now comes word from Tiajuana that the track has been sold to an American syndicate. The procedure of expropriating a piece of American-owned property, then reselling a part of it to another American syndicate is extraordinary, to say the least."

Many newspapers in the United States are moved by circumstantial reports from Mexico of financial embarrassments and economic depression. "Mexico is in a bad way," notes the Boston *Herald*. It is all very well for President Cardenas to make optimistic and patriotic speeches, "but defiant words will not solve the troublesome economic problems confronting the country," remarks the Houston (Texas) *Post*. The people of Mexico, as the New York *Daily News* phrases it, "are twirling down the vicious spiral of depression which we came to know so much about in 1929-1933." The St. Louis *Globe-Democrat* sees Mexico "in the throes of one of the worst economic depressions in its history," while the San Francisco *Chronicle* beholds her "in a state of dire economic need." Such characterizations might be repeated almost indefinitely.

Although the present crisis in the peso was precipitated by the seizure of the oil properties, "its underlying causes go deeper," explains the New York *Times*. They include:

"The Government's program of public works, which has necessitated large imports of special materials and equipment; the labor program, which has resulted in higher costs; droughts and the failure of the agricultural program to bring about increased or more efficient production, which have made necessary increased imports of food, and, finally, the flight of capital induced by the program of expropriation of land and other measures hostile to capital."

A similar review is made by the New York *Herald Tribune*:

"The economic and financial difficulties of Mexico started long before March 18, 1938—date of the seizure of the foreign oil companies—but it was then that the situation attracted attention abroad. The depression's roots go back at least to 1935, the result largely of a series of crop failures, strikes, increased labor costs, and skyrocketing rises in the costs of essential commodities.

"Long before March 18th, the Bank of Mexico's weekly reports showed how its gold and silver reserves were being eaten up to keep the peso pegged at 3.60 (3 pesos and 60 centavos) to the dollar. Upon expropriating the oil companies, the Government itself cut the peso loose from its fixed rate, and left it to find its own level. The dollar is now about five pesos."

Mexico's financial position borders on bankruptcy, declares the Omaha *World-Herald*:

"According to figures presented in *Collier's* by George Creel, Mexico had a recognized foreign debt of $510,000,000 at the end of 1936; has an internal debt of more than $35,000,000; a national railway debt near $466,000,000; faces claims of $450,000,000 expropriation damages by 17 oil companies; agrarian claims of $125,000,000 to $250,000,000; and additional millions owed to the United States and Great Britain for damages awarded by special claims commissions. *Balance those figures with Mexico's meager national income of $122,000,000 in 1937—and the expenditure of nearly all of that without payment of a debt.*"

With affairs in such a condition, President Cardenas's expropriation policy seems to dozens of our papers to be simply "killing the goose that lays the golden egg." It means, writes General Hugh S. Johnson in his syndicated column, "complete collapse of the present economic and political internal Mexican structure." What bothers the Cardenas Government most, remarks the Portland *Oregonian*, "is that the very act which was expected to bring prosperity has brought depression instead." As the Colorado Springs (Colo.) *Gazette* notes, "confiscations have meant loss of revenue, declining economic strength, unemployment, decreased pay, increased debt." To the Minneapolis *Journal*, "a singular feature of the seizure is that Mexico is working herself financial injury. For the taxes and royalties which the American, British, and Dutch oil companies paid the Mexican Government were a big factor in keeping Mexican exchange stabilized."

"Mexico has cut off a large proportion of her income, with no immediate prospect of replacing it," explains the Baltimore *Sun*. The properties of foreign oil companies, the San Diego (Calif.) *Union* understands, "had been virtually sustaining a large part of the population in the drilling region for many years." In a Mexico City dispatch to the New York *Times*, it is estimated that "direct and indirect taxes accruing to the Mexican Government from its natural resource industries account for almost 60 per cent of tax receipts of the country."

In Mexico, the newspaper *El Mundo*, of Tampico, has this to say of the recent rise in living costs:

"As a consequence of the increased cost of living estimated at an average of 30 per cent in relation to prices during the first months of the year 1938, the majority of the inhabitants of Mexico have cut down their expenses to the most indispensable needs, so that the greatest number are able only to provide food for themselves and their families and have to dispense with new clothes and shoes, prolonging to an impossible point the life of their old clothing.

"This rise is due mainly to the decline, greater day by day, of national production; to high freight rates and tariffs for the handling of merchandise because of higher wages; to heavy taxes that are necessary to support a bureaucracy that grows more numerous every day; to the fall of our currency, and to strikes and conflicts which have increased so tremendously in the last three years."

"The misery being endured by the Mexican people as a result of this situation is well-nigh desperate and tragic," reports *El Telegrafo*, of Guayaquil, Ecuador.

Many observers anticipate a civil war in Mexico. The Houston *Chronicle*, in the border State of Texas, makes this observation: "When the loss of revenue, due to seizure of the oil properties, is added to the previously existing causes of unrest, the danger of an uprising by dissatisfied elements is magnified." The Car-

Pig in a Poke

—*Reprinted from the Providence Bulletin.*

denas Government, notes the neighboring *Post*, "has bogged down in a morass of financial and economic difficulties," and the present difficulties, "are precisely of the kind which have led to revolutions in Mexico in the past."

President Cardenas has damaged several once-profitable Mexican businesses—oil, cotton, mining, railroads—by his expropriation policy. And now that program has acted indirectly to reduce drastically the nation's once lucrative tourist trade. The Cincinnati *Enquirer* reports this trade "dropping off rapidly as disorders and threats of worse disorders discourage visitors." In fact, declares the Council Bluffs (Ia.) *Nonpareil, "citizens of the United States are no longer popular in Mexico. The country is not safe for American tourists."* There was a time, writes C. William Duncan in the Philadelphia *Evening Public Ledger,* "when Mexico depended heavily on our tourist trade, and a fine business was built up. But this has been hurt badly, as a result of the Mexican Government's expropriation of oil properties, and tourists are staying away." And we read in the Houston (Texas) *Post* that:

"Thousands of Americans who formerly spent their vacations in Mexico decided this year to see their own country. Confiscation of American oil and agricultural lands; and reappearance of an attitude of hostility toward Americans, prevented many tourists from returning to the pleasant land to the south. They decided it would be wiser to spend their money at home, in a more friendly atmosphere."

About this situation some pertinent statistics are in order. According to the Pasadena (Calif.) *Star-News,* "ninety-eight per cent of Mexico's tourists are from the United States." The Pensacola (Fla.) *News* reports that the expenditures of 122,466 classified American tourists amounted to $18,105,000 in 1937.

But when anti-United States feeling grew after northern protests against the expropriations of agrarian lands and oil properties, a radical change was to be seen. Reports from the American Automobile Association representatives at Laredo, Texas, we read in the Madison *Wisconsin State Journal,* showed that for the first eight months of 1938, "only 16,474 cars crossed the border into Mexico for touring purposes, as compared with 21,467 cars during the corresponding period in 1937, a decrease of more than twenty-three per cent."

Such leading papers as the Chicago *Tribune*, Rochester (N. Y.) *Democrat and Chronicle*, and Philadelphia *Evening Public Ledger* agree with the Tulsa (Okla.) *World* when it utters this warning against Mexican vacations:

"Without any violent desire to go to Mexico, and without any control upon individual readers, we suggest that going to Mexico is a matter for thought. Maybe the 'Mex' will expropriate automobiles.

"Until the Mexican Government formally backs down from its seizure of United States property, we are not going to advocate any tourist invasion of Mexico."

Mexico has suffered greatly from loss of revenue since the oil-expropriation order was issued, reports a California paper, the Anaheim *Bulletin*. Wells were shut down; markets lost; storage tanks filled with crude oil that could not be moved because the Government had no tankers. A week after the Cardenas decree went into effect, the St. Louis *Globe-Democrat* observed:

"The oil industry is paralyzed. The foreign market holds no hope for immediate activity even though normal production is resumed. Oil workers face decreased wages instead of increased pay.

"Mexican trade is in a stalemate. Foreign business men are taking huge losses as the banks suspend dealings in foreign exchange. The peso has dropped, and will doubtless go lower. Deflation of the peso will hit especially hard installment houses dealing in automobiles, radios, refrigerators, and tires. To bolster the faltering peso the Government has issued paper money which may be exchanged for minted silver, but Mexico has had memorable difficulties with such currency and a test of Cardenas's strength may well come if he puts the nation on a 'paper' basis.

"Food prices increased up to twenty per cent over the week end. Hoarding has already started."

Additional facts were set forth in a later editorial:

"The Mexican President's expropriation policy has deprived his Government of millions of dollars in taxes from mines and oil fields, and has not provided increased employment or higher wages for labor, as he promised. Because of the uncertainty of the economic situation, commodity prices are going up—and wages are not keeping step. Such barter arrangements as it has made to dispose of expropriated oil, add little or nothing to the national exchequer.

"In short, Mexico faces an economic crisis which President Cardenas deliberately augments by his blind devotion to the flamboyant ideals of his socialization program. The United States has long been sympathetic with Mexico. It still is. We have tried to play the part of a 'good neighbor', but Cardenas prefers to rebuff good intentions. He has displayed a haughty attitude at a time when he might well make good use of American friendship. In so doing he has threatened the stability of his own Administration."

"It looks as if expropriation has not solved the Mexican workers' problems, and it may have made them worse," reflects the Des Moines *Register*. And a number of our editorial observers seem to have reached the same conclusion, judging from remarks made by the Buffalo *News*, Cincinnati *Enquirer*, Louisville *Courier-Journal*, Springfield (Mass.) *Union*, Bridgeport (Conn.) *Post*, Norfolk (Va.) *Ledger-Dispatch*, and Augusta (Ga.) *Chronicle*. "The workers, for whose sake the Government ostensibly closed in upon the British, Dutch, and American oil companies and prostrated the industry, have been betrayed," declares the Tulsa (Okla.) *World*. "The workers expected to own the companies, and now they find that the Government 'owns' them," remarks the Youngstown (O.) *Vindicator*. This last statement is made a little clearer by a paragraph from a Mexico City dispatch to *The Christian Science Monitor:*

"They find they cannot wrest from government managers the same rights they wanted from the foreign companies. In their demands to the latter, they could always turn to the Government for help, but now that the Government itself is managing the petroleum industry, they must abide by its rulings whether they like them or not."

The Mexican oil workers have been receiving a series of jolts, the Paterson (N. J.) *News* observed soon after the Cardenas decree went into effect:

"Not only has the Mexican Government been unable to pay the increases in wages which had been ordered by the Mexican Supreme Court, but it has actually been obliged to cut the prevailing wages paid by the American companies and to lay off a large number of oil workers.

"Their first jolt came when they were told by the Government that they would have to continue working 44 hours a week, instead of a 40-hour week which had already been granted by the oil companies. Their next jolt came when the Government raised the cost of food and supplies needed by the workers in all of the oil fields. The third came in a series of lay-offs."

But what is "most grinding the Mexican patriots in the oil fields," the Wichita (Kan.) *Eagle* learns, "is the appearance of class distinctions." According to *The Eagle:*

"The labor leaders have appropriated the clubs once maintained by the private companies and can wine, dine, and lounge there. The common laborer is not permitted within these sacred precincts. The leaders also ride around in company cars—which were confiscated.

"Free speech is gone, of course. If a common laborer criticises his superiors, his membership in the union is cancelled, and without it he is out a job."

And Henry J. Allen, in his Topeka (Kan.) *State Journal,* reports older and more thoughtful oil workers as feeling that "they would be safer as employes of the oil companies than they will be as employes of the Mexican Government, with all the uncertainties of political administration."

So what have "the grandiose Socialistic schemes of Cardenas actually accomplishd for the little fellow?" After putting the question, the Syracuse (N. Y.) *Post-Standard* answers it:

"They have increased the little fellow's cost of living and decreased the amount of work available for him. He is worse off than he was before. It is the inevitable result of Socialistic dreams."

This being the case, the Saginaw (Mich.) *News* wonders if Cardenas "will turn back before it is too late, or if he will persist in a course that is bound to lead to economic ruin." Well, concludes the Hartford (Conn.) *Courant*, "let the sentiment grow among the workers that they are worse off now than ever before, and the Government, despite the cheers that it received for its policy of 'Mexico for the Mexicans', may be obliged to readjust its policies."

IV

MEXICO'S BREAK WITH GREAT BRITAIN

Great Britain's Note to Mexico—Mexico's Reply—Stand of The Netherlands Government—Principles of the Oil Companies—Effect of Expropriation on United States Exports—On the Monroe Doctrine—Our Duty to Great Britain—International Law—Expropriation Without Compensation Spreading—The Danger to World Trade.

Great Britain's first note to the Mexican Government was written three days after the oil properties of the Mexican Eagle Oil Company, in which British investors are largely interested, were expropriated by promulgation of the Cardenas decree of March, 1938. Three weeks later—three weeks of silence on the part of the Mexican Government—the British Minister at Mexico City delivered another document to Mexico's Foreign Secretary. This note said, in part:

"The British Government do not question the general right of a government to expropriate in the public interest and on payment of adequate compensation; but, this principle does not serve to justify expropriations essentially arbitrary in character. In the present case, expropriation was the culminating point in a series of events, and the question of its validity cannot be separated from these.

"The Mexican Eagle Company were, as a result of various proceedings in law, confronted with an award rendered by the Labor Board and confirmed by the Supreme Court, which was not, in the view of His Majesty's Government, justified on the facts.

"Passing from the award and its confirmation by the Supreme Court to the decree of expropriation, His Majesty's Government find that one injustice becomes the basis for others.

"His Majesty's Government are fully satisfied that the conditions following from non-compliance with the award were not such as have warranted the adoption of such a drastic and far-reaching measure as expropriation. . . .

95

"In the face of considerations such as those set forth above, His Majesty's Government find difficulty in escaping the conclusions that the real motive for the expropriation was a political desire to acquire for Mexico, in permanence, the advantages of ownership and control of the oil fields; that expropriation was tantamount to confiscation, carried out under a veil of legality formed by basing it upon labor issues; and that the consequences have been a denial of justice and a transgression by the Mexican Government of the principles of international law.

"His Majesty's Government see no way in which this situation can be remedied but by the restoration of its properties to the Company itself."

To this note, Mexico replied that the Government considered both the Labor Board award and the judgment in question to be in strict conformity with the laws of the Republic of Mexico. And it added: "The firm determination to pay for the properties expropriated has been declared before the entire world, and the republic's capacity to pay is a real and certain fact." Mexico also reminded Great Britain that the company in question is a Mexican legal entity, and therefore the British Government was precluded from intervening on its behalf. To which the British Government replied on April 21, 1938:

"His Majesty's Government are not intervening on behalf of the Mexican Eagle Company, but on behalf of the very large majority of shareholders who are of British nationality. They are perfectly well aware of the Mexican nationality of the Mexican Eagle Company itself, in the sense that it is incorporated under Mexican law, and in no way seek to deny this.

"But the fact remains that the majority of shareholders who are the ultimate sufferers from the action of the Mexican Government are British, and the undertaking in question is essentially a British interest. For this reason alone His Majesty's Government have the right, which cannot be affected by anything in the Mexican Constitution, to protest against an action which they regard as unjustified, and to request the restitution as being the only practical means of avoiding serious injury to extensive British interests.

"If the doctrine were admitted that a government can first make the operation of foreign interests in its territories depend upon their incorporation under local law, and then plead such incorporation as the justification for rejecting foreign diplomatic intervention, it is clear that the means would never be wanting whereby foreign governments could be prevented from exercising their undoubted right under international law to protect the commercial interests of their nationals abroad.

"His Majesty's Government cannot admit such a doctrine as debarring them from intervention."

The Netherlands Government took an attitude identical to that of Great Britain, in respect to the expropriated oil properties of her nationals. In a note to the Mexican Government, The Netherlands Government said the expropriation of Dutch oil properties in Mexico, and the points of view stated by Mexico's Foreign Secretary, were matters of "grave concern." Moreover, it maintained, the expropriations were in violation of the fundamental rules of fair dealing between governments, and in a brief note it demanded that the oil properties be returned to their Dutch owners.

Great Britain also questioned Mexico's ability to pay in a note dated May 11th, and declared in no uncertain terms that Mexico therefore was not justified in carrying out its expropriation program:

"According to the best information, Mexico's public external debt (excluding all foreign claims not represented by Mexican Government securities) amounts to $243,000,000 of principal and $267,000,000 of accrued interest to which must be added about $240,000,000 principal and $226,000,000 interest in respect to foreign debt dependent on railways, for which the Mexican Government assumed responsibility when they expropriated them on June 24, 1937. A substantial proportion of this debt is held by British subjects, who in the last quarter of a century have received no interest in twenty of these years, and only part of the interest due in respect of five of them. There are also outstanding against the Mexican Government claims amounting to approximately $45,000,000.

"In addition to the internal debt, the Mexican Government have assumed very extensive internal obligations, . . . and have expropriated the properties of seventeen oil companies.

Mexican "Seeing Eye"

—*Reprinted from the Newark, N. J., News.*

According to their own statement, they consider themselves to have incurred an additional financial liability.

"His Majesty's Government cannot but regard the failure of the Mexican Government to discharge even their existing obligations as in itself rendering unjustified an expropriation, an essential condition of the validity of which would be the payment of full and adequate compensation, amounting, in this case, to a very large sum."

But the roar of the British lion had no effect, so far as could be seen, upon the Mexican Government. The Cardenas Administration was sufficiently nettled by Great Britain's sharp words, however, to suspend diplomatic relations and to recall its Minister from London. Great Britain thereupon withdrew her Minister from Mexico City, pending a disposition of her protest, and placed a ban on the purchase of Mexican oil throughout the Empire.

The suspension of diplomatic relations between Mexico and Great Britain over the expropriation of British oil properties in Mexico, and the refusal of the Mexican Government either to return them or to pay for them in cash, intensified, so far as the United States was concerned, an already bad situation. The use of force by Great Britain, while it might have been justified, would mean the occupation of non-British territory in the Western Hemisphere, i. e., Mexico. And the United States, bound as it is by the Monroe Doctrine, could not tolerate that. *Yet that same Doctrine required the United States to represent and protect British interests.*

"In suspending diplomatic relations with Great Britain, Mexico acted indiscreetly, if not rashly," thinks the Springfield (Mass.) *Republican.* What was the motive? In the opinion of the Hartford (Conn.) *Courant,* "the break may be explained, in part, by the disclosure that the Cardenas régime was faced with a revolt from within. Confronted by a threatened domestic uprising, President Cardenas apparently resorted to the familiar tactics of seeking to head it off by creating a foreign diversion." "His defiance of Great Britain," notes the Boston *Herald,* "helped to rally the Mexican people behind him." "Moreover, recalls the New York *Sun:* "When American oil properties were seized,

99

President Roosevelt and Secretary Hull showed no great interest or resentment. If the 'Colossus of the North' had become so amiable, why should not the British lion's tail be twisted?"

However, "Mexico has not helped herself by this hasty action," thinks the Los Angeles *Times*. Her motive is clear to the Washington *Star:* "Unable to pay claims for damages inflicted upon British citizens during various uprisings, and in addition the amount due on the expropriated oil properties, Mexico has taken the easiest—and least honorable—way out."

In judging the respective attitudes of the United States and Great Britain in the Mexican crisis over expropriation, it is necessary to take into consideration two different points of view.

The United States is bound by President Roosevelt's "good neighbor" policy, which precludes any use, or even threat, of force in a Latin American situation. President Cardenas, according to Baroness Adda von Bruemmer-Bozeman, writing in the Dallas (Texas) *Dispatch*, "must have reckoned with a comparatively lenient attitude of the American Government. This feeling was probably intensified by what the Mexican Government thought to be one of the principal aims of the Roosevelt New Deal policy—a curtailment of the powers of big business."

But Britain had no such policy to handicap her diplomacy, notes the Atlanta *Constitution*. In this Georgia paper's opinion:

"Great Britain is not primarily concerned over possible commercial losses of her citizens, although she is historically famous for protecting her nationals' rights in all parts of the world.

"What Downing Street is primarily concerned over is the possible importance of those Mexican oil fields in event of any war involving the British Empire. She visualizes a situation where, with other sources of supply (such as Roumania, the Near East, or the Dutch East Indies) blocked, the oil wells in Mexico might become an Empire life-line of supply of the essential commodity.

"Britain, too, has other tremendous investments and interests in raw material supplies all through South America. She sees, in the Mexican seizure, a possible precedent imperiling her interests in other countries on this side of the South Atlantic."

"England," points out the St. Louis *Globe-Democrat,* "has no territorial desires in Mexico; she is not an aggressor nation. On the other hand, she has valid claims for damages, and she is not the nation to allow herself to be pushed around indefinitely." In a New York *Times* article, J. H. Carmical tells us more about British interests in Mexico:

"For about a hundred years British capital and technique have been an important factor in the development of the resources of Mexico. A large part of these investments was made when the United States was seeking capital abroad for the development of her own resources, and had not yet become an investor in foreign enterprises.

"Partly in recognition of what British interests had accomplished in Mexico, President Porfirio Diaz, soon after the opening of the twentieth century, invited Lord Cowdray to undertake the development of Mexican oil resources. Millions of pounds were invested. It was not until about 1913 that they found sufficient oil to justify huge exploitation expenditures.

"The firmness of Great Britain in her dealings with the Mexican Government with respect to the seized oil properties of British subjects is due largely to a desire to keep inviolate the time-honored principles of international commerce, and to the necessity of maintaining adequate oil supplies for her navy, both of which are absolutely essential to the well-being of the British people.

"With no oil production in the British Isles, and with her citizens dependent almost entirely upon international trade for a livelihood, Great Britain can hardly afford to abandon any basic principle of foreign commerce which would lessen the respect for property rights, for this would mean a severe loss of prestige and might seriously endanger her vast foreign investments, which are sizable in virtually every country.

"For these reasons the position of Great Britain in the controversy over the foreign-owned oil properties seized by the Mexican Government is slightly different from that of the United States."

To a newspaper in the Oklahoma oil country, the Tulsa *World:*

"The crisis in the diplomatic relations of Great Britain and Mexico is an illustration of the potency of oil in international affairs. It is evident that, as the world is now organized, no

101

war can be fought anywhere without oil supplies. The oil supply is a mighty consideration with nations disposed to war, fearing war, or absolutely peaceable in intent.

"Mexico, having taken over the foreign oil holdings, must have a wide market. Great Britain sees potential enemies getting vital supplies; her civil commerce is also greatly affected. The British 'stake' in Mexico has long been very great. The rebellion of Mexico against the foremost European Power is most significant. It can have very serious consequences."

The reaction among American newspapers to the break between Britain and Mexico is that a suspension of diplomatic relations, rather than a rupture, has resulted, since neither country requested the withdrawal of credentials. The majority of American newspapers seem to sympathize with Great Britain in the emergency. To the Minneapolis *Tribune*, Mexico's "gesture of defiance is that of a distracted Government indulging in theatrics for the benefit of the home audience because it can think of no better way out of its impasse." As for our own diplomatic exchanges with Mexico over the country's expropriation of farm lands and oil properties, as compared with Great Britain's, the Hartford (Conn.) *Courant* explains:

"The United States has formally granted that Mexico has the legal right to expropriate foreign holdings, and has shifted the issue to the question of proper compensation.

"The British Foreign Office, on the other hand, insists that Mexico had no legal right to take over the properties as it did. Not only is it on legalistically weak ground in making such a declaration, but it apparently committed a grave error in diplomatic strategy, leaving neither itself nor Mexico room for retreat. The Foreign Office cannot use force or the threat of force to carry out its demand for the return of the properties without encountering effective opposition from the United States."

The principles to which the oil companies themselves have steadfastly adhered are given by the New York *Journal of Commerce:*

"1. That they are entitled to the protection of their property rights under international, rather than Mexican law.

"2. That they should receive, in accordance with established precedents of international law, reasonable compensation for their property, without undue delay.

"3. That compensation must be paid in cash, not confiscated oil.

"4. That, because of the patent inability of Mexico to pay such compensation, a settlement should be negotiated on the basis of a return of the properties to their owners.

"5. That, once the properties are returned, the companies will make every effort to settle outstanding differences with the Mexican Government.

"If the oil companies do not stand firm in their insistence upon these reasonable principles, then an unhealthy precedent will be established that will militate against our economic interests throughout Latin America. Other governments may feel encouraged to expropriate American property—and negotiate compromise settlements thereafter."

The suspension of diplomatic relations with the British Government was a more serious development than Mexico could have anticipated. It means, among other things, the loss of British trade, amounting to upwards of $70,000,000 a year. On the other hand, the loss of Mexican trade to the British, notes the Albany (N. Y.) *Knickerbocker News,* "is trifling by comparison."

According to *The Lamp,* published by the Standard Oil Company (N. J.), the oil expropriation decree "paralyzed an industry that paid the highest wages in Mexico, gave its workers an improved standard of living; and that in taxes, royalties, employment, social benefits, and stimulation of foreign trade and local business, created a new fountain of national wealth and current income." "Coming at a time when Mexico's financial and economic conditions were at a critical stage," observes the Louisville *Courier-Journal,* "the British boycott on Mexican imports became a most effective weapon." Continues the Kentucky paper:

"As these imports amount annually to twice as much as the American nation buys from Great Britain, the break in diplomatic relations may prove as costly to Mexico as the expropriation of the foreign-owned oil properties.

"President Cardenas has united a large part of his country behind him by his dramatic break with Great Britain—and this no doubt was the object of his spectacular diplomacy—

but he has weakened his position, if he has not made it untenable."

"Unless we are much mistaken," remarks the Chicago *Daily News:*

"All this will end badly for Mexico. It is at best a relatively poor country, which must export its raw materials in order to get the manufactured goods it needs. For its continued development, it must have foreign capital. What chance is there that foreigners will again risk their savings in Mexico after this present act of brazen confiscation?

"The two chief victims of Cardenas's great grab are Great Britain and the United States. In a world racked by Fascist aggressions, to whom would Cardenas look now for support? To Italy, Germany, and Japan? They have not enough capital for themselves, let alone Mexico. To Russia? Between Germany and Japan, it has its hands full.

"In short, Mexico could hardly have chosen a worse time to pick a quarrel with its American and British friends."

"If Mexico is determined to ignore what other nations consider to be their rights, she will have to accept the consequences—the avoidance of Mexico by foreign capital and business enterprises, which that country now needs more than ever before," declares the Savannah (Ga.) *News.*

From the beginning it was realized by American newspaper publishers and their correspondents in Mexico that the Cardenas Administration would pay heavily for its hasty action in taking over the British, Dutch and American oil properties; also that the wells and refineries would deteriorate for lack of competent engineers and mechanics. As the Wilmington (Del.) *News* remarked a few days after the Cardenas decree went into effect: "Mexico lacks the money, the organizing genius, the trained technicians to develop its wealth of natural resources. Judging by the conditions of its nationalized railroads, the Government's administration of the oil fields will be on a highly inefficient plane."

Among the immediate results of the Mexican Government's expropriation of the foreign oil properties, the Houston *Chronicle* reported the virtual revolt of part of the very workers concerned

Internal Strife

—*Reprinted from the Houston, Texas, Chronicle.*

with this industry. "Rioting and fighting are said to be due to the failure of the workers to receive their pay. Part-time workers are losing their jobs, whereas they had been led to expect higher wages and a voice in the control of the industry." This Texas daily made a prediction at the time that:

"A nationalized Mexican oil industry is likely to prove a drain on the Treasury, instead of an asset. This is so because Mexicans lack experience in operating the properties and selling the product. The Mexican Government is not likely to be able to market its product as efficiently as are the well-organized foreign firms with world-wide connections. And the powerful labor unions will be in position to make such exactions from the industry as to render profitable operation impossible."

Still another problem was listed by the Cincinnati *Times-Star*: "To operate great enterprises such as the Mexican Government has seized, requires both skill and capital. Mexico has neither." As the San Francisco *Chronicle* saw the situation:

"The Mexican Government has bitten off quite a mouthful. Mexico lacks a number of facilities and qualifications possessed by the former British, Dutch, and American owners. Mexico has had no experience in the oil business.

"Mexico is totally without a selling organization to handle her oil abroad. Such an organization can be built, but the state of Mexican finance and certain commitments she has made seem to demand cash returns at once for the oil."

Or, to quote the Louisville *Courier-Journal*:

"The nation is not prepared to enter the industrial field; it is still a backward country. Even if it were able to operate the oil properties efficiently, it is unable to sell the product; it is lacking in both markets and ships."

The Mexican policy in regard to oil has had three general effects which must be kept in mind in evaluating the significance of events since March, 1938. They are:

1. Closing the door in the face of Mexico's best friends and customers, the United States and Great Britain.

2. General trade dislocation.

3. Opening of new sources of supply to totalitarian Powers, with which a Leftist Administration, such as that of General Cardenas, would seem to have little in common.

In recent years political and economic relations between the United States and Mexico have steadily deteriorated. This is apparent not only in the high-handed manner in which the oil properties were expropriated, but in the imposition, more than a year ago, of prohibitive tariffs on goods from the United States.

Besides the oil and land expropriations, other Mexican moves against commerce with the United States and the United States program for removing trade barriers are listed by the New York *Times* as follows:

"Establishment of prohibitive import duties, the fall in the value of the peso, the cutting of imports for which cash payment is required, and the establishment of export duties, affecting chiefly the mining and banana industries, which are still largely United States-controlled."

A year ago last January the Mexican Government announced a list of tariff increases, in certain cases as much as 200 per cent, amounting in many cases, according to the New York *Herald Tribune*, "virtually to an embargo against goods entering from the United States." In May there were slight reductions from these rates. Then in August import duties on a long list of products, chiefly raw materials, were reduced, while those on automobiles, buses, and certain other manufactured products were put back on the January level or higher.

During the months that followed expropriation of the oil properties, United States exports to Mexico shrank from $10,000,000 in July, 1937, to less than $3,000,000. Last October, United States sales to Mexico were running about 30 per cent below last year.

In October it was learned that the Mexican tariff rate on rayon yarn had been raised by 680 per cent. In 1937 about 43 per cent of Mexico's imports of rayon came from the United States. According to a New York *Times* Mexico City dispatch, "the new tariff is expected to eliminate all except Italy from this business."

These tariff plans, the Washington *Post* regrets to note, fly rudely in the face of the friendly trade relations between the

United States and Mexico; "far from encouraging co-operation between the two countries, increased trade barriers will tend to drive them apart."

Criticism of the Mexican Government's import and export taxation policy "does not all come from the outside," the Houston (Texas) *Chronicle* discovers, for "the National Chamber of Commerce of Mexico City, in a circular sent to its members, contends that imports will diminish; that prices will advance and leave the Government with but small revenue in relation to the damage which will be done to the principal sources of production."

Even more important to Mexico itself than the indignation abroad over expropriation, is the serious food shortage, which, at least in part, stems from the same source. The Government, reports Jack Starr-Hunt in a Mexico City dispatch to the New York *Herald Tribune*, is marshaling all its forces to solve this most serious problem. "Corn," he writes, "is being imported from the United States."

The mention of corn is significant, for corn, the Minneapolis *Journal* reminds us, "means more to Mexico than to any other country in the world." In fact:

> "Corn is more important, perhaps, than corn, wheat, and hay combined to the United States. It occupies two-thirds of the crop land, and supplies more than one-half of the people's food."

This necessity for importing food is "putting more strain on Mexico," adds Frank L. Kluckhohn in the New York *Times,* and the St. Louis *Globe-Democrat* reminds us that:

> "Since Mexico is not self-sustaining in food crops, the wisdom of President Cardenas may be doubted when he arbitrarily cuts off the Treasury's largest source of revenue—the oil industry. His grandiose scheme of nationalization may possess elementary popular appeal to a people which can know nothing about economics, but in its practical workings it appears to be heading Mexico merely toward economic chaos, the concomitant of which is social upheaval."

But even more interesting and pertinent are the reactions of the Mexican press to this vital subject. Says *La Prensa,* of Mexico City:

"Prices of articles of prime necessity increased from January to September, 1938, and the working and middle classes are seriously affected. Prices have increased in the following proportion in the period named: Choice meats, 55 per cent; second-class meat, 100 per cent; third-class meat, this being the class generally used by the public, 150 per cent; red beans, 71 per cent; black beans, 50 per cent; first-class rice, 66 per cent; sugar, 37 per cent; milk, 75 per cent; lard, 125 per cent; corn meal for making tortillas, 100 per cent. Notwithstanding the fact that the Government named a Price Regulating Committee, it has been a complete failure.

"Present wages and salaries have lost 40 per cent of their purchasing power with relation to the dollar, which in turn has fallen off 40 per cent. Corn used to sell for five and six cents a kilo; now the price is twenty-five cents. This excessive cost of corn and its products is the most eloquent accusation against the agrarian system."

El Mundo, of Tampico, Mexico, informs us that:

"There is no doubt but that the intentions of General Cardenas have been good; he has done everything possible to improve the economic and social conditions of the Mexican proletariat. However, results have not been up to his expectations.

"No matter what the organ of official optimism may say, there has never been more poverty and more hunger in the country than at present."

Mexico's food troubles are partly attributed by the Newark (N. J.) *News* to such factors as general depression and crop failures. The Dayton (O.) *Journal* has another explanation:

"Mexico's troubles are largely attributable to the fact that foreign capital is avoiding the country (as a result of expropriation policies), and Mexican capital is fleeing abroad."

Whatever the entire list of causes may be—and certainly there are more than one—there could be no doubt as to the ultimate effect reported by *The Christian Science Monitor:*

"A survey of social conditions in the country reveals an extreme restlessness which is attributed to hunger. The high cost of foods during the past year, and the simultaneous decline of employment and income, has created a serious condition in many parts of the country."

The Laguna district, a great cotton-growing region in the northern States of Durango and Coahuila, was divided by President Cardenas two years ago. Once one of the finest cotton regions in the world, since the partition, production has declined. Some of the details of this change are given by Henry J. Allen, former Governor of Kansas, as quoted in the Santa Monica (Calif.) *Outlook:*

"Governor Allen cites the seizure of the cotton-growing industry in the Laguna district as an illustration of what is occurring under President Cardenas. This district has about 1,000 square miles and was reclaimed from the desert, partly by Mexican industry and partly by American finance. Cotton and wheat were raised under irrigation. The cotton crop has run approximately 250,000 bales annually.

"This highly developed area was confiscated, the owners being permitted to retain only 20 per cent of their holdings, the other 80 per cent being given to the workers. This year the workers' production on their 80 per cent fell to less than 80,000 bales of cotton. Inspection of the district by former Governor Allen showed that the irrigation ditches were badly cared for and the entire district was retrograding steadily."

Not only have large estates been taken over, but small proprietors have been squeezed out as well. That the situation thus produced is as bad for the Mexican workers as for American business men is shown in a description of conditions by Frank L. Kluckhohn, former Mexico City correspondent of the New York *Times:*

"In La Laguna, 30,000 farm laborers were working last year under government supervision and with satisfactory government pay. Today the labor union officials say half of those workers are unpaid and in serious plight."

According to Betty Kirk, in a *Christian Science Monitor* analysis of the situation:

"The *hacendados* managing the land operated on a big scale, with large profits and losses expected, but always with credit at the private banks. With the bank credit withdrawn, the small farmers and communal operators have had to depend upon government funds to finance their crops, their machinery, and their harvestings.

"At the beginning of the experiment, ample funds were provided by the Government for this financing. The subsequent economic decline has limited these funds and consequently restricted planting and cultivation. Grave charges have also been made that money provided by the Government for the farmers has been misappropriated by officials of the *ejido* (the communal farm village) and agrarian banks. Accordingly, the combination of circumstances has had an adverse effect upon the whole development.

"It is therefore apparent that while 'justice' is being done to the peons, much injustice has been caused to the owners. Yet no power has been able to stop this process, for in its extreme it merely represents the historical swing of the pendulum to the left."

Secretary of State Hull has emphasized the fact that Mexico's internal affairs, agrarian or otherwise, are none of our business —unless and until Mexican governmental policies, such as expropriation, deprive British and American citizens of their rights and property under international law. In fact, intervention by the United States would be contrary to the basic policy of this country and also to the non-intervention pledge negotiated at the Pan American Conference at Montevideo in 1933. Having renounced intervention as an instrument for dealing with Latin American countries, the United States has only two weapons for dealing with the Mexican Government—diplomatic argument and economic pressure. The "Big Stick" of former days created resentment, admits the Washington *Star*, "but its use may be necessary if President Cardenas is unable to pull his Government out of the morass of financial and economical trouble." To quote the Colorado Springs (Colo.) *Gazette:*

"We would not have aggression against Mexico. Nor would we argue that intervention is ever wise or profitable.

"*But it has long been apparent where Cardenas was taking Mexico, and it seems that a counsel of restraint by the Wash-*

111

ington Government might at any time have helped to save Mexico from the results of its own imprudence. Such counsel was never given.

"Any who have been familiar with the thought of Mexico during the last four years knows that the silence here in the United States was construed there as tacit approval of a domestic policy that seemed much more likely to dissipate the national substance than to achieve any far-reaching social good."

In the opinion of the Cincinnati *Times-Star:*

"The fact that President Cardenas remains popular amid a scene of growing industrial wreckage is due to the President on this side of the Rio Grande. When the official exponent of our 'good neighbor' policy took this seizure of American property in Mexico as blandly as he took the seizure of American property by sit-down strikers at home, he gave Mexico's Russian-schooled propagandists their opening. The Chamber of Deputies sent him a grateful greeting, and the most was made of his polite reply. Now the Mexican populace believes that the two Presidents stand side by side for a policy of confiscation."

Mexico's break with Great Britain is the most severe test the Monroe Doctrine has faced in many years, believes the New York *Herald Tribune.* This paper then makes an extended historical analysis of the Monroe Doctrine and its successive interpretations. In the beginning, we are told, it was "interpreted simply as a warning to other Powers not to extend their possessions in the west at the expense of free American nations." Narrowly interpreted, we read on, "this statement clearly barred such adventures as that of Napoleon III in Mexico, when he set up an empire during the Civil War." But as time went on, "the simple terms of our early foreign policy became subtler and more complex." It so happened that:

"The republics to the south were notoriously bad managers financially and unstable politically. When they defaulted on a debt, or began to shoot up the Government in the local plaza, it was the habit of the Powers to send a warship or two to protect lives and property of their nationals or hold the custom-houses.

112

"Until Theodore Roosevelt's Administration, American policy permitted such expeditions by European nations, so long as no permanent occupation followed."

But after President Roosevelt had forced Germany to arbitrate in the case of Venezuela, a real change came over the American interpretation of the Monroe Doctrine, with the acquisition of the Panama Canal Zone. While President Roosevelt agreed that an aggrieved nation had the right to take action against a defaulter, such action necessitated a blockade, bombardment, or seizure of custom-houses—"in effect, a possession, even though only a temporary possession, of territory." This meant that European Powers might not collect debts by force. "But as an adjunct to this policy, the United States undertook to police the region and to collect all foreign debts; in a word, America accepted or seized a protectorate over all nations in the area of the Canal Zone defense system." Under this policy, Wilson went into Santo Domingo and Haiti, and Coolidge into Nicaragua.

But in December, 1933, President Franklin D. Roosevelt said: "The definite policy of the United States from now on is one opposed to armed intervention." The United States may be willing enough to forego the forcible collection of overdue debts, but then, concludes *The Herald Tribune:* "It must also persuade European—and Asiatic—Powers to do the same, or face the difficulties that Theodore Roosevelt foresaw."

Thus, under the Monroe Doctrine, outsiders may not intervene, even to protect the property of their nationals. Under the new inter-American policy, the United States Government may not forcibly intervene to protect the property of its nationals in any of these republics. As Secretary of State Hull said at Montevideo in 1933: "No government need fear any intervention on the part of the United States."

"Thus a radically new Latin American policy was created," reflects the Easton (Pa.) *Express;* "and it is reasonable to believe that Mexico's expropriation of American oil properties and her defiance of the United States Government may be traced to that utterance." This new policy, as the Dayton (O.) *Journal* sees it, "has almost amounted to an invitation for unstable govern-

113

ments to take what they want in the form of foreign-owned property."

When Mexico joined the League of Nations eight years ago, it did so with the proviso that it did not recognize the validity of a certain "regional understanding"—meaning the Monroe Doctrine —mentioned in the Covenant. "Mexico, like some South American republics, resented the notion that it should have to lean on the United States for protection," but in the present crisis, continues the Savannah (Ga.) *News*, "it is glad of that backing." But what of the victims of expropriation? As Carlos J. Videla points out in a *North American Newspaper Alliance* article:

> "Many European nationals have invested great sums in building railroads, ports, public utility enterprises, and radio and cable networks, as well as manufacturing plants, in the countries south of the Rio Grande. The Monroe Doctrine, which in fact makes the United States a guardian of the American republics, has precluded the forcible intervention of European governments on this side of the Atlantic.
>
> *"By the same token, the Doctrine has, to some extent, made the United States responsible for the conduct of the Latin Americans toward European interests."*

The combination of Mexico and the Monroe Doctrine makes a "ticklish proposition" for the United States, writes Charles P. Stewart from Washington for *The Central Press*:

> "We can be patient, but we can't compel Europe to be patient likewise. And if Europe refuses to be patient, we're bound to be placed, under the Monroe Doctrine, in the position of defending Mexico—making us, in a sense, responsible for Mexican obligations to Europeans.
>
> "In this particular matter we're not much in sympathy with Mexico, either. We ourselves have talked pretty sharply to the Mexican Government. Yet we can't afford to be overly rough with Cardenas. If we are we inevitably will encourage the anti-Cardenas faction to attempt his overthrow. Then we'd have, in our own door-yard, a reproduction of Spanish civil war conditions, and heaven knows we don't want that."

Recalling the saying: "Spare the rod and you spoil the child," the Tucson *Arizona Star* believes "it would be an easy matter for the American Government merely to stand aside, and let some

Careful, Young Fellow!

one else—Great Britain, for instance—do the spanking." And Alan Barth writes to much the same effect in the Fort Myers (Fla.) *News-Press*:

"Whether a blockade of Mexican ports by British warships, or seizure of Mexican customs, or even bombardment of Mexican cities should be viewed as 'interposition for the purpose of oppressing them' would constitute a knotty problem for the State Department to solve. In well informed quarters it is believed that the British can proceed to do anything they please, so long as they don't try to retain control of Mexico after their legitimate claims have been satisfied."

The difficulties raised by the expropriation of British, Dutch, and American oil properties in Mexico are more international than domestic. Since we do not allow foreign Powers to interfere with republics below the Rio Grande, we must assume responsibility for the interests of those Powers in the Western Hemisphere. As the Boston *Post* puts it:

"Under the Monroe Doctrine, we cannot let England seize a Mexican port to enforce payment for confiscated oil properties. By the same token, we cannot allow one of the Latin American nations to cheat or affront a foreign Power."

Meanwhile, explains the Brooklyn *Citizen*, Mexico apparently is relying on the Monroe Doctrine to protect her from any use of force by Great Britain. "Under the protection of the Monroe Doctrine, Mexico manages to escape the punishment she invited," agrees the Salt Lake City *Tribune*.

"The challenge to the Monroe Doctrine," asserts the New York *Enquirer*, "is much more serious than has been the case heretofore." What we must do, believes the St. Louis *Star-Times*, is to demonstrate to the Old World that we can protect its legitimate interests in the Western Hemisphere. The Detroit *News* offers a suggestion:

"Intervention in Mexico over the expropriation issue is out of the question, but consultation—with a view to presenting a united Pan American front both to Mexico and to the British —would seem a course thoroughly worth considering. Indeed, it would seem an opportunity to demonstrate that the Monroe Doctrine, as interpreted at Buenos Aires, is really an instrument of peace—and not one of United States domination in this hemisphere."

At Buenos Aires, it will be recalled, the Monroe Doctrine of the United States was transformed into a multilateral policy of all American nations, by declaring that an external threat to one nation is a threat to all, and that all will unite in a common resistance to any intervention by a non-American Power. "In other words," claims the Louisville *Courier-Journal,* "under the 'good neighbor' policy enunciated by President Roosevelt, no American nation can intervene in the domestic affairs of another country in the Western Hemisphere. Under the Monroe Doctrine, no outside nation can interfere. That puts the Washington Government in an embarrassing position, since Great Britain will expect her interests in Mexico to be looked after by the United States." Moreover, maintains the Grand Rapids (Mich.) *Press,* if this country fails to insist upon the observance of international principles, it cannot object to the invasion of this sphere of influence by others. It is quite possible, believes the Port Arthur (Texas) *News,* that Great Britain "may weary of inaction and take measures to protect her nationals owning property in Mexico." Continues this paper:

"The Monroe Doctrine does not prohibit the use of force by European Powers against the Central and South American nations. It functions only against any attempt on the part of foreign Powers to extend their system to any portion of this hemisphere.

"This being so, there is nothing to prevent Great Britain from taking such action as she believes necessary to satisfy her claims, except that of outright control of Mexico."

This somewhat unusual interpretation of the Monroe Doctrine is further discussed by the New York *Sun.* "Suppose," says the New York paper, "the British decide to blockade Mexican ports, or bombard Mexican cities in the event of Mexico's refusal to pay full price to the British owners of expropriated oil properties?" In the opinion of *The Sun:*

"If President Cardenas thinks that the United States will fly to his rescue, he misunderstands the Monroe Doctrine.

Only thirty-five years ago Great Britain, Germany, and Italy, failing to collect certain debts and compensations owed to their nationals by the Government of Venezuela, blockaded Venezuelan ports and bombarded two fortified towns. President Castro persuaded the American Minister to help in negotiating a settlement; and this was effected through The Hague Tribunal, with a verdict in favor of the European Powers.

"When Santo Domingo's debts to foreign Powers got it into hot water, President Theodore Roosevelt stated the American case briefly and clearly:

" 'An aggrieved nation can, without interfering with the Monroe Doctrine, take what action it sees fit in adjustments of its disputes with American states, provided that action does not take the shape of interference with their form of government or of the despoilment of their territory under any disguise.'

"Or, to put it in the words of that veteran expert on international law, John Bassett Moore:

" 'We have not assumed to forbid European Powers to settle their quarrels with American states by the use of force any more than we have hesitated to do so ourselves.'

"To tell a European Power that it must not cross the boundary lines drawn before Monroe's time—as President Cleveland told Great Britain—is one thing. To tell it that it cannot collect its honest dues from a delinquent South American republic is quite another thing. Even the New Deal may not dare to monkey with the Monroe Doctrine."

The Manchester (N. H.) *Union* indulges still further in speculation when it says:

"Suppose Britain declares that oil from British-owned properties belongs to the owners until it is paid for, and takes steps to seize Mexican tankers bearing that oil. Suppose this leads to a clash with Mexico, and the British fleet is sent across the Atlantic to back up the British demands.

"What are we going to do about it? We will be required to either take a stand with Britain in her demand for a just settlement of the oil controversy; or support Mexico in a policy that is unjust and unfair to both Britain and ourselves. The Monroe Doctrine alone would make neutrality impossible.

"The Mexican situation arising from the illegal seizure of American and British oil properties threatens to put the United States in an embarrassing position. Our own Govern-

118

ment has tacitly condoned this seizure, although there is no prospect that dispossessed Americans will receive fair compensation."

"It is just possible," reflects the New Haven (Conn.) *Journal-Courier*, "that a firmer attitude at Washington in the beginning would have made consideration of any of these contingencies unnecessary."

In addition to the serious question involving the rights of American investors in Mexico, there is another important obligation that American newspapers do not overlook, especially in view of the present world situation—our duty to Great Britain. Since Mexican diplomatic relations with Great Britain have been suspended, "an awkward situation faces the United States," so the Birmingham *Age-Herald* observes. And it adds: "This country is eager to maintain the 'good neighbor' policy in this hemisphere, and especially in Mexico, but it is loath to do anything that would disrupt its virtual unity of action with Great Britain in international affairs."

It should not be forgotten that the Dutch are interested financially in one of the companies affected by the Cardenas decree, the Mexican Eagle Company; and The Netherlands Government has taken a position parallel to that of Great Britain in demanding the return of the properties. In the opinion of the Worcester (Mass.) *Gazette:*

> "The United States Government should now add its voice to those of the British and Dutch Governments, and make specific demands for a return of the seized oil properties. We owe it to these countries to avoid taking any stand that encourages confiscation of the property of their nationals in Latin America, owing to our peculiar responsibility under the Monroe Doctrine, which both Britain and Holland respect.
>
> *"We would doubtless look to similar British co-operation should American oil interests in the Near East ever be threatened."*

The prestige of the United States is at a very low ebb, according to John W. White of the New York *Times*, because of "its failure to take a stronger stand on the confiscation of American oil fields." It is known, says Mr. White, that several other Latin

American countries contemplated similar seizures as soon as they could be sure that neither force nor diplomatic action would be used to protect American property. This is confirmed by the Detroit *Free Press*, which adds:

"The failure of the Administration in Washington to take a sufficiently firm stand in connection with the seizure of American-owned oil fields appears to have reduced American prestige in Mexico to a very low point.

"American properties in Mexico have not been the only sufferers from the Administration's policies; American trade with Mexico is also suffering from them."

The New York *Daily News*, noting the damage to our reputation, points out that "sagging prestige means sagging foreign trade eventually; and sagging foreign trade means fewer jobs at home."

Frank L. Kluckhohn, former Mexico City correspondent of the New York *Times*, adds some sidelights on the situation:

"At a moment when European dictatorships seek aggressively to extend their commercial and political strength in Latin America, the prestige of the United States in Mexico has fallen close to the lowest ebb in twenty-eight years.

"During the last two years, investments of the United States in many fields, and valued at hundreds of millions of dollars, have been expropriated or dissolved by the Mexican Government. With the loss of investments, the trade of the United States has fallen to less than half the level of a year ago, and Mexican barter deals with the world's three great dictatorships threaten it further."

Among the press comments on the way the Roosevelt Administration has handled the Mexican crisis is the following from the New York *Enquirer:*

"No nation as powerful as ours, with justice so completely on its side, would have tolerated for twenty-four hours the challenge to international honesty which the 'red' Administration at Mexico City has flung in the face of Uncle Sam, if its foreign affairs were conducted with true statesmanship."

The Washington bureau of the New York *Herald Tribune* reports Representative Hamilton Fish, Jr., as blaming the Roose-

velt Administration for not registering a protest when President
Cardenas first began the seizure of American holdings in Mexico.
The Congressman is quoted as saying:

"The Administration at Washington is largely to blame for
not protesting vigorously three years ago. The delay was
unfortunate, and gave color to the claim that the New Deal
at Washington was sympathetic to the plans for a Socialized
state in Mexico."

And *The Herald Tribune* adds, in an editorial:

"How the United States can expect to obtain the co-operation and respect of the rest of the Western Hemisphere, to
say nothing of the rest of the world, so long as she permits
this expropriation to continue without effective protest, and
allows its citizens to traffic in the products of expropriation,
is a question that should be answered."

Similar views are expressed by the Berkeley (Calif.) *Gazette,*
the San Bernardino (Calif.) *Sun,* and the Dayton (O.) *Journal.*
According to the New York *Times:*

"A point has now been reached at which the situation holds
disturbing possibilities. What answer is our Government to
make to Mexico's rejection of our claim that the accepted
principles of international law call for prompt payment of
adequate compensation to foreigners whose property is
seized? Our Government, of course, can sidestep the whole
issue if it chooses to do so. It can go through the motions of
maintaining its position as previously stated, but actually
let the oil lands wait, accept direct negotiations in so far as
agrarian lands are concerned, and meantime seek to effect
some arrangement by which independent companies in this
country would take the oil which the Mexican Government is
producing from the wells which it has seized. This would
save face for the 'good neighbor' policy by stretching out
negotiations over a considerable period of time, and it would
also ease the economic situation in Mexico, and thereby lessen
the consequent risk of Fascism by getting money into the
hands of the hard-pressed Mexican Government.
"But is there any reason to believe that expediency of this
kind would in the long run accomplish any good result? It
would amount to a poorly concealed surrender, on our part,
of principles which we believe ought to guide the conduct of

121

One Moment Please!

—*Reprinted from the Washington Post.*

friendly nations. And it would establish a precedent that might readily encourage other countries to follow Mexico's example. Sooner or later it must be made clear to the Mexican Government that while the United States looks sympathetically on the development of a program of social justice in Mexico, it has certain rights which it cannot consent to waive; rights which Mexico herself cannot reject without destroying the investment of foreign capital on which the prosperity of the Mexican people so heavily depends."

The controversy with Mexico about expropriation of oil properties is joined sharply and unequivocally over a point of international law. A point which all civilized nations have long accepted, and to which Mexico herself agreed, as the Houston (Texas) *Chronicle* reminds us, in the Warren-Payne negotiations of 1923. But now the Cardenas régime denies that such a point exists.

The point, briefly, is this:

Expropriated property (and the right to expropriate is universally recognized) must be paid for in cash at or before the time it is taken.

To reminders of this fact from Secretary Hull, the Mexican Government replies with a complete rejection of this premise. It insists that there is nothing in international law which requires a government to make any compensation whatever for expropriated property, provided the expropriation is of "a general and impersonal character."

In other words, Mexico and other nations are seeking radical revision of international law. According to the Worcester (Mass.) *Gazette:*

"What these nations want now is an international law which would place the foreign owners of seized property on the same basis as domestic owners. That is, the foreigners could appeal to the local courts, but could not appeal to their own governments to redress their wrongs."

As H. V. Kaltenborn, the noted commentator, explains:

"Mexico is seeking to set up a new principle of international law which this country cannot accept. If we did accept it, we could not afford to invest a dollar in any foreign country."

123

Even in South America the danger of the Mexican President's course is recognized, and in *El Telegrafo* of Guayaquil, Ecuador, we read:

"The entire press of the South American continent has given its opinion concerning the difficulties between Mexico and the United States which have resulted from the expropriations; and the unanimous opinion is that the Government of General Cardenas is treading upon the most sacred principles of international law."

To the Baroness Adda Von Bruemmer-Bozeman, an authority on international law, writing in the Dallas (Texas) *Dispatch,* it seems that Mexico has broken, not only international law, but her own law as well. For:

"Similar to the American practice, the Mexican Constitution provides that private property may only be expropriated for purposes falling under the general head of public welfare. This covers what in Anglo-Saxon law is known as the power of eminent domain. The 1936 Act for the first time authorizes the Government to expropriate property whenever it is necessary, in the opinion of the Government, for the economic and social benefit of a particular class, or for the people as a whole. This is, of course, obviously an entirely different concept from the generally accepted theories of eminent domain.

"As to the expropriation of the property of its own citizens, the Mexican Constitution itself provides that indemnity must be paid immediately upon expropriation. As to the foreign-owned property, not only does the same constitutional provision apply, but any action on the part of the Mexican Government expropriating foreign property without immediate payment is contrary to the well recognized principle of international law, that payment must be made either before or at the · time of the seizure.

"In reading the Mexican Constitution, one comes across another provision under which the action of the Government may be questioned.

"*The Government is strictly limited with respect to the scope of its activities. It can do nothing unless there is an express authorization for its action. Not only is there no authorization for its action, but there is an express provision preventing the Government from maintaining a monopoly, which, according to most leading Mexican lawyers, prohibits the Government from operating the oil fields.*

124

"It appears furthermore that the application of the 1936 Act to the oil case is contrary to the Mexican law of labor. Numerous irregularities in the proceedings before the Labor Board could be quoted. The workers petitioned the Board under a special section of the Labor Act which deals with 'economic issues' and demanded an investigation into the economic capacity of the oil companies. This move on the part of the unions was probably suggested by the Government, which feared the consequence of a continued strike.

"The leading Mexican economist, Prof. Jesus Silva Herzog, was charged with the investigation. He came to the conclusion that the oil companies were financially strong enough to meet the demands of the workers' syndicate. His report was based on the profits of the years 1934 to 1936. The plea of the companies that those years were commonly regarded as an exceptional era of prosperity, and that it would be more correct to base the investigation on a period of ten years, was disregarded. Nor did the investigators accept the data found in the companies' books and balance sheets, because, allegedly, the corporate books were only kept for the purpose of concealing profits and evading taxes.

"After reading the bulky files of the proceedings, one is left with the definite impression that, not only have the companies been unduly deprived of their legal rights throughout the investigation and the following proceedings, but that the experts and the Labor Board were from the beginning distinctly in favor of the syndicate and against the corporations.

"The partial tendency of the investigation may be explained by the fact that Professor Herzog is officially a member of the Communist Party.

"The award was incorporated into the decision of the Board. The Court confirmed the decision of the Board.

"Nobody in Mexico seems to dispute that the syndicates and their powerful leader, Vicente Lombardo Toledano, succeeded in bringing a certain amount of pressure on the Court so as to make it sustain the award.

"The demands of the syndicate of oil workers which were thus sanctioned by the Court are so exorbitant that it seems difficult to see who could have ever accepted them. Only one interpretation is left: The decision was purposely made unacceptable in order to force the oil companies out of the country.

"The Labor Board, the Supreme Court, and the Chief Executive have unquestionably, according to all authorities, acted illegally in their proceedings against the oil companies. They have not only infringed commonly accepted doctrines of international law, but have also violated their own Constitution and laws. There is no doubt but that the legal proceedings were just a sham in order to achieve a premeditated end."

According to the Fort Smith (Ark.) *Times-Record:*

"Mexico's expropriation of the oil properties is the climax of a number of acts carried out since President Cardenas assumed office, in which the Mexican Government has violated its own laws as well as the laws of international relations. Of course, any foreign investor who enters any nation must accept the laws of that nation. But he has a right to expect that such laws will be maintained and that any rights he has under those laws will be respected. In the expropriation of oil properties and in the similar seizure of farm lands belonging to Americans and other nationals, the Government of Mexico has violated its own Constitution, its own laws governing expropriation, and the consistent decisions of its own Supreme Court."

Of course, admits the Covington *Kentucky Times-Star:*

"Secretary Hull has made a sound and strong assertion of American property rights abroad under international law. But why was not such an assertion made when Cardenas seized American-owned oil wells? True, Mr. Hull then sent a cautious note of protest, and the Treasury temporarily suspended purchases of Mexican silver. But these were mere diplomatic slaps on the wrist, and statements by President Roosevelt in press conference and by his potent advisers off the record made clear that no stronger action would be taken against Mexico. That country was, in effect, encouraged to interpret the official American attitude as approval of the oil seizures."

Secretary Hull, explains the San Diego (Calif.) *Sun*, "is fighting for more than just a settlement of claims; he is fighting for a principle of international law." In fact, declares the Youngstown (O.) *Vindicator*, "the whole American effort toward reliance on friendship and international law breaks down if Mexico is permitted to violate international law with impunity." In the opinion of the Hartford (Conn.) *Courant*, "no principle of international law is more firmly established than the right of a citizen of one country to be compensated when his property is taken over by another nation." And the Dallas (Texas) *News* reminds us that:

"Over a hundred years ago, Chief Justice Marshall fixed this country's policy on international honesty. He said: 'That sense of justice and right which is acknowledged and felt by the whole civilized world would be outraged if private property should be generally confiscated and private rights annulled.'"

There is no disposition to deny Mexico the right to run her own affairs. "Resumed ownership of an important natural resource is, of course, a right of the Mexican nation, but fair dealing and plain honesty, as well as the practice of international law, require remuneration to the foreign owners for property taken from them," says the Dallas *News,* while to the Duluth (Minn.) *News-Tribune* it seems:

"Mexico could have legislated that no alien could buy oil lands in Mexico. It did not do this. It permitted many purchases of such lands. Hence it may not expropriate them now."

The low estate to which international morality has come is revealed in the answers which Mexico made to the British note. The only way that a number of American newspapers are able to construe the arrogant Mexican attitude is that the Government has repudiated ancient standards of international morality, and is preparing to embark on an outlaw career. Mexico apparently has taken the position that she is above international law and international morality. But, points out the Louisville *Courier-Journal,* "since amicable international relations are based on good faith, there can be no such relation where there is not that good faith."

President Cardenas, remarks the Indianapolis *Star,* may very properly figure that taking British and American oil wells is no worse than sending an army into Ethiopia, China, or Czecho-Slovakia. But, it adds, "the answer is that two wrongs do not make a right. It is high time for the world to get back to the solid foundation of honesty and decency, and away from the idea that might makes right."

At present, protests the Danbury (Conn.) *News-Times,* "expropriation without compensation is quite the fashion. Another method is simply not to pay." In fact, observes the Mobile *Register,* "this is all too obviously an era in which debts between nations are treated as lightly as treaties between nations." Continues this Alabama daily:

"In Mexico's defense, it must be acknowledged that it did not originate the principle, or attitude, which governs the course it is taking in the farm and oil lands expropriations. It is imitating, in some measure, the attitude of the leading European nations on the war debts of the U.S.S.R. on the Czarist debts; and of Germany on the Austrian debts. There are signal differences between each of the debt instances cited here, but in every case the argument expounded by the debtor has been that a national objective justifies international anarchy."

In the past, notes the Miami (Fla.) *News,* "nations have had two reliances where other nations were in their debt. The first was national honor. The second recourse was force." But, we read on:

"The World War and the rise of the Fascist state revolutionized the situation as to international debts. The defeated nations in one way or another repudiated their debts. The Allied nations in one way or another virtually repudiated their debts to their good angel, the United States. The dodging of debts became the regular thing. National honor stood aside. Repudiation is no longer disgrace, but, rather, the vogue.

"When England spoke up saucily to Mexico regarding payment for English oil, the Mexican Government retorted with remarks about other nations which seemed in no hurry to pay their debts. There was nothing for England, in debt to its ears to the United States and making no effort to pay, but to blush and go back and sit down."

It was different in the old days, when the oldest of all republics, prior to the present British democracy, was in flower. According to the Raleigh (N. C.) *Times:*

Upon My Honor!

—*Reprinted from the Philadelphia Inquirer.*

"Rome's attitude was that a Roman citizen was the world's aristocrat. Not a hair on his head could be rumpled, wherever he might be. Behind him, his life, his property, stood the Roman legions. And if his rights were endangered the legions marched.

"It is different now. Particularly in China. The Japs have given cause for a dozen wars, according to old standards. American and British ships have been bombed with loss of life. But do the two greatest nations—the two nations that assume the role of preserving law and order—assume to act in the old forthright fashion? Not so one would notice it!'"

Over in Europe, the Brooklyn *Eagle* informs us, "the non-observance of treaties and covenants has gone to the point where a general conflagration is threatened, and the future of mankind hangs in the balance; and it adds: "It would be doubly unfortunate if such breaches of faith were to endanger the future of the nations of the Western Hemisphere." If, points out the El Paso (Texas) *Herald Post,* "the people of the world expect to have business relations, they must have and observe a code of fair dealing. Otherwise the whole structure of international economics will break down.

"If that happens—if world trade collapses—then, as Secretary Hull reminds us, international relations will end in chaos."

And, believes the New York *Herald Tribune,* "the total disappearance of individual liberty and private property is in the offing unless a sudden revival of morale is established." As David Lawrence points out in one of his Washington dispatches:

"When a sovereign country of Mexico's stature starts confiscating the property of larger nations, the day is not far distant when the policemen of the seas—the navies—will be quietly stationed off the seaports to prevent products from being exported which were illegally taken from their owners. In these days of undeclared war, there are undeclared blockades, and Mexico is making a big mistake in stirring up international friction at a time when she needs international cooperation to help her conquer her economic woes."

In view of the progress made by Fascism, Nazism, and Nipponism, the Greensboro (N. C.) *News* is convinced that:

"The effect which the rapidly changing European situation has had in the United States makes all the more imperative the settlement of differences which exist between Washington and Mexico City in order that solidarity of the Western Hemisphere may be attained and strengthened.

"Back of the crises which have kept Europe and the world teetering on the brink is a collapse of treaties, of international law, of collective security. Such agreements and committals, in all that they symbolize, are no stronger than the will and the character of the nations behind them.

"The base therefore, becomes comity, understanding, friendship, and co-operation. Great progress has been achieved in the furtherance of such a spirit and its more or less tangible application. But at present there is a disrupting factor, one breach which has not only its material but its ideological aspects; that is, the difficulties which have arisen with Mexico over that country's expropriation of American-owned properties.

"Here we get back to the heart of international law, breakdown of which did as much as any other one factor to bring Europe's tragedies. Seizure of the property of subjects of another nation, especially a nation which is trying to be a better neighbor, by a government, without restitution, is anything but an observance of the amenities. In such a light, revealed as the possible beginning of disregard of an implied, if not an express, international obligation, the Mexican attitude takes on new meaning and new importance. It is not the sort of conduct that can be depended upon; it is not the sort of spirit upon which to build good-will, understanding, or commercial relationships, in which faith is the backbone of credit."

Under the old rule of international law, explains the Dayton (O.) *News:*

"England and the United States would be justified in collecting from Mexico at the point of a gun. Neither will take this course.

"International law is now as dead as the Locarno Agreement, the Nine-Power Treaty, and the Kellogg-Briand Pact; and that is dead indeed.

"With nations—notably Italy, Germany and Japan—and now Mexico, insisting on doing what seems right in their own eyes, international law gives way to the international claw.

"First, insane nationalism set the nations to cutting off international trade. Now an extension of that mania makes it impossible for international investment to go on. The allied nations repudiate, in effect, their debt to the United States. The Soviets confiscate private property in Russia. Japan makes a raid on China, with but a sketchy regard for foreign property interests there. The thing we used to call honor as among nations, with rules gaining the status of international law, has virtually vanished from the face of the earth.

"It will return. Human societies cannot long maintain themselves without some trace of ethics and honor in their common relations. That return waits the discovery anew that men, to thrive, must recognize some level of action above the beast now dominant in the earth."

V

SECRETARY HULL'S NOTE ON THE LAND SEIZURES

Secretary Hull's July Note—A Portion of the Text—Brazil Follows Mexico's Example—Danger to Foreign-Owned Property—Mexico Spreads the Expropriation Gospel—Pressure Upon Mexico Advocated—The "Good Neighbor" Policy Strained—Oil Properties Not Mentioned in Hull Note.

The expropriation by the Mexican Government of oil properties belonging to seventeen British, Dutch, and American corporations, brought to a dramatic climax the long-standing discussion over wages and working conditions.

In the month that followed, Mexico learned a painful lesson in economics. By the middle of the following July, the republic was in the throes of the worst depression in its peace-time history —at least in modern times. The shorter hours, higher wages, and other considerations which the Mexican Labor Board ordered the private oil companies to give the workers, were still unrealized. The Mexican Government was trying to force unbacked fiat money into circulation. Foreign trade had fallen off from 30 to 50 per cent. Many companies and individuals made no attempt to meet their financial obligations, and some small concerns even went into bankruptcy. As the Dayton (O.) *Journal* remarked at the time:

> "We in the United States have been taught that the way of the transgressor is hard. In Mexico they are learning that the way of the expropriator is just as difficult."

To add to all the other difficulties, the price level rose alarmingly in those first four months. The peso, worth 28 cents when the oil properties were expropriated, went down to 20 cents. The substantial payment of taxes by the foreign oil companies ceased altogether. The status of 18,000 workers in the oil fields was lower than it was before the expropriation. Even raising the tariff to a degree that threatened trade with the United States did not produce the desired results. As the Dayton *Journal* remarked in a second editorial: "One of the principle difficulties of

We'll Know the Contents Tomorrow

—*Reprinted from the New York Journal of Commerce.*

Mexico's New Deal, as personified by President Cardenas, is that it seeks to kill the very goose whose financial egg makes its 'Mexico for the Mexicans' program possible." Continued the Ohio paper:

> "It has attacked foreign-owned oil companies from two angles—increasing taxes and aiding labor in demands for higher wages. Yet taxes on this type of industry are needed to carry out the agrarian program which is the corner-stone of the Cardenas régime. To buy the extensive landholdings of native and foreign investors for distribution among the peons, the Government must obtain money from taxes on industrial interests."

Neither party to the controversy was happy. The American and other oil companies had lost their properties. The Mexican Government had lost essential tax revenue. Oil production was cut to about 65 per cent to its formal level. Thousands of jobs had been lost. Business was stagnant. Now, observes the Ansonia (Conn.) *Sentinel:*

> "If these matters concerned only the oil companies and the Mexican people, they would not disturb the average citizen of the United States. Unfortunately, part of the cost of Mexico's action falls on us.
> *"There are some 300,000 investors in the United States who are the real owners, through their companies, of the oil properties. They have a right to demand that Mexico return the properties.*
> "There are a larger number of citizens engaged in the production and manufacture of products going into the export business, who are likewise losers. Unable to sell the seized oil in the United States, Mexico has been trading it to foreign countries for equipment and supplies formerly bought in this country."

On June 29th, a detailed communication was addressed to the Mexican Government by the Acting Secretary of State, setting forth the amount of the claims for expropriated agrarian properties owned by American citizens, and containing suggestions for determining the value of the properties. On July 21st, we read in the New York *Journal of Commerce:*

"Secretary of State Hull sent an ably worded note to Mexico pointing out that expropriation of foreign-owned property by a government unable to pay was tantamount to confiscation, and urging arbitration of the claims of American owners of expropriated farm lands. However, not a single mention was made in this note of the seizure of American-owned oil properties.

"The reasons why the State Department thus concentrated its efforts upon obtaining compensation for American farmers who were evicted from their lands in Mexico are obvious. The protection of small farmers was expected to have a far greater popular appeal in this country. Also, it is doubtless assumed that a settlement of the claims of expropriated farmers would furnish a precedent for clearing up the oil issue.

"However well meant the efforts of the State Department in this matter have been, and despite the clear and able reasoning which marked Secretary Hull's note to Mexico, it becomes increasingly apparent that a mistake in strategy has been made.

"In the first place, the impression has been spread in Mexico that failure even to allude to the oil seizures in the American protest note concerning seized farm lands reflects a lack of interest on the part of the American Government in the fate of the American-owned oil properties. As a result, business and other interests in Mexico who have recognized the suicidal aspects of the expropriation policy and have warned against it feel that there is little that can be done, since the American Government itself seems to be uninterested.

"Secondly, by placing exclusive emphasis upon cash payment in the case of the expropriated farm lands, the State Department fails to point to the one practical solution of the oil problem. Mexico cannot pay for the expropriated oil lands. She can only correct her confiscatory action by returning these properties to their rightful owners, under reasonable conditions such as those which, in the past, have proved highly beneficial to Mexican economy.

"*By discussing only cash payment, the State Department has failed to insist upon the only possible method of correcting the injustice involved in the confiscation of the foreign-owned oil properties.*

"The Mexican Government should be given to understand that the State Department is keenly interested in obtaining

justice for the expropriated American owners of oil properties, and that the return of these properties intact under
reasonable conditions is the only possible way to undo the
confiscation. The Mexican Government could rescind its
action in short order through administrative action or by a
decision of the Supreme Court holding that the expropriation
decree was invalid."

If this is discounted as a "Wall Street" reaction, let us see what
a Texas daily, the Corpus Christi *Caller*, has to say:

"President Cardenas insists on the right of confiscating
private property whenever his Administration thinks that
policy desirable.

"This is a defiance of the United States and of international law in practically every particular. He overlooks the
fact that international law is binding on all states, and that
a minimum of protection for foreigners is an elementary condition of admission to the family of nations. Protection
against confiscation is among these minimum requirements.

"Mexico's financial poverty is no excuse for confiscation.
Mexico invited foreign capital and promised it the protection
of law; its extermination now cannot be permitted.

"As to the oil properties, for twenty years the United
States has maintained that subsoil petroleum on land owned
or leased by American companies prior to May 1, 1917, the
date of the Mexican Constitution, belonged to the surface
owners.

"*The Mexican Supreme Court in five successive decisions in
1921, thus constituting established law, held that this subsoil petroleum was the property of the surface owners. This
was confirmed by the Warren-Payne negotiations and recognition by the United States of President Obregon's Government in 1923. It was again confirmed by the Mexican Supreme Court in 1926, and was the basis for the Morrow-
Calles Agreement of 1927.*

"Although Mexico has tried to confiscate the oil properties
indirectly by making operation extremely difficult, if not impossible, this is the first time that the Mexican Government
has openly undertaken unilaterally to abrogate the international agreements between the United States and Mexico
of nearly twenty years' standing and to over-rule the Mexican Constitution and decisions of the Mexican Supreme
Court confirming it. This is a flagrant confiscation of the bulk
of the oil values."

The Hull note, remarked the Washington correspondent of the New York *Herald Tribune*, "brought to a virtual showdown the Roosevelt Administration's long diplomatic feud with the Cardenas Government over the latter's land expropriation policies." Among other things, the note reminded the Mexican Government that the taking of properties without compensation "is not expropriation, but confiscation." Said the State Department communication of July 21st, in part:

"During recent years the Government of the United States has upon repeated occasions made representations to the Government of Mexico with regard to the continuing expropriation of agrarian properties owned by American citizens, without adequate, effective, and prompt compensation being made therefor.

"The issue is not whether Mexico should pursue social and economic policies designed to improve the standard of living of its people. The issue is whether, in pursuing them, the property of American nationals may be taken by the Mexican Government without making prompt payment of just compensation to the owner, in accordance with the universally recognized rules of law and equity.

"My Government has frequently asserted the right of all countries freely to determine their own social, agrarian, and industrial problems. This right includes the sovereign right of any government to expropriate private property within its borders in furtherance of public purposes.

"Agrarian expropriations began in Mexico in 1915. Up to August 30, 1927, 161 moderate-sized properties of American citizens had been taken. Not a single claim has been adjusted and none has been paid.

"Subsequent to 1927, additional properties, chiefly farms of a moderate size, with a value claimed by their owners of $10,132,388, have been expropriated by the Mexican Government. None of them as yet has been paid for.

"The taking of property without compensation is not expropriation. It is confiscation. It is no less confiscation because there may be an expressed intent to pay at some time in the future.

138

The Better Word in This Case

—*Reprinted from the Houston, Texas, Chronicle.*

"If it were permissible for a government to take the private property of the citizens of other countries and pay for it as and when, in the judgment of that government, its economic circumstances and its local legislation may perhaps permit, the safeguards which the constitutions of most countries and established international law have sought to provide would be illusory.

"Governments would be free to take property far beyond their ability or willingness to pay, and the owners thereof would be without recourse.

"We cannot admit that a foreign government may take the property of American nationals in disregard of the rule of compensation under international law.

"We are entirely sympathetic to the desires of the Mexican Government for the social betterment of its people. We cannot accept the idea, however, that these plans can be carried forward at the expense of our citizens.

"The whole structure of friendly intercourse, of international trade and commerce, and many other vital and mutually desirable relations between nations indispensable to their progress, rest upon the single and hitherto solid foundation of respect on the part of governments and of peoples for each other's rights under international justice.

"*The right of prompt and just compensation for expropriated property is a part of this structure. It is a principle to which the Government of the United States and most governments of the world have emphatically subscribed, which they have practised, and which must be maintained.*"

The reaction of other American newspapers to the Hull note was immediate and severe in condemnation of the Cardenas Government. "The farm land owned by Americans in Mexico is real property, for which payment has been made," declared the Philadelphia *Inquirer*. In the opinion of this paper, the seizure of farm land by the Mexican Government without indemnity was "an act of the greatest injustice." The Minneapolis *Journal* recalled that the Hull note was "the harshest that has gone to Mexico for many a day—but fully justified." *The Star-Times*, of St. Louis, considered it a "gem of thoughtful and enlightened statesmanship."

The Hull note, to quote the Boston Herald, was "firm and blunt. It did not deal with the expropriation of oil properties, but the

*principle at stake is precisely the same, and the State Department
will surely invoke that principle in treating with President Cardenas over the oil question."*

In the case of the expropriated land, the St. Louis *Post-Dis-
patch* informs us, Mexico did not question the title of American
owners. It took the land from them, as it took other land from
Mexican owners, to distribute among the people. "Mexico's right
to undertake social experiment is undeniable," admits the Mis-
souri paper, "but the obligation to make payment for seized property is that of elementary honesty, the first rule in private business as in international relations." For, points out the Ansonia
(Conn.) *Sentinel:*

> "If it is established in the Mexican instance that a Latin
> American government can arbitrarily confiscate the property
> of American companies and American investors without pay-
> ing for it fully and promptly, this will give collectivists in
> those countries such a powerful weapon that collectivist poli-
> cies, whether Fascist or Communist, will become almost
> general throughout Latin America. And that will mean eco-
> nomic retrogression of a kind and to an extent that will affect
> the prosperity of the entire Western Hemisphere—and even
> of the Old World. Moreover, it will spell the doom of democ-
> racy in many countries."

Already, says the St. Louis *Globe-Democrat:*

> "The Costa Rican Congress by a vote of 40 to 1 has author-
> ized the Government to expropriate the properties of the
> American and Foreign Power Company, an affiliate of the
> Electric Bond and Share Company, a United States concern.
> Costa Rica, however, included in its expropriation measure a
> grant of power to negotiate a loan to pay the indemnity,
> which leaves the American investors no complaint, if com-
> pensation is paid, other than that they have been ousted
> from a profitable business. Indemnification by Mexico is still
> awaited.
>
> "As Secretary Hull has pointed out, Mexico or any other
> country may expropriate properties for the general welfare
> as it sees fit, provided it indemnifies the owners. We cannot
> quarrel with the Constitution of Mexico or Costa Rica. But
> not all nations may be competent, as we hope Costa Rica is,
> to pay for the properties they seize. In which event foreign

141

investors face confiscation without compensation, in the Mexican manner."

The Danville (Va.) *Bee* probes a little deeper into the Costa Rica situation, when it says:

"The little Central American Republic of Costa Rica is evidently taking a leaf from Mexico's book. The Costa Rica Government has decided it would like to take over and nationalize the electric plant in San José, the capital, which now belongs to a subsidiary of Electric Bond and Share.

"Costa Rica's approach is much less crude than Mexico's. The Government's position is that it wants to pay a fair price for the property. In order to do so, it proposes to float a bond issue in the United States.

"The joker is that Costa Rica has long since defaulted on all her foreign obligations. Her credit rating is well below zero. Financial men figure that Costa Rica is only going through the motions."

On February 11th last, it was announced in a Mexico City dispatch that Colonel Fulgencio Batista, head of the Cuban army, after a visit to Mexico, was prepared to "nationalize" the sugar industry of Cuba. And a few weeks after the oil properties in Mexico were seized, the St. Louis *Globe-Democrat* said editorially:

"An echo of Mexico's oil expropriation policy is heard in Brazil, where President Vargas, in his new role of Dictator, has decreed that the Government shall assume immediate control of all refineries in the nation, which henceforth will be operated by Brazilians. The inexplicable feature of his action is that Brazil produces no oil of its own and depends exclusively on imports for such commodity. The Army suggested the decree to Vargas, and also sponsored the law passed by the controlled Legislature which provides that all petroleum deposits, if any, shall be exploited exclusively by the Government. The law also regulates imports, exports, transport, and distribution—a blanket measure that places the Government in sole control of the industry.

"Although the steps taken in Brazil are not immediately important, they set a precedent for other South American countries that may give foreign operators considerable trouble in the future."

142

Carlos J. Videla, an authority on Latin American affairs, writing for the *North American Newspaper Alliance,* associates the seizure of foreign-owned oil properties in Mexico with a general attack on American investments in Central and South America. He reports "a wave of nationalistic movement throughout Latin America, aimed primarily against foreign holdings." His dispatch brings this comment from the Kansas City *Star:*

"Mr. Videla cited, in particular, the expropriation of American oil companies in Bolivia, the threat of similar treatment for a mining enterprise and the United Fruit Company in Ecuador, the forcing of the Standard Oil Company out of Argentina, and discriminatory action against American interests in Colombia.

"In Mr. Videla's opinion, these developments derive more or less directly from a growing belief in Latin America that the United States will no longer protect its investments. There is widespread resentment, he explained, over contracts and concessions granted to American companies by various South American governments in the past, on the ground that their terms were far too favorable to the companies. And now that the threat of intervention appears to have been removed, according to him, it is to be expected that many of these agreements will be drastically revised."

South of the Rio Grande, "the fires of social revolution burn with increasing vigor," notes the Savannah (Ga.) *News.* "Moreover, if these fires are not checked, they might spread southward to other countries which, like Mexico, are relatively poor and in debt."

"Once the principle is accepted that foreign-owned property can be taken over indiscriminately, all of our vast holdings in Latin American countries are at the mercy of those governments," declares the Rochester (*N. Y.) Democrat and Chronicle.*

Already, we are reminded by the Milwaukee *Journal,* Mexico has hinted broadly to all other Latin American countries, as she did to Colonel Batista on his recent visit to Mexico, that they ought to try the same arbitrary procedure of seizing foreign-owned property. According to the Atlanta *Constitution,* President Cardenas has sent envoys to Cuba, Argentina, Brazil, Venezuela,

143

Salvador, Nicaragua, Guatemala, and Colombia "to develop sentiment for expropriation in these countries." And we must not
forget, warns the Louisville *Courier-Journal*, "that across the sea
there are land-hungry nations who look to the Western Hemisphere for future expansion."

It is not the governments of Central and South American republics, as they now exist, that are to be feared. But, as *The
Texas Weekly*, of Dallas, explains: "To permit the Mexican Government or any other government to seize American property
without making full, prompt, and effective payment for it would
be equivalent to an invitation to collectivists in other countries,
whether Communists or Fascists, to ride into power on the *promise* to expropriate foreign-owned properties and turn them over to
workers. This would be the surest way to promote the interest of
collectivist parties in all countries in which there is any considerable amount of foreign investment."

In California, Chester Rowell, writing in the Long Beach *Sun*,
agrees that:

> "If we concede, as a matter of law and of right, that any
> nation is entitled to confiscate without compensation the
> property of Americans having investments or doing business
> in that country, it means an end of business or investment by
> the nations of any country within the territory of another.
> The exchange of credit and of goods, on which the very life
> of modern civilization depends, would simply cease to exist."

"What is the United States to do in the present circumstances?" asks the Boston *Herald*. As it goes on to explain:

> "We are anxious to preserve the friendliest relations with
> all our neighbor republics. But can we afford to allow the
> establishment of such an unfortunate precedent as the
> acceptance of the Cardenas doctrine would constitute? The
> principle at stake is fundamental in international relations.
> The alternative is international chaos."

In his note of last July, Secretary Hull proposed arbitration of
the claim under the Pan American Arbitration and Conciliation
Treaty of 1929. This, believes the New York *Herald Tribune*,
was a "fair and friendly offer." But Secretary Hull's note found

its chief significance, thinks *The Herald Tribune,* as the "entering wedge of an adjustment of the larger oil problem." As this paper points out:

"Once an international tribunal upheld the principle of payment upon expropriation in this case, it would have provided both the State Department and the oil companies with some measure of protection against a wave of confiscations by other countries, and so might conceivably have opened the way to a settlement of the oil problem on the basis of something less than outright return of the properties."

"The future of the controversy," believes the Boston *Transcript,* "lies in the forcefulness which may be exhibited by Secretary of State Hull." Continues *The Transcript:*

"Mr. Hull is regarded throughout the world as a statesman of first rank, and in Latin America, his prestige is of unprecedented importance. But there are conservatives in Latin American countries who see Socialism on the horizon.

"If a forceful word is not spoken now against confiscation, whether in the domestic or international sense, the way is opened to a dislocation of the whole economic system in Latin American countries.

"Secretary Hull's job is a painful one, but it will have to be performed. To shirk it would be to evade a plain international duty. Mexico must be made to understand that it cannot ignore its recognized obligations without losing its standing in the company of nations and without subjecting itself to the risk of costly reprisals.

"In the larger sense, it is not simply an American-Mexican issue. As a result of the attitude of the Cardenas Cabinet, a question of government morality is raised. The matter now to be determined is whether any country may seize the property of foreigners and, on the plea that it is trying to promote the welfare of its own citizens, escape the consequences of its illegal action. Obviously it is of high importance to the whole world, including the United States, that this destructive theory be destroyed before it becomes common practice. Let it once gain a foothold, and only chaos could result. Let it be accepted doctrine, and debts would lose their sanctity and treaties their binding force."

The fear that Mexico has set an example that will result in the expropriation of foreign-owned property in other Latin Ameri-

How to Start Your Car These Cold Winter Mornings?

—Reprinted from the Plainfield, N. J., Courier-News.

can countries is echoed in the following United States newspapers: Dayton (O.) *Journal,* Youngstown (O.) *Vindicator,* Detroit *Free Press,* Providence *Journal,* Richmond (Va.) *Times-Dispatch,* Portland *Oregonian,* Louisville *Courier-Journal,* Cleveland *News,* St. Paul *Pioneer Press,* San Francisco *News,* Indianapolis *Star,* New York *Enquirer,* Washington *Post,* Brooklyn *Citizen,* New York *Journal of Commerce,* Washington *Times,* Lynchburg (Va.) *Advance,* and Philadelphia *Inquirer.* Yet, admits the Boston *Herald:*

"It is difficult to see what our State Department can do. Secretary Hull at Montevideo in 1933 went on record for the 'absolute independence, the unimpaired sovereignty, the perfect equality and political integrity of each nation, large and small'. The Mexican Administration has not overlooked this guarantee."

"Nevertheless, something will have to be done," asserts the Atlanta *Constitution.* The obvious step, thinks this Georgia paper, "is a severance of diplomatic relations between the two countries. This would make an already difficult problem still more difficult for the Cardenas régime." Dr. Roscoe Pound, Dean Emeritus of the Harvard Law School, on his return from a tour of the principal South American republics, is quoted as saying "the only weapon that can be used against Mexico is the application of what might be called financial sanctions. My guess is that Mexico would give way if strong pressure were applied to the Central Government there." "The United States Government should take a realistic position and demand the immediate return of the expropriated properties," maintains the Worcester (Mass.) *Gazette.*

Bertram D. Hulen, in a Washington dispatch to the New York *Times,* explains that the Department of State preferred to move first with reference to the agrarian cases because they "were clear cut, contained no complicating collateral circumstances, and presented the same principle as the oil expropriation." In the opinion of the Wilmington (Del.) *Journal:*

"Mr. Hull's proposal that the issue be submitted to arbitration under the treaty signed in 1929 was a shrewd stroke. Property of the citizens of other Latin American nations is

147

involved in the Mexican land expropriation. If these nations put themselves on record as opposing such seizures without full, immediate payment, the tendency of expropriation policies to spread may be stopped.

"What is puzzling, however, is the fact that Mr. Hull fails to mention the recent oil expropriation. Exactly the same principles are involved in the oil property seizure as in the seizure of land.

"Suggestion has been made by persons close to the Administration that the Government press for full indemnification of those who had invested small savings in Mexican farm lands, but that the oil companies be left to shift for themselves. However, it is incredible that Secretary Hull should consent to any procedure so utterly unjust and so completely violative of democratic principles."

It was obvious to practically all of the Latin American republics that Secretary Hull's note to the Mexican Government was addressed to them, as much as to Mexico. To the Detroit *Free-Press*, the stand taken by Mr. Hull "was important, not only because it was for the protection of American property in Mexico, but also because it was for the protection of American property owners everywhere in the world." The Hull communication also had the complete approval of the Washington *Star*, which said at the time:

"The note was a masterpiece of paternal advice from a world Power to one of its satellites. Secretary Hull wrote like a father would to a son, pressing upon him the right course, and offering him persuasive arguments for that course. To the last period the note was courteous and friendly, and bore a stamp of sincerity.

"There is much to be gained by the adoption of such a tone in international correspondence, and particularly as it is carried on with the nations within the sphere of the 'good neighbor' policy, for it is a serious question whether that policy can be preserved without winning our neighbors to the south to the realization that it is by its very nature reciprocal, as Secretary Hull took pains to point out. 'Good neighborliness' cannot be entirely on one side."

"For more than twenty years," recalls the Philadelphia *Inquirer*, "Mexico has been addicted to the peculiar practice of seizing land owned by Americans, with the vague promise that compensation some day would be forthcoming. It is reassuring to know that Washington is now taking a decisive step for the settlement of that account." "The Hull note put Mexico on the spot," remarks the Louisville *Courier-Journal.* To the New Haven (Conn.) *Journal-Courier,* "Secretary Hull's note implies a definite stiffening of the Administration's attitude.

"The oil cases are not mentioned, but the implication is that the Administration is to establish a precedent in the clear-cut agrarian dispute before proceeding to others."

"What Mr. Hull says boils down to this," explains the New York *Herald Tribune:*

"That while the right of a government to expropriate property is not challenged, the failure to make proper restitution to the owners for the seized property results in what is nothing less than confiscation, and hence is in violation of accepted practices in international law.

"Two points in connection with Mexican expropriation of foreign-owned property have been badly confused in the American mind. The first, pushed by the Mexican Government and eagerly supported by American radicals and sentimentalists, is that the purpose for which expropriation has been resorted to has some sort of bearing on the legality of the act. The second is that the final settlement of this issue concerns only the American and the Mexican Governments.

"The first point is answered by Secretary Hull in his statement to the effect that the purposes of the program of expropriation—i.e., the social betterment of the masses of the Mexican people—'however desirable they may be, are entirely unrelated to the real issue under discussion'. This issue is not whether the Mexican Government should pursue social and economic policies designed to improve the conditions of the Mexican people, but rather whether, in pursuing them, the Mexican Government may take the property of American nationals without making prompt payment of just compensation to the owners. This payment has not been forthcoming on any of the properties seized.

"The second point overlooks the fact that other nations are watching closely the result of the negotiations about Mexico's policy of expropriation and that if the Cardenas Government 'gets away' with it, other governments will be

149

tempted to expropriate American—and other foreign—property in other countries. As a result, not only may the losses to Americans with foreign interests be very large, but the entire structure of international law will be still further weakened.

"This is why Mr. Hull's note is so important. It has crystallized the issue in unmistakable terms."

As the Austin (Texas) *Times* observes:

"Protection of foreigners against confiscation is an elementary requirement of international law and an understood condition of international recourse. Recognition of Mexico as an equal member of the family of nations carries with it the understanding that Mexico will respect the principles of international law. It is her right to limit or forbid the acquisition of property by foreigners coming within her borders, but she cannot allow them to acquire property and then take it away from them without compensation.

"The rights which Mexico has violated in confiscating farms, ranches, and oil properties were acquired in accordance with Mexican law and at the invitation of then existing Mexican Governments. Those rights must be respected in any change of Mexican policy. If Mexico wants to develop her resources without foreign aid, that is her right. If she wants to acquire for herself properties held by foreigners, she may do that, too, but not by the simple, savage process of taking them without compensation."

This, it might be added, is also the view of the Manchester (N. H.) *Union*, New York *Daily News*, Hartford (Conn.) *Times*, Philadelphia *Bulletin*, San Francisco *Chronicle*, Los Angeles *Times*, Brooklyn *Eagle*, Washington *Star*, Chattanooga (Tenn.) *Times*, San Diego (Calif.) *Tribune*, St. Louis *Globe-Democrat*, St. Paul *Pioneer Press*, Salt Lake City *Deseret News*, New York *Journal of Commerce*, Minneapolis *Journal*, New York *Times*, San Diego (Calif.) *Union*, Norfolk (Va.) *Ledger-Dispatch*, Sacramento *Bee*, Baltimore *Sun*, Houston *Post*, Memphis *Commercial Appeal*, Kansas City *Star*, Newark (N. J.) *News*, Peoria (Ill.) *Journal-Transcript*, and Washington *Post*.

William Allen White, editor of the Emporia (Kan.) *Gazette*, believes that Mr. Hull, "by patience, forbearance, and a kindly attitude, has earned the right to talk plainly to Mexico." According to the Miami (Fla.) *Herald,* "the United States has been easy with Mexico. But the calm Secretary of State is now tired of this utter disregard of American rights. The Roosevelt Administration has strained the 'good neighbor' policy to the limit." Moreover believes the Hartford (Conn.) *Courant:*

"Mexico would be running grave risk of damaging not only itself, but all of Latin America if it consistently refused to grant the fair and just demands of the United States.

"Mexico has more to lose than has the United States if it persists in denying the rights of American citizens under international law. This country can afford the resulting loss of trade; Mexico cannot. Worse, should the United States formally renounce its friendship, a tacit encouragement, no matter how little intended, would be given the internal opponents of the Mexican régime. Revolution is not far from the surface there."

Like most newspapers which comment on the Mexican situation, the Augusta *Chronicle* eventually gets around to comparing the oil claims with the land claims. Says this Georgia daily:

"One aspect of Secretary Hull's note should not pass unnoticed. In its whole length it does not contain a single mention of the seizure of American-owned oil properties. We are thus put in the position of insisting vigorously on compensation for land seizures amounting in value to about $10,000,-000, while ignoring seizures of British, Dutch, and American oil properties of an estimated value of $450,000,000.

"There are several possible reasons for this omission. One is that our State Department believes a demand for compensation for American farmers and other landowners will find popular support here, but that demands for similar compensation for the oil companies would be criticized as Dollar Diplomacy. Yet many stockholders in oil companies are persons of moderate means.

"Another reason why Secretary Hull may have omitted mention of the oil companies is that it is necessary to settle one question at a time; and that, if the principle of just compensation is established in the case of land, its application must necessarily follow in the oil fields.

"But there are serious objections to this strategy. If the oil claims are not publicly pressed, the impression must grow both here and in Mexico that our Government is not seriously concerned about them."

The Good Neighbor

—*Reprinted from the Columbus, Ohio, Dispatch.*

VI

MEXICO'S REPLY TO THE HULL NOTE

Mexico Refuses Arbitration—Hull Note Upheld by Latin American Press—Secretary Hull's Final Note—The Joker in the Settlement—Mexico's Annual Revenue—Worthless Mexican Bonds—The History of Land Seizures in Mexico—Mexico's Expressed Intention to Pay for Seizures—Restoring Oil Properties to Corporations Held Proper Solution.

In his reply to Secretary Hull's July note on the land claims, Eduardo Hay, Mexico's Secretary of Foreign Affairs, admitted that under her own laws Mexico is bound to make adequate indemnification. But she alone would decide the time and manner of payment. Mexico intimated that payment at this time, or on any terms which were not suitable to the Mexican Government, would jeopardize President Cardenas's agrarian program. In fact, remarked the Washington *Post* at the time, "the Mexican reply to the Hull note is a curious mixture of eloquence and evasiveness."

For example, the Mexican Government declared it could take possession of any lands if they were deemed necessary to carry out social reform. The Government might pay for them, if it could. If it could not, the right of expropriation, in their estima- tion, was not for that reason impaired. In other words, President Cardenas took the authoritarian view: The Government could do as it pleased with the property of its citizens—and it could not treat foreigners with any more consideration than it did its own people.

The Associated Press thus sums up the reply, on August 3rd, of Foreign Secretary Hay to Secretary Hull's note of July 21st:

"The reply refused arbitration; suggested discussion to determine value of the farm land; acknowledged the debt, but held there was no legal obligation to make prompt or even deferred payment; said indemnification would be under Mexican law on the basis of the nation's ability to pay; insisted that inability to pay could not be accepted as a valid reason for delaying the program of social reform by which land is being turned back to the peasantry; said flatly these reforms would be continued."

To quote a portion of this Mexican document:

"My Government maintains that no principle, universally accepted in theory or realized in practice, is found in international law which makes obligatory the payment of immediate compensation, or even deferred compensation, for expropriations of a general and impersonal character, such as those which Mexico has carried out in effecting the redistribution of land.

"Nevertheless, Mexico admits, in obedience to her own laws, that she is bound to make adequate indemnification; but the doctrine Mexico maintains in the premises, upheld by most authoritative opinions of writers on international law, is that the time and manner of such payment should be determined by her own laws."

Secretary Hay's refusal to submit the case to arbitration suggests to the Newark (N. J.) *Star-Eagle* that "Mexico regards its case as too weak to stand a disinterested scrutiny." Certainly, observes the Hartford (Conn.) *Courant*, "if Mexico's response to Secretary Hull's demands for 'adequate, effective, and prompt compensation' for the expropriated agricultural land was designed to embarrass the Administration, it has succeeded." The most charitable thing to be said about the Mexican note, believes the San Bernardino (Calif.) *Sun*, "is that Mexico's Foreign Secretary was probably considering the effect on the home audience."

Be that as it may, "in rejecting the arbitration offer, the Mexican Government has not helped its case before the bar of public opinion," maintains the Washington *Post*. The Mexican Government, notes the Galveston (Texas) *News*, "takes the position that expropriation is incidental to a program of social betterment, and that the right of property owners must be subordinated to the claims of that program." Secretary Hay also refers to Mexican law (which requires payment in agrarian bonds), and asks whether Americans think they should be favored over Mexicans. This, of course, is but a pleasant evasion of the question, because

Mexico's agrarian bonds are just about worthless, and pay no interest. As the Deadwood (S. D.) *Pioneer-Times* points out:

"The argument that Mexico cannot indemnify the landowners whose property she seized because she is at present heavily in debt is held to be neither logical nor reassuring. There are a number of nations heavily in debt just now. This kind of reasoning would give all of them a splendid excuse to take over all foreign investments without any compensation."

To the St. Louis *Star-Times* it seems that:

"Mexico is confusing international law with home economics. International law does obligate nations to compensate foreigners for property expropriated. True, there is no super-state to enforce international law, and if Mexico wishes to flout it she may do so. Then the only way the United States could collect would be by force or by seizing the property and funds of Mexicans in this country. In view of the Administration's 'good neighbor' policy, measures of this sort are not even contemplated.

"From the standpoint of international law, Mexico's domestic situation has nothing to do with the case. Mexico may be financially embarrassed as a result of her agrarian reform program, but that embarrassment should not be used as an excuse to embarrass in turn those Americans who invested their life's savings in Mexican farm lands."

"Mexico does not question the validity of the land claims," points out the Springfield (Mass.) *Republican.* In fact, reflects the Buffalo (N. Y.) *News*, "it would appear that the Government of President Cardenas is using the expropriation method to make Americans and other foreigners owning property in Mexico pay for his program of social reform, the economic soundness of which is open to question."

We find many newspapers, including the Los Angeles *Times*, criticizing Mexico for its unwillingness to arbitrate matters. As the Los Angeles paper points out:

"The Treaty of 1929, signed by Mexico, the United States, and twelve other nations of the Western Hemisphere, is fairly specific. It lists among matters subject to arbitration between signatories 'the existence of any fact which, if established, would constitute a breach of international obligation' and 'the nature and extent of the reparation to be made for the breach of an international obligation.' "

On the matter of arbitration, the Detroit *News* has this to say:

"Secretary Hull asked arbitration of American claims arising from the expropriation of farm lands, and Cardenas answered that the claims will be paid when Mexico is allowed to sell its oil abroad. From the Mexican viewpoint, that may be an apt reply, but in our language, it doesn't make sense.

"For one thing, it is evasive, in that it confuses two issues which are separate and distinct; and because the President of Mexico is aware that the foreign oil market is not subject to the action of this Government. The fundamental differences between the legal questions in the land claims and the oil expropriation have been repeatedly cited by the Mexican courts. Which fact the President must know also.

"Secondly, when viewed as a plea of necessity, the Cardenas reply calls into question the economic practicability of the revolution. It tacitly acknowledges that the agrarian action is not self-sustaining. If the agrarian claims are to be satisfied via the oil seizure, then some equally abortive move will be necessary to satisfy the oil claims, and the result will be a pyramiding of the indemnification problem."

While American newspapers, in their attitude towards Mexico, cannot by any stretch of the imagination be called vindictive, the Nashville *Tennesseean* asks us to remember that "it would be possible for the United States to seize all Mexican property in this country, and refuse to pay for it." But that, it adds, would be neither a proper act nor an indication of the "good neighbor" spirit. This paper and others fail to see what President Cardenas has to gain by creating ill-feeling and distress in the United States at this time. As a result of Mexico's evasiveness, the New Haven (Conn.) *Journal-Courier* is convinced of one thing:

"That nations investing in colonial countries like Mexico will not, over the long future, take confiscation, or expropriation at Mexico's price, lying down. True, it is inconceivable that the United States will send ships or soldiers to collect for this property; not even the most exasperated American capitalist would think this course wise in the present state of world opinion. But Britain and France and The Nether-

156

lands, all heavily involved in Mexico, will surely re-examine the Monroe Doctrine, in the face of this new threat to international law in the matter of foreign investment.

"And whether such re-examination leads to military measures of any sort, the Mexicans, at the very least, will find it difficult from now on to get capital."

As S. L. A. Marshall reviews the situation leading up to the Mexican note in a comprehensive article on Mexico:

"The question which our State Department is now facing is this: Can the United States Government afford to leave American property abroad to its own devices, thereby placing in jeopardy billions of dollars invested by our citizens in other countries? Or would it more advisedly insist on compliance with the recognized principles of international law that there be 'no expropriation without compensation,' even at the risk of provoking a situation which will destroy the 'good neighbor' policy?

"Let us first see why the question arose, and then examine whither it is leading and what are its implications as to Mexico's domestic situation.

"The claims which Secretary Hull urged be submitted to arbitration total about $10,000,000. The land owners were Americans, some wealthy and in no need of the land, some not. Much of the land was in production, and contributed importantly to Mexico's agricultural wealth. It was farmed by Mexican peasant labor, which in some cases was exploited, and in other cases, well-paid.

"These lands were taken from their owners under laws which recognized their title to compensation. They were then given to *ejidos* or groups of peasant farmers, who held and worked the land communally, with the financial support and guidance of the Mexican Government. Land distribution made little headway under President Alvaro Obregon. While Dictator, General Plutarco Elias Calles renounced it as economically unsound.

"But under President Cardenas, more land has been expropriated and given to the *ejidos* than during the administrations of all other revolutionary Presidents. He has made it in practice, as well as theory, the basic reform of the revolution.

"What that reform will yield Mexico fifty years hence is a matter for conjecture. Theorists, and the régime, see in it the salvation of the masses.

157

"On the evidence that I have seen throughout Mexico, the utter failure of the agrarian program would appear to be the one unmistakable fact in the national economy. Agricultural production has retrogressed in proportion as land distribution has speeded.

"Mexico is now an importer of a number of its basic subsistence commodities. Unemployment in the farm areas is more general than ever before, and the drift of rural populations from one section to another is more pronounced.

"I have repeatedly asked of government officers, but have never found, in one instance in which the agrarian cycle had been completed, that the land was continuing to produce as fully as it had before expropriation, and the *ejido* had begun to turn revenues to the Government which might be used in payment for the land.

"Thus the domestic significance of Mexico's reply to Hull, refusing arbitration, claiming its right to adjudicate the land claims, and contending that compensation should be subject to ability to pay, is that it tacitly admits the failure of the agrarian program. However dubious may have been the circumstances in which many foreigners acquired land, division must be a social and political fraud on the Mexican people if its prospect for a future increment is no brighter than the Mexican note would make it appear.

"Mexico, in effect, is pleading: 'We cannot pay you because of the cost of a program which will make it impossible to pay you.' "

Secretary Hull's note to Mexico of July 21, 1938, conceded Mexico's legal right to expropriate land belonging to foreigners, but insisted that such lands must be paid for; and asked Mexico to take adequate steps toward meeting claims of American citizens covering a twenty-year period and amounting to $10,132,888. To American newspapers this seemed quite justified. But Mexico's reply of August 3rd was evasive. The Mexican Government enunciated the startling proposition that there was neither law nor practice that made "obligatory the giving of adequate compensation for expropriations of a general and impersonal character."

The Mexican position was virtually that, as the American property had been taken in the execution of a program for the benefit of the Mexican people, there was no reason why the Mexican

Government should take any steps toward compensation as long as its fiscal condition made it inconvenient. The American reply to this in August was a sharp challenge of the Mexican contention that compensation was not due under international law, and a declaration that the policy followed by the Mexican Government was equivalent to bald confiscation. Secretary Hull also hinted rather strongly that this Government had become tired of the manner in which long-drawn-out discussions over methods of compensation had apparently been used to postpone settlement for properties taken over by the Mexican Government in recent years.

Perhaps the dominant note of editorial comment at that time was one of friendly warning to Mexico. The Minneapolis *Tribune* was glad that American handling of the situation had been free of jingoism. The New York *World-Telegram* was quite willing to admit that "as a sovereign State, Mexico has the same right to take possession of land within her borders as our Government asserts in respect to privately owned land in the United States." Indeed, it added, "it is almost a daily occurrence for our Government to take over private property—for conservation of soil or natural resources, for reforestation or parks, for slum clearance and rehousing. Yet our Government compensates dispossessed owners, both citizens and foreigners, immediately and in cash." Or, as the Houston (Texas) *Post* argues, "the fact that the Mexican Government claims to be pursuing this policy in connection with the working out of a social reform does not justify or excuse the failure to make recompense for the property taken." "The implication that the American Government, in applying its New Deal, would likewise fail to pay if this country were less wealthy, is," in the opinion of the Texas paper, "simply begging the question," and "lacks little of being a gratuitous insult." Then comes this warning to Mexico:

"Our Government and our people are committed to a policy of cultivating friendly relations with Mexico, but the patience of neither will stand the strain of a willful disregard of obligations to American citizens by a Mexican régime that is

It Takes Two to Make Good Neighbors

—*Reprinted from the Hartford, Conn., Courant.*

frankly Communistic, and, as such, disdainful of the right of private property as a fundamental."

But it took the Hull note of August 22nd to call forth the full volume of editorial applause. This 5,000-word note was called the strongest sent to anyone by our State Department since the Wilson pre-war notes. Secretary Hull renewed the proposal Mexico had rejected, of arbitrating under existing treaties, but offered an alternative of a special commission. Under either plan Mexico was to make no more seizures, and was to deposit sums of money *in escrow* to meet future payments agreed upon by the negotiators. The Secretary repeated his earlier statement:

"The taking of property without compensation is not expropriation. It is confiscation. It is no less confiscation because there may be an expressed intent to pay at some time in the future."

He called attention to this assertion in the Mexican note:

"There is in international law no rule universally accepted in theory or carried out in practice which makes obligatory the payment of immediate compensation, or even of deferred compensation, for expropriations of a general and impersonal character like those which Mexico has carried out for the purpose of the redistribution of the land."

In other words, Secretary Hull went on to say in his note of August 22nd:

"The Mexican Government now advances the surprising contention that it may expropriate property and pay therefor in so far as its economic circumstances and its local legislation permit, but that if these circumstances and legislation do not make possible the payment of compensation, it can still take the property.

"If such a policy were to be generally followed, what citizen of one republic making his living in any of the other twenty republics of the Western Hemisphere could have any assurance from one day to the next that he and his family would not be evicted from their home and bereft of all means of livelihood? Under such conditions, what guarantees or security could be offered which would induce the nationals of one country to invest savings in another country, or even to do ordinary business with the nationals of another country?

"If this theory were sound, the safeguards which the fundamental laws of most countries and established international law have sought to provide for private property would be utterly worthless. Governments would be free to take private property far beyond or regardless of their ability or willingness to pay, and the owners thereof would be without recourse. This, of course, would be unadulterated confiscation.

"Reduced to its essential terms, the contention of the Mexican Government is this: That any government may, on the ground that its municipal legislation so permits, or on the plea that its financial situation makes prompt and adequate compensation onerous or impossible, seize properties owned by foreigners within its jurisdiction, utilize them for whatever purpose it sees fit, and refrain from providing effective payment therefor, either at the time of seizure or at any assured time in the future.

"I do not hesitate to maintain that this is the first occasion in the history of the Western Hemisphere that such a theory has been seriously advanced.

"In the opinion of my Government, the doctrine so proposed runs counter to the basic precepts of international law and of the law of every American republic, as well as to every principle of right and justice upon which the institutions of the American republics are founded.

"The Government of the United States maintains that in the treatment accorded its nationals by the Government of Mexico, as set forth in my note of July 21st, the Government of Mexico has disregarded the universally recognized principles of international law, and that its failure to make adequate, prompt, and effective payment for properties expropriated constitutes the breach of an international obligation.

"The statement in your Government's note to the effect that foreigners who voluntarily move to a country not their own assume, along with the advantages which they may seek to enjoy, the risks to which they may be exposed, and are not entitled to better treatment than nationals of the country, presupposes the maintenance of law and order consistent with principles of international law. Actually, the question at issue raises no possible problem of special privilege.

"The plain question is whether American citizens owning property in Mexico shall be deprived of their properties and,

162

in many instances, their very livelihood, in clear disregard of their just rights.

"The Government of the United States merely adverts to a self-evident fact when it notes that the applicable precedents and recognized authorities on international law support its declaration that, under every rule of law and equity, no government is entitled to expropriate private property, for whatever purpose, without provision for prompt, adequate, and effective payment therefor.

"Specifically, it is proposed to replace the rule of just compensation by the rule of confiscation. Adoption by the nations of the world of any such theory as that would result in the immediate breakdown of confidence and trust between nations, and in such progressive deterioration of international economic and commercial relations as would imperil the very foundations of modern civilization."

"This is a firm note, but a just one," was the Providence *Journal's* prompt characterization. The logic of the note seemed "so devastating" to the New York *Times* as to leave the Mexican Government's position "without legal or moral support." Similar praise came from the New York *Herald Tribune*, Philadelphia *Inquirer*, Hartford (Conn.) *Courant*, and Manchester (N. H.) *Union*, while the Milwaukee *Journal*, New Haven (Conn.) *Journal-Courier*, and Norfolk *Virginian-Pilot* found the firm tone of the communication most gratifying. "A masterpiece of candor," the El Paso (Texas) *Times*, on the Mexican border, called it. Though it was "firm in tone," the Scranton (Pa.) *Times* could find "nothing of the mailed fist about it." To the Kansas City *Times* our demands seemed most reasonable and quite in the spirit of the "good neighbor" policy.

In the opinion of the Louisville *Courier-Journal*, "Washington can sympathize with the hard-pressed Cardenas régime, which has been rushed into extreme measures by a radical following and now occupies none too firm a position. Hull, therefore, has been sympathetic but firm."

There is more than dollars and cents, more than land and oil, involved in this controversy, observes the Milwaukee *Journal*. Secretary Hull was addressing the whole southern half of this hemisphere, concluded the Washington *Post:* "The whole tenor of the message was that of a Dutch uncle explaining a delicate matter to a family—in this case the twenty-one other American republics."

The Boston *Globe* found the note "a persuasive and powerful argument for the establishment in this part of the world of an orderly method of settling the claims that citizens of one nation may have against the government of another." This is the policy the United States Government must follow, reasons the Evansville (Ind.) *Courier;* "any other course would create chaos in the Western Hemisphere and ultimately bring on foreign intervention."

According to Gardner Harding, *Scripps-Howard* correspondent, it was understood in Washington that the principal Latin American diplomats were consulted and none of them had any fault to find with the Hull note.

The Boston Transcript even checked to find that a large section of the Central and South American press upholds the position of the United States. "In numerous countries—Brazil, Argentina, Chile, Colombia, Ecuador"—it says, "newspapers voice their astonishment over the stubborn insistence of the Cardenas Government."

In his speech before the Mexican Congress on September 1st, President Cardenas insisted that the Mexican attitude would not be changed. This created a feeling of disappointment among American newspapers. The Mexican note of September 3rd accepted the proposal for a joint commission to determine the value of the lands in question, but upheld the earlier Mexican position in all other respects. The explanation was made that the rights of Mexican society, in the case of division of lands under its agrarian law, are so urgent that the necessity for satisfaction of such rights cannot be subordinated to possibilities of immediate payment for lands seized. The paragraph which seemed to draw the most editorial fire, however, was the following:

"There are numerous examples of nations whose cultural progress is beyond discussion, which have seen themselves obliged, without repudiating the right of property in the

164

abstract, to issue laws which have signified expropriation without immediate payment and sometimes without later compensation. Countries might be mentioned which, under pressure of reasons considered to be of public necessity, have forced private individuals to exchange their gold and their gold certificates for money which has already been depreciated, or which was depreciated immediately afterwards. Those countries have also been under necessity to require private persons, without distinguishing between nationals and foreigners, to receive in payment of obligations, which had been contracted in gold, the already depreciated currency of the country. Because appropriation was indirect in these cases, it was none the less effective, since the owners of gold and gold certificates in the first example, or of credits payable in gold, in the second one, have seen their property diminish without receiving adequate compensation in return."

To the argument of President Cardenas that nations which devalued their currencies really expropriated property without compensation, the New York *Times* replied:

"In an attempt to buttress the position he has taken, President Cardenas argues that the United States also expropriated property belonging to foreigners when it forced foreign holders of American gold certificates to exchange them for depreciated bank notes. This argument doubtless has an element of truth in it. But it overlooks several important considerations.

"In the first place, Mexico left the gold standard long before that step was taken by the United States. In the second place, from the time we left the gold standard until March, 1938, the Mexican peso was pegged approximately to our dollar, thus equalizing the exchange of currencies. In the third place, the value of the peso has fallen still further since March. And in the fourth place, Mexicans living in the United States who received depreciated dollars in exchange for gold certificates suffered no actual loss in the purchasing power of their money, whereas Americans in Mexico have suffered a heavy loss indeed through the confiscation of their properties, in many cases without any compensation whatever."

165

In the Oklahoma oil country, the Tulsa *World* also has something to say about the attempt of the Mexican Government to justify the seizure of lands and other property by citing the action of the Roosevelt Administration in "nationalizing" gold. As a matter of fact, avers the Oklahoma daily:

> "The Mexican Government is shystering on the demonetization issue. The United States called in the gold and instantly paid the owner of that gold the face value. That's all there is to it. The Mexican Government now pleads that action of taking over of the gold as justification for its taking over of lands and other properties owned by foreigners.
>
> *"If, as is claimed, the Mexican Government is imitating the United States, it should pay for the properties taken over."*

The Topeka (Kan.) *State Journal* goes a little deeper into the subject, in reply to this question by one of its subscribers: "Has the United States ever reimbursed the foreign holders of gold-clause bonds which it arbitrarily devalued; and if not, is there any essential difference between our treatment of those foreigners and the Mexican treatment of foreign oil companies?" Says this Kansas daily:

> "Without taking up any defense of the Government's policy in regard to the gold clause bonds, it may be stated that there is no similarity in the treatment of foreign bondholders by the United States and the Mexican treatment of foreign oil companies.
>
> "The bondholder has his bonds. The interest is being paid on them. He can sell them today for coin of the realm with which he can purchase food, clothing, or property—anything that could have been purchased with the interest money he obtained before the present price of gold was set and the present gold policy adopted. He can sell the bonds if he desires, and get his money out of them—possibly with a premium.
>
> *"It wasn't gold that the investor desired when he bought the bonds. Otherwise he should have bought bar gold. What he desired was safety for his capital, and interest upon his investment. He has both. The foreign oil companies who made their investments in Mexico have neither."*

166

In the two months that followed receipt of the Cardenas note, the Mexican Ambassador at Washington, to use the words of the San Francisco *Chronicle*, "went shuttling back and forth by air from closeted discussions in Mexico City to intimate chats in Washington." But after two notes out of Washington, and two replies from Mexico, the situation still was at deadlock.

On November 9th, Secretary Hull produced a final note—and received an immediate and amiable reply from President Cardenas. Said Secretary Hull, in part:

"My Government has a particular desire to safeguard friendship with Mexico, not only because Mexico is one of its nearest neighbors, but on account of the many ways in which ever-improving relations, in the fullest sense, between the two countries could be complementary and mutually beneficial. It has, therefore, spared no effort to arrive at prompt, friendly and satisfactory solutions of problems as they arose. . . .

"Last November my Government urged, in accordance with the principle of just compensation, the desirability of a comprehensive agreement providing for the compensation of the American citizens whose properties had been seized by the Mexican Government.

"Both our Governments are in accord that the value of the American-owned agrarian properties expropriated since August 30, 1927, be determined by a commission composed of one representative of each of our Governments, and, in case of disagreement, by a third person selected by the Permanent Commission.

"My Government believes it important, and understands that your Government is in accord in this regard, that a time limit be established for the completion of the work of the commissioners. It is, therefore, proposed that the commissioners be instructed that they must complete the determinations of value by not later than May 31, 1939."

Both countries stood firm on the ground previously taken, as far as general principles were concerned. Both agreed on setting up a special joint commission to determine the value of the properties. Mexico agreed to start periodically setting aside sums to create a fund for the future payment of American claims. And in fixing the compensation, the value of the property is taken into

167

"Do You Still Find This Seat Comfortable?"

account, and also the fair return from the property during the period between seizure and compensation.

The terms of the agreement which finally resulted from the negotiations carried on by Secretary Hull and Mexico's Ambassador are thus summarized by John C. O'Brien in the New York *Herald Tribune:*

"The value of the expropriated American lands is to be determined before May 31, 1939, by commissioners, one appointed by each Government.

"The Mexican Government is to make an initial payment of $1,000,000 on May 31, 1939, and a payment of not less than $1,000,000 annually thereafter until the full award of indemnities is paid.

"Both Governments agree that all claims which the two commissioners fail to adjust are to be referred to a third person who is to be selected by the Permanent Commission in Washington."

The agreement terminating the land expropriation controversy was embodied in two notes, one from Secretary of State Hull, and the other from Eduardo Hay, who acts in a similar capacity for Mexico. These followed an exchange of notes that seemed, for a time, to have led to an impasse. During this exchange, explains a Washington correspondent of the New York *Times:*

"Mr. Hull insisted that the Mexican Government was obligated to make fair and prompt payment to American citizens whose lands it took over, basing his contentions on what he considered to be the accepted principles of international law. The Mexican Government denied that any such obligation existed under international law, on the ground that the lands had been taken over pursuant to the terms of the Mexican Constitution, and that the matter was one of domestic legislation permitted to any sovereign state."

As the settlement is appraised by the St. Louis *Star-Times:*

"Secretary of State Hull gets what he demanded, rather sharply on one occasion, in the promise of Mexico to pay for expropriated farm lands on a definite schedule. Claims of Americans whose property has been taken will be adjusted by an arbitration board, representing the two nations.

169

"President Cardenas avoids, however, any agreement to pay in full. He avoids any commitment to halt his seizures of land for distribution among Mexico's peasants. Mexico specifically states that settlement of the agricultural expropriation problem is not to be considered a precedent for other expropriation claims—that is, oil properties."

The settlement of the question probably is satisfactory as far as it goes. At least, says the Austin (Texas) *American,* it "represents a decided improvement over Mexico's former attitude of defiant indifference regarding claims for expropriated property." And the Kansas City *Star* agrees that:

"By undertaking to pay $1,000,000 a year until all adjudicated agricultural claims have been satisfied, the Government of Mexico made an important contribution to international confidence in the entire Western Hemisphere.

"As these claims piled up, year after year, without any real attempt on the part of the Mexican authorities to meet their obligations toward the owners, an impression began to develop in the United States that co-operation with a country like Mexico was impossible—unless supported by some kind of force. That impression was greatly strengthened when the State Department reminded the Mexican Government that payment was long overdue, and was virtually told that nothing could be done.

"Here, some Americans began to say, is what may be expected from the 'good neighbor' policy. As soon as the other Latin American governments see Mexico successfully accomplish the confiscation of foreign property, the practice will spread like an epidemic.

"But Secretary Hull and his associates continued their patient negotiation within the framework of the new policy, only becoming progressively firmer. And their efforts have finally been rewarded."

The settlement with Mexico, in the opinion of the Elmira (N. Y.) *Advertiser,* "should make the South American countries feel all the more certain that Uncle Sam is a friend." Mr. Hull, says the Washington *Star,* "has stood resolute in his faith that sincere arguments, based on logic, and clearly and forcefully presented, are more effective than threats and bluster."

While it admits that the agreement is "fair enough," the Houston (Texas) *Chronicle* sees possible trouble ahead in Mexico's reaffirmation of the justice of its position and its failure to promise to discontinue seizures:

"Taken together, these two facts mean that Mexico is free to seize all remaining American properties, without intention of paying for them until after years of negotiations and perhaps pressure on the part of this country."

The Manchester *Union* also calls attention to the refusal of the Mexican Government to consider the settlement as a precedent; and to the non-settlement of the judicial question involved. Furthermore, explains the New Hampshire daily:

"The joker in the whole transaction is the source from which the Mexican payments are to come. This is not in the agreement, but it is well understood that the indemnities are to be taken from revenues obtained from new taxes on American mining properties in Mexico."

The "profit" here mentioned is explained in a New York *Times* Mexico City dispatch as coming from "Washington's tacit approval of new taxes on American companies in Mexico, from which revenues for the agrarian payments to the United States will be taken." This tax is said to be bringing in a minimum of $6,000,000 a year, from which the $1,000,000 annual land indemnity payment will be made. American business men in Mexico consulted by this correspondent admitted that Secretary Hull's concession had aided his general Latin American policy. But they felt that there had been no settlement of any basic problem, such as the increasing elimination of United States trade, now at a third of its former level, as a result of the Mexican Government's general program.

Ultimate analysis of the Mexican scheme for payment shows, in the words of the New Haven (Conn.) *Journal-Courier*, "that the United States Treasury is financing the Mexican Government's remuneration of American farmers whose lands it has seized; therefore, so far as the internal economy of Mexico itself goes, the effect is practically nil." The New York *Journal of Commerce* recalls that Mexico's promises of payment are made

171

subject to the reservation that such payment must reflect the economic possibilities of Mexico.

"In other words, if we stop buying Mexican silver, or some other unfavorable economic development occurs, presumably payments would be halted."

This settlement "does not wholly get away from the idea of confiscation," declares the St. Paul *Pioneer Press,* for "by any standard of justice, when a government takes private land or any other property for a national purpose, the former owners are entitled, not only to an adequate compensation, but a prompt one." And several Texas papers, close to such controversies with Mexico, feel that the settlement is inconclusive. It really settles nothing, declares the El Paso (Texas) *Herald Post,* "because the principle involved is left still in the balance."

Many impartial observers doubt that the former owners of expropriated farm lands will be compensated. The value of this land was set at $10,000,000, which Mexico agreed to pay in ten installments of $1,000,000 each. But, warns the Boston *Transcript:*

> "Only by a violent stretch of the imagination is it possible to think of the United States-Mexican land pact as 'a settlement' of this vexatious question. What the agreement does —and all that it does—is to remove the matter temporarily from the arena of discussion."

Both the declaration of principles in the Hull notes and the land claims settlement are held to have significance far transcending the intrinsic importance of the land obligations. Secretary Hull's note in reply to the Mexican note of August 3rd refers only to the seizure of agricultural lands. But the demand he makes in the case obviously provides a basis for dealing with the British, Dutch, and American oil properties which Cardenas seized. As the New York *World-Telegram* explains:

> "Mr. Hull's note does not mention the expropriated oil properties. But it is clear that the policy he has laid down in respect to land seizures is one which our Government intends to follow in regard to all expropriation of properties

172

belonging to American nationals, by Mexico or by any other government."

In the opinion of the conservative Cincinnati *Times-Star:*

"The oil controversy, of course, is much the more serious of the two. The property involved is many times more valuable than the agrarian lands, and the political issue has wider ramifications. The Cardenas régime has seized British and Dutch oil properties, as well as American. Since the United States claims special rights in Latin America under the Monroe Doctrine, it can hardly ignore injustices suffered there by foreign countries.

"To make a bad matter worse, the Mexican Government has lately been selling the product of the confiscated wells abroad—at a very low price—in competition with American, British, and Dutch oil companies. While most foreign countries have refused to buy the 'hot' oil, regarding it as stolen goods, Mexico has found a ready market in Germany, Italy, and Japan.

"Admittedly, Secretary Hull has a delicate task in dealing with the Cardenas Government. But at least the State Department can make clear that the settlement of the agrarian land question does not prejudice the oil claims of American citizens."

Now, the Mexican note agreeing to settle the land claims included the definite statement that this settlement shall not constitute a precedent in any case or for any reason. "Notwithstanding the official Mexican reservation to the contrary," emphatically declares the Norfolk *Virginian-Pilot,* "the land settlement *does* establish a precedent." "Whether a legally binding precedent or not," asserts the Washington *Post,* "the adjustment of the land dispute *does* suggest a way out for the settlement of similar disputes over the expropriation of other types of American-owned properties by Mexico." Similar statements are made by the Washington *Star,* Asheville (N. C.) *Citizen,* St. Paul *Pioneer Press,* Kansas City *Star,* and Louisville *Courier-Journal.* Says the Louisville daily:

"Property is property; and derricks, wells, and tanks are no different from land. If compensation must be made in the case of one, it must be made in the case of the other."

The important difference between the land expropriations and those involving the oil properties is that most of the seized agricultural tracts belonged to Americans. The oil properties, on the other hand, were owned by British and Dutch interests, as well as American. According to the New York *Journal of Commerce:*

"Mexico claims that immediate compensation need not be paid for seized property where the expropriation is 'of a general and impersonal character.' The seizure of the oil properties, however, was definitely not of such a character. It was directed only against foreign-owned companies, and was clearly discriminatory in its application. Also, it was not done to carry out a broad social purpose, as was the case with the farm lands, but resulted from a labor dispute where sharp wage increases were sought for a group of employes already the best paid in the country.

"The State Department, therefore, would do well to emphasize the settlement of the oil controversy as the paramount issue in our relations with Mexico. A solution of this conflict would definitely open the way to a settlement of the other problem involved, as well as a restoration of our trade with the neighboring republic."

In the opinion of the Covington *Kentucky Times-Star:*

"Secretary Hull knows perfectly well, and his note implies, that oil wells and farm lands, big property-owners and little property-owners, are on precisely the same footing in international law. No doubt he also knows, if his Chief does not, that the quickest way to break down respect for American property rights abroad and to start a wave of confiscation is to make class distinctions as between Americans."

Within the last two years, declares Henry J. Allen, former Governor of Kansas and Editor of the Topeka *State Journal,* the Mexican Government has confiscated nearly $1,000,000,000 worth of American property. In connection with the expropriation of American-owned oil properties, notes the Houston (Texas) *Post:*

"President Roosevelt said payment should be based upon the amount of money actually invested in the properties, and not upon their potential value, based upon underground oil reserves. *That gave the Mexican Government moral support in Washington.* Now the Mexican authorities have gone

174

much further. They have seized property without troubling themselves to provide even the fiction of legality."

In appraising the oil properties, the Mexican Government apparently did not take into consideration the millions of dollars spent in discovering oil wells; yet, maintained the Dallas (Texas) *News*, "under any just theory, the expense of exploration is a part of the actual investment in the property." For example, says the New York *Times:*

"The discovery of the prolific Poza Rica field in Mexico was accomplished by the Mexican Eagle Company, controlled by British and Dutch capital, only after probably $20,000,000 had been expended before a barrel of oil was produced.

"Executives of the United States oil companies whose properties were expropriated by the Mexican Government do not believe that it would be fair to their stockholders to accept in payment for these properties only the amount of their original investment, less depreciation. Because of conditions peculiar to the oil industry, they consider such a yardstick of valuation as being quite unfair. They believe that the valuation should be left to independent oil experts.

"The application of such a principle of valuation for oil properties, it is further argued, might result in the sacrifice of the huge investment made by the United States oil companies in foreign countries. It is contended that all the risk of business would be thrown upon privately-owned foreign oil companies, and, if and when success has been achieved after years of effort, the foreign country could then take over the successful venture, pay the cost of the investment in that successful venture, and thus discharge its international obligation."

Let us see what the record shows about Mexico's custom of "honoring" her obligations. Mexico started borrowing in 1821. By 1824, she had borrowed $32,000,000 in London. But it was not until 1888, *63 years later,* that the debt was finally paid by the Diaz Government. According to the Milwaukee *Journal,* the interest rate on this debt was 1.7 per cent, and it was not until the debt was paid that Mexico was able to borrow abroad once more. But the interest rate had gone up to 8 per cent. Continues the Milwaukee paper:

"After Diaz, things went rapidly from bad to worse. In 1922 the international banking committee came to an agreement with the Calles Government whereby the Mexican foreign debt was scaled down from $725,869,000 to $445,101,000. Mexico agreed to pay off interest arrears over a period of 40 years, beginning in 1928. Meanwhile she was to make partial payments. These were made in 1923, 1924, and 1925. Then the Mexican Government shrugged its shoulders—pointed to 'uncontrollable conditions'—and that was that.

"On July 1, 1938, Mexico's foreign debt was about $1,053,000,000 (railway debt principal $240,000,000, arrears $258,000,000; other foreign debt principal amounted to $275,000,000, arrears $280,000,000).

"All of this debt is in complete default. Some bonds are worth less than Czarist Russian bonds.

"In addition to this, there is a $400,000,000 internal debt of bonds issued by the Government for expropriated lands. This, too, is in default."

"Add up these amounts," suggests George Creel, in a *Collier's* article, "and contrast the staggering total with Mexico's income of $122,000,000 in 1937, and expenditures of $121,000,000, without the payment of a debt!" Continues this experienced writer:

"What adds to the gravity of the situation is the manner in which Mexico is turning assets into liabilities. One out of every seven pesos of Mexican income came from the oil companies—about $19,000,000 a year—and it was this same source that provided $5,000,000 for the construction of the Pan American Highway from Laredo to the City of Mexico."

The British, Dutch, and American-owned oil properties which were seized in March, 1938, are valued at $450,000,000. If we add this sum to the Milwaukee *Journal's* staggering total—$1,053,000,000—we find that Mexico, with no money in the Treasury, with revenues dwindling, and with its bonds a drug on the market, is, to quote the Louisville *Courier-Journal,* "confronted with total foreign debts of more than $1,500,000,000. And the greater part of this is due to the 'Mexico for the Mexicans' program of President Cardenas."

"It is a waste of time to even talk of Mexico paying for the 60,000,000 acres of farm lands and the $450,000,000 worth of oil properties which have been expropriated," thinks the Denver *Post,* for "she is notorious as a debt dodger." Mexico is "proud, progressive—and broke," remarks the Pittsburgh *Press.* In fact, says the Cincinnati *Times-Star:*

"Mexico's bonds have been in default for a long time. The government paper which is given in exchange for expropriated land is little better than if nothing were written on it.

"Mexico has no credit on which she could borrow the $450,000,000 or any considerable fraction of that amount.

"In the meantime, the Mexican Government has promised the workers all the profits of the oil industry. Just now there are no profits, and it is unlikely that under native management there ever will be profits to amount to much. So what good is all the talk of payment?"

The history of land seizure under the Cardenas Administration and the régime of his immediate predecessors offers no basis for hope that his promises to pay for expropriated oil properties can or will be carried out. This is the conclusion of the New York *Times.*

Almost four years ago, we read in the Manchester *Union,* the Mexican Government confiscated a million acres of land owned by Americans and valued at $80,000,000. What happened? According to the New Hampshire paper:

"For a time the Mexican Government made some payments for this land in its own bonds—which today are practically worthless. Then two years ago it ceased even this form of payment, in spite of the representations of our State Department."

The report of the Foreign Policy Association says, in part: "Since 1933, Mexico has suspended both issuance of new agrarian bonds and service on existing bonds." "The entire external debt of the Mexican Government is in default, and all but a small segment of its internal debt, as well," adds the St. Paul *Pioneer Press.* What the investing world thinks of Mexico's good faith and ability to pay is reflected in the fact that its bonds are going —when they *do* sell—for about two cents on the dollar.

Meanwhile, observes *The Christian Science Monitor*, "many Americans whose properties were seized have been waiting from eleven to twenty years for payment."

Moreover, says a Washington dispatch to the New York Times, "no Mexican Administration feels compelled to honor commitments of its predecessors."

In view of the above, the owners of the expropriated oil properties certainly would not consider accepting Mexican Government bonds as adequate payment. "Paying for lands with bonds that are virtually worthless is not expropriation; it's confiscation," declares the Houston (Texas) *Chronicle*. So the Minneapolis *Tribune* is convinced that:

> "The promise of President Cardenas that Mexico will pay for the expropriated properties would be more reassuring if it were accompanied by details as to the manner, the amount, and the time of payment. The record of Mexico so far as indemnification is concerned is unfortunately not of the best.
>
> "Under the circumstances, it is not surprising that this country should press Mexico for some definite guarantee that adequate compensation will be made for American oil holdings. As Secretary Hull points out, it is in accordance with every principle of international law that the properties so expropriated be paid for by compensation representing fair, assured, and effective value. At the moment, Mexico seems to have no lack of good intentions with regard to payment, but the fact remains that it has given not the slightest hint as to how these intentions are to be fulfilled."

President Cardenas has said many times that the expropriated oil properties of British, Dutch, and American companies would be paid for. But the question of just how, when, and on what basis is a serious one to the companies directly concerned, as well as to banks, insurance companies, corporations, and individuals with investments in any foreign country.

In March, 1938, when the oil properties were confiscated, *The Associated Press* reported efforts by the Cardenas Administration to float a domestic bond-issue of 100,000,000 pesos to help pay the owners. The blunt comment of the Cincinnati *Times-Star*,

Now What?

—Reprinted from the Brooklyn Eagle.

upon reading the bond-issue story, was: "Mexico has no real ability, and no intention, of paying for the oil properties."

The properties were valued at $450,000,000. If every bond had been sold; and if the money had been used for the purpose intended, the owners of the oil properties would have received $20,000,000—approximately one-twentieth of their value. But let us see what happened to the fund-raising campaign—and the funds. According to Henry J. Allen, former Governor of Kansas, writing in the Topeka *State Journal:*

"Soon after the oil properties were taken over by the Mexican Government, Mexico began loudly to announce its intention to raise a fund to pay for the confiscated properties. The Government arranged elaborate public meetings; people paraded the streets with banners which declared the intention of the marchers to raise the money to liquidate the debt for the stolen properties.

"Finally, as not a word arrived from Washington, they counted up the contributions. These amounted to some $200,000.

"Instead of paying this, as an earnest of their intention to liquidate the oil debt, they followed the advice of the President, who told them the money should be used on the highways and that donors could accept highway bonds."

As the St. Paul *Pioneer Press* pointed out at the time:

"The Mexican Government does not deny that it is obliged to pay for the properties, but insists upon its own methods of valuation and form of payment. What these methods come down to is sufficiently clarified by the fact that the Mexican Government, in direct contradiction of agreements made with the United States in 1923 and 1927, refuses to recognize subsoil petroleum as part of the properties. This principle, if accepted, would wipe out 90 per cent of the value of the properties. Even this sum would not, however, be paid in cash, but in oil at Mexico's convenience."

The reaction of the St. Louis *Globe-Democrat* to this suggestion was as follows:

"Aside from the fact that this would mean that the original owners are merely reimbursing themselves out of earnings from properties which are rightfully theirs, the amount

180

received would be so small, compared to the total debt, that even under the best of circumstances the account could not be liquidated within the next half century.

"Restoring the properties after reaching an agreement on taxes and reasonable wages for labor is the logical solution."

VII

THE SILVER PURCHASE ACT, AND HOW IT FAVORS MEXICO

History of Our Silver Purchase Program—How Mexico's Export Tax on Silver Helps to Sustain the Government—Our Silver Purchase Agreement with Mexico—How the Silver Purchase Program Adversely Affected China—How the Treasury Continues to Buy Mexican Silver—How the Workers Get Control of Mines—Our Stupendous Silver Hoard—Repeal of the Silver Purchase Act Advocated.

The belief is widely held that the Silver Purchase Act, as well as the Government's entire silver-purchase program, will expire on June 30, 1939. Nothing could be further from the truth. The Roosevelt Administration will have full power to continue buying domestic-mined silver, along with other silver, unless and until the Act is repealed. As George Crane points out in the Gary (Ind.) *Post-Tribune:*

"These purchases have been made for the last five years under authority of the Silver Purchase Act of July, 1935. It created a bonanza for domestic silver producers and speculators. Guaranteed a price of 64.64 cents an ounce (troy), they received as high as 81 cents per ounce in 1935.

"Our six silver-producing states of the Rocky Mountain region will clamor for an extension of this Act. If they win, it will be one more subsidy for the taxpayer to carry.

"Since 1934, in addition to domestic purchases, the Government has made foreign silver purchases amounting to approximately 1,650,000,000 ounces. The price of this imported metal has varied from 43 cents to 81 cents an ounce. The chief foreign beneficiary of all this enormous buying has been the great silver-producing country of Mexico, which produces more silver annually than the United States.

"The United States now possesses in silver bullion about 2,500,000,000 ounces. This includes the old stocks and the new purchases made since 1934.

"The direct objective in passing the Silver Purchase Act was to increase the monetary stocks of silver in the Treasury until the ratio became $1 of silver to $3 of gold.

182

"One indirect purpose was to revitalize silver as the secondary metal base of our monetary system. This in turn would provide a healthy price and a permanent market for our own western silver.

"In August, 1934, the President by decree nationalized all silver stocks at $1.2929 per ounce—in other words gave it a bookkeeping price at this figure. In turn, there has been about $1,000,000,000 issued in silver certificates.

"But if it were possible to demand bullion for paper money, a one-dollar silver certificate today would draw from the Treasury less than one ounce of silver, which would be worth on the world market about 33 cents.

"Also it is to be held in mind that even this world market price is sustained artificially by the United States; and should it stop buying and begin selling, silver would drop to the price of copper.

"A second indirect purpose behind the buying policy: At the darkest period of the depression (1933), economists thought that an increase in silver stocks would supplement a shortage of gold stocks. This increase in silver would permit a much larger currency circulation, leading in turn to cheaper money and consequently higher commodity prices. There were two errors subsequent to this policy. We have never at any time, since 1934 at least, needed more bullion to cover our circulating currency. For the Government began gold-buying, and at the same time it began silver-buying.

"The gold reserves have more than covered all the paper currency that the country could absorb.

"In fact, the Treasury report for December 31st last showed total circulating currency to be $6,912,000,000; total gold stocks, $14,508,000,000. So it doesn't look as though our paper money will soon be used for wall-paper. Nor does it show much need for our silver reserves other than the 40,000,000 ounces we need annually for commercial purposes. In this writer's opinion, a second error was made in regard to this 'high circulating capital' theory. The error was made by the economists who held that higher commodity prices would lift the depression and cure unemployment. The British still hold to this viewpoint. But it is maintained here that America seems to be swinging around to the economic philosophy that higher wages and lower commodity prices is the way out.

183

"A third indirect purpose behind all this silver and gold-buying: The dollars paid out for the metal would remain in this country for the purchase of American goods. To a certain extent this has been true; particularly with China, Japan, Mexico, and Latin America. But not with England. For England, like the United States, is a creditor nation and doesn't need capital; it needs markets.

"Whatever Congress does about the problem will make little immediate difference in our money system. But it may make a great deal of difference in our national debt and tax burden."

Under a proclamation issued by President Roosevelt at the beginning of the year, the subsidy which the Government has paid to domestic silver producers since December, 1933, will be continued in operation—at least, until June 30th, next. Thus the Treasury will pay 64.64 cents for every ounce of newly-mined silver offered at any United States mint.

This price, remarks the New York Herald Tribune, "is probably three times as high as could be obtained were the Government to withdraw its support from the market." The world price, says the Philadelphia Bulletin, "is about 43 cents. The difference is an outright subsidy to the silver producers."

"Under the terms of the Silver Act," explains the Pontiac (Mich.) *Press*, "the Treasury is at liberty to purchase silver when, where, and as it likes." It is the theory of Secretary of the Treasury Morgenthau that purchases of foreign silver by the United States has stimulated the buying power of such silver-producing and holding countries as China, Mexico, Canada, Peru, Chile, and the Philippine Islands. According to *Editorial Research Reports,* of Washington:

"The United States Treasury, under the Silver Act of June 19, 1934, buys silver at two different prices. Foreign silver is bought at 43 cents an ounce, in amounts determined by the Secretary of the Treasury. Under these circumstances the market price is bound to be around 43 cents or slightly less. Prior to the inflationary legislation of the Roosevelt Administration, the market price of silver was around 33 cents.

"Domestic silver, newly produced from mines in the United States, is bought at 64.64 cents, one-half of the statutory value of $1.2929 for silver coined at the mints. This was the price fixed in the President's proclamation of December 30, 1937. For 1937 the price had been 77.57 cents, so that at the end of last year the subsidy enjoyed by the domestic producers was cut by about 40 per cent.

"The Silver Act of 1934 calls upon the Treasury to acquire, from domestic or foreign sources, large additional stocks of silver, and to issue a specified mimimum of silver certificates against these stocks. The purchases are to be suspended whenever the market price of silver reaches $1.29 an ounce, or when the ratio of the value of silver to the value of gold in the monetary stock becomes 1 to 3.

"This latter goal is still distant, not because the silver purchases have not been made, but because the gold stock has been steadily increasing."

Under the Treasury program, notes the New York *Times,* "domestic producers are receiving for their silver an amount nearly 50 per cent higher than the world price, and the world price is itself an artificial one, held up principally by Government purchases." In the opinion of *The Times:*

"Not a single contention made in favor of this silver policy at the time of its initiation has proved to be correct. It was argued that it would strengthen the silver standard in the countries where it already existed, and encourage more countries to adopt it. Its effect was to throw China, the only important country in the world on a silver standard, off it."

Speaking of the subsidy which will be continued until June 30th at least, the New York *Herald Tribune* says:

"The most interesting aspect of this newest proclamation is the reason advanced for its continuance: It is deemed advisable, to 'keep American silver out of the world market.' By doing so, it seems, the Administration 'hopes to thwart efforts of the dictator nations to bring the silver-producing countries into their orbit.'

"Here is a perfect example of the *ex post facto* rationalization that has accompanied every inflationary episode in history. Going back to the origins of the Silver Purchase Act, one will search in vain for any reference to this theory of 'saving the silver-producing countries from the dictators.'

185

Hoping He'll Take the Hint

—*Reprinted from The Christian Science Monitor.*

"The original justification for the program, as set forth by the President himself, was that it would 'assist in increasing and stabilizing domestic prices, augment the purchasing power of people in silver-using countries, and protect our foreign commerce against depreciated currencies.'

"These arguments have subsequently been so thoroughly discredited, not merely by argument but by events, that no one would dare to advance them seriously today. But the silver subsidy must be continued if the Administration is to assure itself the support of the silver-minded Representatives and Senators in Congress. So the 'dictator nations' are dragged in by the scruff of the neck to make the action appear rational.

"Even if this argument had any merit, it would not explain why it was necessary to maintain a domestic price more than 20 cents above the world price of 43 cents. All that would be necessary to prevent the dumping of American silver on the world market, obviously, would be to guarantee a price, say, two cents an ounce above the world price."

The fact that the Treasury buys Mexican silver at artificially high prices, and that the Mexican Government then places an export tax on the silver, thus compelling American-owned mines in Mexico to pay about $6,000,000 a year to support the Mexican Government, is severely criticized by the New York *Mirror*. And the Roanoke (Va.) *World-News* has this to say in an editorial headed "Subsidizing Mexico":

"At the very time the American State Department is engaged in a bitter controversy with the Government of Mexico over expropriation without compensation, the United States Treasury is subsidizing the Mexican Government through its silver purchase policy. For the United States buys Mexican silver as produced at 43 cents an ounce, and by that purchase is holding up the world price.

"Out of this payment a direct subsidy goes to the Mexican Treasury. Of every 43 cents this country pays for Mexican-mined silver, eight cents goes directly to the Mexican Government, besides the other taxes that Mexican mining companies pay, and the new export duty.

"The American subsidy on Mexican silver was sharply criticized when Mexico seized American and British oil properties in Mexico, and made no compensation to the oil companies. The Treasury then announced that it had abrogated

187

the agreement to buy silver direct from the Mexican Government, *but continued to buy it from silver producers in Mexico.* In fact the amount of silver purchased has increased month by month since that announcement. Purchases are made from Mexican mining companies after they have paid the eight-cent production tax to Mexico.

"Silver-producing states of the west support the Mexican subsidy on the theory that if this country stopped buying, the world price of silver would immediately drop, and that it would then be difficult to justify a continued subsidy such as is now being paid to American silver miners for silver the Government does not want and for which it has no special use."

As for the theory of the Secretary of the Treasury that purchases of foreign silver would stimulate the buying power of silver-producing countries, trade statistics supplied by the United States Department of Commerce show that exports to several silver-producing countries of Latin America are not much more than half of what they were in 1929, and imports are less than one-half in comparison with the same period.

According to the Acting Director of the Budget, the Treasury has bought in the open market, since the silver purchase plan went into effect, between $1,500,000,000 and $1,750,000,000 worth of silver.

Moreover, notes the Massillon (O.) Independent, "he has said that if the metal were sold today, it would bring only $1,000,-000,000.

As if this were not enough, we read in the Savannah (Ga.) *News* that:

"The whole six-year $60,000,000 silver subsidy program of the Government is without legal authorization, according to Neil Carothers, Dean of the College of Business Administration, Lehigh University, in the last of six articles on silver in the current issue of *The Annalist* (New York).

"The domestic subsidy and the general silver purchase program are two entirely different things, according to Professor Carothers, and a suit by some harried taxpayer to stop the subsidy might have some exciting consequences.

"Congress never has passed a subsidy law, he points out. It has never specifically approved the subsidy.

188

"The general public, after six long years, is gradually coming to understand the character of our monetary measures, and any member of Congress who votes for a continuance of this subsidy will very likely find himself before the bar of public opinion."

It is the buying of foreign silver, rather than the metal produced in the United States, that meets with the greatest amount of editorial disapproval. In the United States, explains the Dubuque (Ia.) *Telegraph-Herald*, "the subsidy was excused in the beginning as a concession to our silver-producing states, in the same way that a bounty to farmers is justified. But the same reasoning cannot hold for Mexican mines, for example."

Under the Silver Purchase Agreement concluded with Mexico in January, 1938, the United States undertook to buy, at an artificially high price, 5,000,000 ounces of Mexican silver each month. In addition, it was to take some 35,000,000 ounces of the metal during the year from Mexico's accumulated reserve. The Secretary of the Treasury reserved the right to cancel the agreement at the end of any month.

The money we spent for Mexican silver was, in effect, a subsidy. This subsidy, says the Houston (Texas) Chronicle, amounted to $30,000,000 a year, this being the difference between what our Government had been paying for Mexican silver and its value in an unpegged market.

Now, Mexico yields over a third of the world's total production of silver. For several years the United States has bought virtually the total output. Our agreement with Mexico was understood to be intended to arrange our monetary relation with that country satisfactorily; and also to give stability to Mexican currency by assuring that country of a steady market for its silver. The Government's silver policy has, from the first, been a mysterious one, outside of its purpose to subsidize mining in a few western states. As the New York *Herald Tribune* explains:

"Not long after the Roosevelt Administration took office, silver discovered that it had a warm friend at court. With the United States taking the lead, the so-called London Silver Agreement was negotiated at the London Economic Confer-

189

ence in July, 1933. On December 21, 1933, President Roosevelt moved to put the provisions of that agreement into effect, so far as the United States was concerned. He fixed at 64.5 cents an ounce the price which the United States Treasury would pay for domestic newly-mined silver.

"On June 19, 1934, the Silver Purchase Act became law, requiring the United States Treasury to buy one-third as much silver as it had gold, or to keep buying silver in world markets until the price reached $1.29 an ounce.

"The Treasury began its silver buying with a burst of enthusiasm. It bought all of the silver which the mines in this country could produce, and it bought such silver as it could get abroad."

The Des Moines *Tribune* also informs us that:

"The New Deal started buying silver as part of its plan to boost farm prices, and to increase employment in the mining states of the west. Last year the Treasury paid 77.57 cents an ounce for domestic, and 45 cents an ounce for foreign silver. This year it paid 64.64 for domestic and 43 for foreign metal, although Congress said in 1934 that silver should be valued at $1.29 an ounce for currency purposes.

"Except for small amounts used in minting coins, the Treasury has no direct use for silver.

"It has issued only enough 'silver certificates' to pay for the metal, and has not tried to spend the apparent 86-cent profit on foreign, and 64-cent profit on domestic silver indicated by current prices.

"It is these 'profits' that Republicans have attacked as 'fictitious' and 'dangerous.' They argue that the soundness of the currency would be imperiled if it were based on silver at $1.29 an ounce, when other countries are glad to get rid of silver at 43 cents, less shipping charges.

"Silver-state lawmakers, particularly Senators King, of Utah, and Pittman, of Nevada, however, assert that the program is tiding the silver industry over a temporary low-price situation, and is keeping thousands of men at work in mines which could not operate profitably at lower silver prices.

"At the beginning, the other important silver nations agreed to help boost silver prices by limiting sales or buying surpluses, but after the United States found itself carrying almost the whole burden of this 'London Silver Agreement' the plan was permitted to lapse without renewal on January 1, 1938.

"China, for instance, which was the only important nation with a silver monetary base, found that the higher external prices resulting from the 'Agreement' pulled so much silver out of the country that it abandoned its silver standard and turned to gold. Since then, China has shipped large quantities of silver to the United States, both to buy gold and, especially, since the Japanese invasion, to buy airplanes and other goods.

"Mexico and Canada also have used silver shipments as means of getting the dollars to pay for goods they customarily buy in this country. In the first ten months of 1938, silver imports included $100,514,516 from China, $37,862,463 from Mexico, and $11,214,281 from Canada.

"Mexico formerly received definite commitments from the Treasury on how much silver it could ship each month, but this arrangement was voided during the tension last spring over Mexican expropriation of American oil properties and discriminatory tariffs."

The British, Dutch, and American oil properties in Mexico were expropriated, it will be recalled, on March 18, 1938. On March 27th, Secretary of the Treasury Morgenthau announced that beginning April 1st, the Treasury would "defer continuation of the monthly silver purchase agreement with Mexico until further notice." There was no direct statement that might imply retaliation. The United States Government, he said, wished to "re-examine certain of its financial and commercial relationships with Mexico." In Washington, however, the move was regarded as retaliation by the United States against acts of the Mexican Government, such as the raising of import duties and confiscation of foreign-owned agarian and commercial properties. The fact that the Treasury announcement followed the Cardenas expropriation decree within ten days "makes it pretty plain" to the Los Angeles *Times* that our suspension of silver purchases from Mexico was in reprisal for the expropriation of American oil properties. As the California paper pointed out at the time, "there is no other reason for it, and Secretary Morgenthau does not deny it. The only new relationships are those created by the Silver Purchase Agreement, which are less than three months old; and the oil expropriation."

"The purpose of our agreement with Mexico," points out the Rochester (N. Y.) *Democrat and Chronicle*, "was to keep up the value of the Mexican peso, supply an outlet for Mexico's large silver production, and in general play the 'good neighbor' financially to the country south of the Rio Grande. In a word, our Government has been virtually subsidizing the Mexican silver industry, and through that supporting the Mexican monetary structure." "There was no obligation on the part of the Treasury to make these purchases from Mexico," notes the St. Paul *Pioneer Press*, "and nothing to be gained for the United States except the hope that by helping Mexico maintain the value of the peso, our foreign trade with that country would benefit."

"By purchasing Mexican silver at a price much higher than the world market price on silver, the United States has been furnishing a considerable proportion of the operating expenses of the Mexican Government," asserts the Bloomington (Ind.) *Telephone*. The Washington *Post* puts this proportion at about 13 per cent, since that percentage of revenue comes from the mining industry in Mexico. "And the world price of silver," continues the Washington paper, "is maintained entirely by the United States Government, which has been buying for several years more than the total world's production of silver." In fact, observes the Ishpeming (Mich.) *Iron Ore*, "the taxpayers' money has been invested by the Treasury in sustaining the purchase of silver." We read on:

"China has been favored under the theory that if we helped her out by buying her silver, she would buy more American goods. But the futility of this plan is found in the fact that China has gone off the silver standard. Another optimistic scheme of ours was to stablize the Mexican peso, but the peso sank to new lows."

"The Roosevelt Administration policy of subsidizing silver producers, not only in this country but also abroad, has long been widely criticized," reports the St. Louis *Globe-Democrat*. "Its first great result," the Des Moines *Register* informs us, "was to force a major depression upon China, forcing it to substitute gold for silver as a backing for its currency."

It also furnished Mexico with much-needed funds to carry out its social reforms, under which American-owned farm properties, railroads, sugar plantations, and oil wells were confiscated.

In fact, we are told by the Framingham (Mass.) *News* that in Mexico, the Government's press and propaganda bureau "argued that the United States must continue to purchase Mexican silver in order to protect its stake in Mexican trade and mining." This, says the Massachusetts paper, "is precisely the calculation that persuaded Mexico to expropriate American-owned properties."

The Southbridge (Mass.) *News* also sees the possibility that if Washington does not continue to purchase silver from Mexico, the Mexican Government may take over the largest American-owned mining companies. What is peculiarly ironic to the Mobile (Ala.) *Register* is that the silver purchases, "which cannot be justified economically, are the very means by which President Cardenas has been able to carry out his revolutionary experiment and take so high-handed an attitude towards the British, Dutch, and American oil interests. So far as the Treasury is concerned, the silver purchases have been nothing more than a drain upon it." In fact, recalls the Dallas (Texas) *News:*

"The Roosevelt Administration has gone to great lengths to hold the friendship of Mexico. The Departments of State and Commerce have done their best to better political and economic relationships. The Treasury has extended what amounted to relief payments to the silver mine workers by purchasing over an extensive period silver for which this country had no need whatsoever. The people of this country showed their interest and friendly attitude toward Mexico by pouring millions of dollars of tourist money into that country. Secretary Hull sought eagerly to have Mexico enter into a reciprocal trade agreement. In return, Mexico has confiscated American property and raised its tariff duties.

"Looking at the whole situation from the Mexican viewpoint, there are answers to these charges, of course.

"Mexico has its tremendous problems to work out, but it will learn that it cannot work them out by entirely disregarding international relationships, especially relationship with its nearest and, potentially, its most valuable neighbor.

"The request of Mexico that the United States renew its silver purchases from that country should be considered only in connection with two broad policies, of which the silver purchases from Mexico constitute only a small part: First, what should be the future of the silver purchase policy as a whole? Secondly, what should be the future of our trade relationship with Mexico as a whole?

"The answer to the first question is not difficult, as determined by the result of the silver program to date. It has failed completely in everything promised except the stimulation of activity in the silver mining industries. In view of the tremendous world surplus of silver, further stimulation of production is entirely without justification.

"Considered solely on its own premises, there is surely no justification for maintaining a relief roll of $30,000,000 a year for Mexican silver mines while there are 11,000,000 unemployed in our own country.

"Neither is continuance of the silver purchases justified by our trade relationship with Mexico on the basis of present conditions. Last year we had an unfavorable trade balance with Mexico, due solely to the heavy purchases of silver, as a commodity, from that country. Despite this fact, Mexico raised tariffs on a large number of our principal articles of export, seeking apparently to further increase her own favorable balance of trade."

The announcement of Secretary Morgenthau, in March, 1938, that the United States would discontinue buying silver from Mexico, under the agreement then in effect, was followed by a reduction of two cents an ounce in the buying price of foreign silver. This not only caused consternation in political circles in Mexico City, but caused a drop in the London silver market. The net result of the refusal of the United States to take more Mexican silver was to intensify the financial difficulties of the Cardenas Administration.

This situation lasted only a short time, however. Reports from Mexico City and Washington agreed that silver was being shipped to the Federal Reserve Bank of New York, where it was sold to the Treasury. The only difference was that the Mexican Government was placed in the same position as all other sellers of silver; it was deprived of assurance of future markets for specific quantities at a definite, agreed-upon price. And the price was

194

One Face North

—*Reprinted from the New York Daily News.*

43 cents an ounce instead of 45 cents. At any rate, Mexico was able to bridge the gap brought about by the reduction in revenues, i.e., royalties and taxes, provided by the expropriated oil companies. Which caused the Philadelphia *Inquirer* to ask:

> *"Could anything be more fantastic? Here we are, loading up on Mexican silver that will never be of any use to us, buying this silver at our own artificially high prices which enrich the Mexican Government, and at the same time financing Mexico's seizure of oil lands that belong to American citizens!*
>
> "Gold buying at inflated prices is bad enough. But silver buying—especially from Mexico, with whom we are involved in land-seizure disputes—is worse. Our excess gold, billions of it, is interred out at Fort Knox, Ky. The surplus silver, which has already cost us more than a billion dollars, is entombed at West Point.
>
> "The silver end of this crazy policy, inaugurated as a lure for Democratic votes in the silver-bloc states, is intolerable nonsense. It should be brought promptly to an end."

An Iowa paper, the Boone *News-Republican*, declares that "out of the billion dollars that have already been spent on silver, three-fourths of the amount, or $750,000,000, has gone to foreign producers and hoarders, including Mexico." As the New York *Times* remarks:

> "We continue to buy from our own producers silver at a price much higher than the market, and we continue to buy from Mexico and other countries silver that we do not need at a price made artificially high by our buying. *Thus we lose money both ways.* If an individual thought that he was benefiting himself by selling his own goods much below the market price and buying other people's goods that he did not need at prices higher than there was any good reason to pay, the authorities would begin to look into his sanity."

By purchasing Mexico's silver output at artificially high prices, maintains the West Palm Beach (Fla.) *Post*, "we are supporting the economic framework of a country that expropriates property of our citizens, wiggles its thumb in our face when asked to settle for them, turns its trade over to foreign Powers, and permits of European political penetration." Mexico would be hard hit if

196

the United States should cease buying its silver, confesses *El Universal,* of Mexico City. Silver prices would tumble, and the "catastrophic decrease in prices would cause a semi-paralyzation of the mining industry." But this would not be all:

"The capacity of Mexico to meet payments would likewise diminish notably. The volume of exports from Mexico to the United States during the first eight months of 1938 was nine million dollars under that for the same period in 1937. However, this decrease was largely compensated by exports of gold and silver.

"Were it not for this fortunate increase we would have felt the consequences of the decrease in oil exports. And undoubtedly we would feel these consequences in the event that suspension of silver purchases should take place. We would not be able to import—since we would not be able to pay for them—many articles such as wheat and corn, which we have imported in large quantities. Local sales would likewise decrease; many factories would shut down, and we would enter into a period of acute crisis."

"By purchasing Mexican silver we sustain the rickety financial structure upon which the whole Cardenas régime depends," agrees the Chicago *Daily News.* Such purchases, explains the Detroit *News,* "not only have afforded Mexico needed foreign exchange, but also provides the actual basis of its currency, serving to tie the silver peso to the gold dollar." In the opinion of the Dayton (O.) *Herald:*

"There is no sound reason for the United States purchasing any Mexican silver. As everyone but certain members of the Congressional silver-bloc knows, the white metal is not accepted for monetary use except as subsidiary coins.

"The 'Silver Senators,' of course, would like to see these purchases continue simply to maintain the pretense of the use of silver for monetary purposes. But why should the United States continue such a buying program in the face of Mexico's expropriations of American oil property and the increasing threat to other American-owned holdings below the Rio Grande?"

"Every week," declares the Charlotte *News,* "this nation buys from Mexico between $500,000 and $600,000 of silver. Now, this silver is of no earthly use to us. We are surfeited with the stuff already. We have to go to the trouble of storing it, guarding it, and taking inventories of it." Continues this North Carolina paper:

"If it maintained Mexico's internal stability and the volume of our trade there, this weekly subsidy of a half-million or so might be worth while. *But it hasn't worked out that way.* Mexico has become more and more unstable, and has almost closed the door to imports from America.

"Why wouldn't it be good sense to apply the half-million on the claims, and let Mexico keep her silver? Better still, why wouldn't it be positively astute to cease buying silver altogether?"

Other newspapers that criticize the Treasury program of purchasing domestic and foreign silver at artificially high prices include the San Francisco *Chronicle, The Wall Street Journal* (New York), Cincinnati *Times-Star,* Troy (N. Y.) *Record,* and the Providence *Journal.* "Foreign silver buying," declares *The Journal of Commerce,* of New York, "should be ended without further delay." In the opinion of this financial daily:

"The futility of making constant additions to the monetary silver holdings at this high cost is patent. If the Treasury wishes to issue more currency, it would be just as well to put out additional greenbacks, which cost merely the paper they are printed on, as it is to issue silver certificates with metallic backing that are worth only a fraction of their face value.

"Furthermore, in view of the vast gold holdings of the Federal Reserve banks, the latter can issue all the Federal Reserve notes that are likely to be required under any conceivable circumstances. Hence, there is no excuse at all for the Treasury to issue any additional currency of its own.

"The sensible thing to do, therefore, would be to work out an arrangement for the gradual curtailment of the domestic silver buying program. This is hardly likely to occur, however. First, it would be politically unpopular in the silver-mining states. Secondly, the consequent break in the market price of silver would attract attention to the failure of the Administration's silver buying program.

"Regardless of what is done about the domestic buying price for silver, however, there can be no reasonable objection to the cessation of purchases of the white metal abroad. If, for political reasons, a market must be provided for domestic silver, that does not justify purchases abroad of foreign silver that this country does not need.

"The fixed price of 43 cents an ounce that is being paid for Mexican silver represents, in effect, a very substantial bonus to that country, which has confiscated American-owned oil properties and farm lands, harassed other American enterprises operating there, and greatly curtailed her imports of American goods.

"The whole silver buying program was conceived in folly, and carried out with primary attention to the political considerations involved."

While the expropriation of British, Dutch, and American oil properties in Mexico has brought the silver issue to the fore, the question is not new. The Macon (Ga.) *Telegraph* reminds us that:

"For more than a generation the representatives from the silver-mining states have used the interests of their constituents in the white metal as an excuse for confusing the monetary standard of this country. The agitation reached its finest flower in the candidacies of William Jennings Bryan for the Presidency. The magic talisman of 16-to-1 was held up as a remedy for all our social and economic ills.

"It was one of the issues on which the American voters turned their backs in refusing to elect Bryan, and for many years we went along in the enjoyment of a sound currency, *the preservation of which was one of the planks in the platform on which Mr. Roosevelt was elected President in 1932.*

"But soon after he came into power he was besieged by men like Senator Key Pittman, of Nevada, whose political theories are dominated by the money interests of their constituents. Congress was induced to give the President authority to buy three dollars of silver for every dollar of gold in the Treasury.

"The immediate effect, of course, was to run up the price of silver far beyond its market value, and today we have millions of dollars of this metal lying sterile in the Treasury. It represents nothing except the margin of profit we have given as a direct subsidy to the silver states, and the continuance in power of the Senators and Representatives from these states."

What appeared to be a first step toward expropriating foreign-owned silver mines, chiefly the property of United States citizens, began in July, 1938. News services and special correspondents reported the introduction of a new 12 per cent tax on all exports; and setting up limits on imports. This was regarded as primarily an anti-United States move because of the dominance in the ownership field of our nationals and the Treasury's large purchases of silver from these sources.

A Mexico City dispatch to the New York *Times* supplied the details of the plan:

"The Mexican Government has announced it plans to put a 12 per cent tax on all exports, including raw materials, leaving Mexico, and at the same time to establish a limitation upon imports, which come largely from the United States, by establishing a double exchange rate.

"At least 75 per cent of Mexican exports normally consist of metals, including silver, gold, and lead; and the production of these metals largely is in the hands of United States firms.

"The new tax plan is capable of operating against United States interests in two ways: "First, through the export tax; and, second, by reducing imports."

Moreover, points out the Passaic (N. J.) *Herald-News*, "the 12 per cent tax on metal exports is based on arbitrary Mexican valuations, rather than world market prices—notably in the case of silver, which Mexico carries at an artificially high quotation. *This is in addition to a 12 per cent royalty which foreign mines must pay to the Mexican Government on all metals taken out of the ground.*"

According to *The Associated Press*, "the mining industry in Mexico is 75 per cent United States-owned; 11 per cent English; 10 per cent Mexican, and 4 per cent otherwise foreign." Gardner Harding, writing in the Toledo (O.) *News* tells that:

"The 12 per cent tax, according to unofficial reports from Mexico City, was directed especially against American mining companies, and the effect has been to complete virtual expropriation of the mining properties.

"New high freight rates from the railway unions, strikes in five mines, and seizures in five more have played havoc with American mining investments in Mexico.

"Over a billion dollars of foreign capital in Mexico is thus threatened with expropriation, under terms never before invoked by any other nation save Russia. These terms make future capital investment in the country out of the question."

Editorials in American newspapers almost universally condemned the 12 per cent export tax. Destructive taxation, pointed out the Boston *News Bureau,* can be just as ruinous as confiscation; "in fact, it is a form of confiscation." The 12 per cent export tax, this paper explains, is intended to make up for the loss of petroleum taxes. Although imposed on all exports, income would come chiefly from products of American-owned mines. The 20,000 miners in Mexico who are operating mines on a co-operative basis, however, reports the El Paso (Texas) *Times,* have "protested to the Government that they could not continue working unless the Government granted them a subsidy." Continues the El Paso daily:

"Mining in Mexico faces a crisis. American investors have a billion-dollar stake in the Mexican mining industry. American skill and courage developed many of Mexico's best mines, American ability has operated them, and the United States has been the principal customer for Mexican metals.

"Today, the industry is faced by measures which amount to confiscation."

Now, the mining industry is the principal source of Mexico's income at the present time. When, therefore, the 6,000 workers in the world's largest silver mine go on strike, as they did in December, 1938, both the Federal Treasury and that of the State of Hidalgo are deprived jointly of approximately $10,000 a day in taxes. "In its present economic condition," writes John M. Verber, Latin American editor for *The United Press,* "the Mexican Government can ill afford to lose its share of that revenue. Noting that there were threatened strikes in twelve other American-owned mining properties in Mexico at the time, the Louisville *Courier-Journal* remarked: "The strike and the threatened walk-outs indicate that the silver mines will follow the oil properties into the hands of the Cardenas Government." Speaking of the Real del Monte mines in the old Aztec town of Pachuca, the Kentucky paper continues:

"The organized mine workers ask for from 4,000,000 to 6,000,000 pesos in wages. The United States Smelting Company, owner of the mine, declares that its net earnings are only 5,000,000 pesos. Plainly it is another case of grab, and the workers threaten the Government that, should it force them to reduce their demands, they will sabotage the agreement by reducing the output 50 per cent.

"Evidently President Cardenas has started something he can't stop. His expropriation policy, as applied to land and oil, has gotten completely out of hand."

Betty Kirk, writing in *The Christian Science Monitor*, declares that "deep concern is felt for the future of the mining industry in Mexico, which is at present beset with two major problems. The first of these is in labor relations, and the second in the increase of government-sponsored workers' co-operatives." Continues Miss Kirk from her vantage point at Mexico City:

"Labor agitation within the industry was rife a year ago as the Syndicate of Mining and Metallurgical Workers announced it would launch a drive for a collective contract for the industry. Following the oil expropriation, the labor troubles subsided, apparently upon orders from the Government to avoid further difficulties until the oil problem was settled. Mining labor remained quiescent until October, 1938, when it broke out afresh with demands which, company officials say, are in excess of anything previously presented.

"Labor contracts have expired throughout the industry, and it is on the basis of new contracts that labor is presenting its demands. Their fulfillment would mean an annual increase at one mine alone of 30,000,000 pesos, and at another smaller mine of 20,000,000 pesos.

"Two strikes have already been called. Strikes are threatened at other mines, and a general strike is a probability.

"Since Mexico is in its gravest financial crisis for any time when there was not actual revolution, this advance by labor upon the Government's most important source of income is hard to explain. One explanation offered is that labor is being backed by the Government, as it has been previously, with the objective of creating a conflict similar to that in the

202

oil industry, and expropriating the mines. The second is that labor is acting in defiance of the Government in an attempt to assert its power and force further concessions of a political nature."

In July, 1938, Frank L. Kluckhohn, at that time Mexico City correspondent of the New York *Times,* reported that five United States-owned mines, together with two British, one French, and seven Mexican-owned mines, had been taken over by the Government. These mines, reported Mr. Kluckhohn, were not expropriated, but turned over to the workers when labor conditions made their operation by private companies practically impossible. In August, *La Prensa,* of Mexico City, reported that the Cananea Copper Company, an American concern, had threatened to dismantle its plant if the workers persisted in their exaggerated demands, saying that new taxes had already made the business unprofitable. As the Austin (Texas) *Times* explained:

"The present Government of Mexico has a very simple solution for wage difficulties. If employers cannot pay any wage demand, however high, they are offered the alternative of surrendering their property to the workers. The Government encourages workers' syndicates to make high wage demands in order to hasten what is euphemistically termed a 'program of socialization.' "

According to the Indianapolis *Star:*

"*An organized drive now is in progress to absorb mining interests. Mexican extremists are taking American-owned mines by the simple process of sabotage. After making working conditions impossible, the Government assumes control.*

"Chief attention has been focused on expropriation of vast oil interests, but the Mexican Government is steadily exerting pressure against other industries.

"The prospect of maintaining cordial relations with Mexico has grown dimmer as it steadily freezes out American investments or forces American-controlled companies to the wall. The speed with which Mexico is decimating our commercial operations below the Rio Grande is amazing to those who have observed its operations since acute trouble began about a year ago."

In Mexico City, *Excelsior* calls attention to the formation of miners' co-operatives to work properties considered unprofitable by their original owners. Declares this Mexican daily:

"It is notorious that this unprofitableness has always been the result of a gradual increase in operating costs, combined in some cases with a fall in the price of metals, or exhaustion of the mines.

"The companies that find themselves in this situation have brought before the labor authorities the dilemma of either reducing costs or suspending operations. As invariably the first of these requests is denied, they have been forced to continue operating at a loss until the limit of their economic capacity is reached.

"*They are then compelled to suspend operations, after assuming legal obligations for payment of wages, indemnities, and other charges. The workers thus become preferred creditors, until finally the business is turned over to them.*

"Once ownership and administration have changed hands, the first step of the new management is to introduce the changes which the company was not allowed to make; that is, to cut down expenses, reduce wages, and so forth, thereby justifying the original position taken by the owners. Had authorization been granted them, the business would have continued, with better prospects of future improvement.

"It is easy to understand that, there being no limit to the progressive increase of demands, the time will come when no company will be able to resist, no matter how rich and powerful it may be; thus the doors will be open to a system of expropriation, not by direct action of the state, but by tacit support of labor demands which exceed the limits of industrial economic resistance.

"There is still another procedure, however, this time one directly employed by the state. This system consists in financing workers' co-operatives, thereby violating the spirit of Article 27 of the Constitution (which expressly prohibits federal and state monopolies), as well as exemptions from taxation granted under the pretext of giving protection to industry or to the interests of a certain class. In brief, the spirit of the Constitution is to prevent the granting of privileges to the prejudice of a third party.

"Nevertheless, workers' mining co-operatives, undergoing no sacrifice in order to insure the survival of a business created and managed by its owners, have demanded and obtained from the state many advantages not enjoyed by the employers. Concessions granted them in the form of subsidies constitute a privilege expressly forbidden by the Constitution.

"We refer to the exemption from the 12 per cent tax on exports of silver and other metals, a burden which these co-operatives expressly stated they would not be able to bear without definitely going into bankruptcy.

"This procedure has the same results as the progressively increasing labor burden, since a company that is unable to pay the new tax will be forced to turn over its properties to workers because of unprofitableness, and then the workers will immediately obtain the exemption denied the company.

"Consequently, it is evident that by different routes we arrive at the same point—expropriation—and it is logical that in the course of time the system will become general.

"The problem becomes extremely serious when one considers that if this threat of expropriation is maintained, no company will invest its reserves in new explorations, or in the acquisition of machinery, or in anything that means progress in the mining industry.

"Ninety-nine per cent of the workers are interested only in the wage scale. It is only the leaders of the labor organization who aspire to intervene and have a say in the management.

"If negotiations could be carried on locally between the workers and the companies, and the workers were kept informed of the progress of these negotiations, many difficulties would be avoided. A recent case of settlement of difficulties which at first appeared insurmountable supports this statement.

"We refer to the case of the Cananea Copper Company where, after failure of all previous conferences between labor leaders, the employer, and labor delegates, and labor authorities, a satisfactory settlement was arrived at as soon as direct contact was made between the workers and the company. The men accepted the original proposals of the company, with slight modification of the only point in which they were vitally interested—increase in wages.

"We may say that the economic situation of Mexico would be greatly alleviated, the conditions of industry would be improved, and the workers would be benefited if, in each case of labor bargaining, the interested parties were given

205

the opportunity to deal directly, without interference of personal politics, in the negotiations."

Secretary of the Treasury Morgenthau's abrogation of the agreement to buy Mexico's newly-mined silver at a price above that of the world market, following the expropriation of British, Dutch, and American oil properties in Mexico, was hailed at the time (March, 1938) by the Springfield (Mass.) *Union* as "an incident that may be used to end a policy that should never have begun." The Treasury's further decision to cut the price two cents an ounce on all foreign silver, remarked the Scranton (Pa.) *Tribune*, "might have been expected as a result of Mexico's arbitrary act." But on consideration, adds the Pennsylvania paper, "one wonders why it has been necessary to buy silver at all, from Mexico or any other country."

A number of economists are considerably worried about the Treasury's program for purchasing monetary gold and silver. According to the Joplin (Mo.) *News-Herald,* "we now have in the Treasury approximately 55 per cent of all the monetary gold in the world." The United States not only has gathered the major share of gold, but, reports the Miami *Herald,* "it has also acquired one-seventh of all the silver produced in 450 years. Financiers are becoming worried. The rest of the world may repudiate the gold and the silver standard—or become so envious of our wealth that we shall be the target of attack." Continues the Florida paper:

"Prompt repeal of the Silver Purchase Act of 1934 is sought by a resolution of the Committee on Finance and Currency of the New York State Chamber of Commerce. It declares that the efforts to widen the use of silver as a monetary metal have failed; that we are the dumping ground for silver; and that it is undermining confidence in the nation's currency.

"A nation may have a surplus of silver and gold, as it may have an excess of wheat and cotton and livestock. The metals are not perishable, but their values may crash on a world market. And buried gold and silver serve no purpose; they cease to be wealth or a medium of wealth. Yet their accumulation piles up deficits, increases the burden of debts and taxes, and weakens the currency."

The Treasury, announces *The United States News,* of Washington, "now holds the largest hoard of silver that the world has ever known." According to this paper:

"This huge amount of silver is buried in a large vault at West Point, N. Y. The vault is 252 feet long, 166 feet wide and 22 feet high, and it will be filled with the precious metal.

"To store slightly more than one-half of the nation's silver supply in the vault, hidden in the hills of New York State, 25 trucks operated five days a week for 10 months to transport the metal 50 miles."

In the opinion of the Manchester (N. H.) *Union,* "the Silver Purchase Act is one of the most costly, useless, and unjustifiable features of legislation passed by the New Deal. The Act was conceived as a political sop to the silver interests, and has never been anything else. There is certainly justification for the demand of the Chamber of Commerce of New York for the end of a policy which is undermining confidence in the nation's currency, both at home and abroad." "Enactment of the Act," declares the Chamber, "was an open invitation to the silver-producing nations of the world to speed up their production—and they lost no time in accepting the invitation."

In adopting the report of its Committee on Finance and Currency, calling for the prompt repeal of the Silver Purchase Act, the Chamber of Commerce warns that the attempt to raise the price of silver has resulted in the accumulation of a hoard of the metal so vast that its concentration in the hands of a single nation constitutes a potential menace to the stability of world prices. And, as the New York *Sun* points out:

"We can't possibly sell any important portion of that metal anywhere, since no country now is on a silver currency standard. We are burying it at West Point, but since paper money can be issued against it at $1.29 an ounce—compared with an average purchase price of 45 cents an ounce—it still can raise hob as an inflationary mischief-maker. As a relief to American taxpayers, as an aid in the upholding of confidence in the dollar, as a means of teaching a salutary lesson

207

to the Communistic Government in Mexico—and as a measure of decency in stopping an exhorbitant tribute to a handful of western silver producers, repeal of the Silver Purchase Act should receive the prompt attention of Congress.

"The 'objectives' of the Silver Purchase Act have for a long time been clearly impossible to reach. That is so clear that the Administration no longer refers to them. It defends the purchase of silver on other grounds. One is the aid to employment in American mines. Another is the stabilizing effect on foreign currencies, notably those of Mexico and China. *Those ostensible reasons for continuing the program are as silly as the original purposes of the Act.*

"Silver has been virtually forced out of use as a currency, except for subsidiary coinage use, in every country (including Mexico, where the fiat paper is in circulation) and in China. No conceivable commercial demand ever will lift the price to $1.29 an ounce. As a currency stabilizer the record in Mexico, where the peso has been sharply cut and greenbacks are being used, illustrates the uselessness of silver purchase.

"As a straight-out bonus to American-owned and operated silver mines, the Act might have some defense. No bones are made about special favors to cotton, wheat, and other producers, and in a period in which the Treasury is disbursing billions, the few millions a year that go to domestic silver producers in the way of a bonus (i. e., the difference between a normal market price and the Treasury's fixed honorarium of 64.64 cents an ounce) might be regarded as small change. *The worst of it is that, of the total silver acquired under the Act, only 13 per cent has come from domestic mines.*

"Most of the benefit has accrued to Mexico, the chief producer, and the principal economic and political developments in Mexico since the passage of the Act in 1934 have been: Abandonment of silver as a currency; seizure of American and other foreign land and properties without compensation; devaluation of the peso and the circulation of greenbacks; and the setting up of prohibitive tariffs against American goods."

It is ridiculous, agrees the New York *Times,* "that under the terms of an economically unsound law, enacted as a concession to special silver interests in this country, the United States should continue to subsidize the Mexican Government, which deprives

—*Reprinted from the Tyler, Texas, Courier-Times.*

American citizens of legally acquired interests of great value."
"This country should abandon its blundering silver policy, not
merely to punish Mexico, but because it is wholly uneconomic,"
declares the Eureka (Calif.) *Humboldt Times*. According to the
New Haven (Conn.) *Journal-Courier:*

"There seems to be some doubt in Washington whether the
United States suspended silver purchases from Mexico in
retaliation or not. Certainly the ground for retaliation
existed; following a decision of the Mexican Labor Board
commanding a wage increase for oil field employes, the
Government took foreign oil properties over for failure of
their managements immediately to meet the Board's award.
An American Government less friendly to much the same
philosophy as actuates President Cardenas would have re-
acted, perhaps with less vigor than did Mr. Coolidge on less
provocation in 1927; but with vigor.

"But Mr. Roosevelt has been so accustomed to strafing big
business at home; and his liberal and leftist allies are so
friendly to wage increases, whatever the extent or difficulty
to management, that open disapprobation was somewhat difficult. So it is, perhaps, that Mr. Morgenthau is unwilling to
join the two incidents, although the suspension of silver purchases from our southern neighbor is rather generally believed to be linked to the expropriation. Granted that, it will
be well to remember that we keep on buying silver in the
world market.

"But so long as we buy in the world market, we shall be
helping Mexico at least indirectly. Where we buy from
another vendor that vendor is open to new offers from Mexico. We can hardly take silver off the world market without
opening a vacuum likely to attract more from Mexican sellers, ultimately if not directly. But why not suspend the
whole silver-buying fiasco—no longer denied, even in Washington, to have been a fiasco.

"*Why not move toward a measure of reason and soundness
in our monetary policy by allowing the silver industry, domestic and elsewhere, henceforth to shift for itself?*"

"The United States Government has no disposition to interfere
in Mexico's internal affairs," observes the Manchester (N. H.)
Union, "but when, in the conduct of those affairs, Mexico deliberately tramples upon American rights, the United States Govern-

ment is certainly justified in ceasing to show further favors." At present, explained the Chicago *Daily News,* "we pay Mexico for her silver. Mexico then uses American dollars to pay American investors for their stolen farm properties. They steal the land. We give them our money. They use our money to pay us for our properties!"

"The sensible thing for this country to do," believes the Indianapolis *Star,* "is to realize that the Silver Purchase Act was a mistake; that it has not produced what was promised, and never will." As the New York *Herald Tribune* puts it:

"Not only has the silver policy failed dismally to achieve its avowed objectives, but it possesses—unlike the gold purchase policy—the additional mischievousness that it is still in effect and that the task of terminating it is fraught with serious difficulty—economic as well as political. The silver purchases of our Government have complicated, rather than solved, the silver problem, since they have resulted in a rise in American production from 33,000,000 ounces in 1933 to 69,000,000 ounces in 1937; and in world production from 190,000,000 ounces five years ago to 276,000,000 last year.

"Last year the United States Treasury bought 313,000,000 ounces of silver—or 37,000,000 ounces more than all the silver mined throughout the world in that period."

Secretary of the Treasury Morgenthau has testified that purchases of foreign silver have stimulated the buying power of such silver-producing or holding countries as China, Mexico, Canada, Peru, Chile, and the Philippine Islands. To stop such purchases, he states, would tend to reduce our exports. But, declares the New York *Times:*

"This is not a good reason for continuing to buy abroad, at a highly artificial price, a metal for which we have not the slightest need. We have accumulated such a surplus of silver that, instead of importing any more we ought to be trying to export it. The silver that the Treasury has in its vaults is a dead burden to us in the same way as the 11,000,000 bales of unsold cotton in American warehouses is a dead burden. If the Secretary were compelled by law to buy foreign cotton at twice as much as it was worth, it is true that the other cotton countries would have more money to buy our automobiles. But this is merely another way of saying that,

211

from a national point of view, we would in effect be giving those automobiles away."

Finally we come to the experts. W. A. Lyon, writing in the New York *Herald Tribune,* maintains that:

"The Silver Purchase Act is open to damning criticism on many grounds. It is open to attack as an outright subsidy to an industry whose importance in American economic life is minor. It is assailable on the grounds that it tends toward inflation and dilution of the currency issue. It is vulnerable on the ground that it has disrupted the currency systems of those countries which a few years ago used silver as a base."

Another point is brought out by Herbert M. Bratter, in the New York *Herald Tribune:*

"The Silver Purchase Act is a mandatory Act, yet it gives complete discretion to the Administration to carry it out. And so, whenever the Administration receives criticism because of its silver purchases, it points to the mandatory feature of the Act, and expects you to forget that it was invested with discretionary power.

"Although the Act is indeed 'mandatory', it does not make the Government buy Mexican silver at a time when Mexico is discriminating against American trade and American investors. There was nothing in the Act or any other law to require or to justify the increase in the price of silver from 64.5 cents to 77.5 cents, which the Administration introduced in 1935. *There was nothing in the mandatory terms of the Act which required extension of the special domestic silver subsidy beyond the expiration in 1937 of the President's original silver proclamation.* In fact, these gifts to the silver interests were granted by the Administration of its own accord, or, at least, not under the Silver Purchase Act."

In another editorial, *The Herald Tribune* reminds us that the Chairman of the Federal Reserve Board, Marriner S. Eccles, declared in March, 1939, that the Treasury's foreign-silver buying policy "has tended to destroy the use of silver elsewhere in the world, and does more, in my opinion, to ultimately destroy the domestic silver industry than anything else I know." When you buy the world's silver, said Mr. Eccles before the Senate "silver committee," you "tend to destroy the use of silver elsewhere in the world." And Mr. Eccles added:

"Practically the only important market is in this country, and the only use we have for the silver is to make more excess reserves, which are already excessive, and more bank deposits, which also are already excessive."

In the opinion of *The Herald Tribune:*

"The silver purchasing program hasn't the slightest justification as a monetary measure, and not even its friends pretend to defend it openly. Nevertheless, because of its political implications, no one in the Administration has had the temerity, in these five years, to challenge, or even question, its economic importance. No one, that is to say, until Mr. Eccles came along.

"From a banking standpoint, Mr. Eccles told the committee, the silver purchase scheme is definitely injurious, since it has the effect of adding artificially to excess reserves at a rate of $400,000,000 to $600,000,000 annually. In addition, he noted, it puts the Treasury in the position of being able to add enormously to these reserves by using its seigniorage profits, profits which amount at the present time to some $1,250,000,000. But quite aside from its banking significance, the Reserve Board Chairman pointed out, the policy, if continued, must eventually defeat the objectives of its supposed beneficiaries.

"The Administration has ignored for five years the arguments of orthodox monetary economists, who have repeatedly and unanimously denounced its silver program. How long, one wonders, can it continue to ignore these arguments, now that they have received the frank and unequivocal indorsement of its own chosen monetary expert?"

"It is well to have these aspects of the matter hammered home from an official source," believes the New York *Times.* No currency has been issued against the billion ounces of silver bullion held idle in the Treasury, *The Times* informs us. Yet, under the law, the Government must go on buying. This conservative daily is convinced that our Silver Purchase Law, "which has failed in every one of its avowed purposes, ought promptly to go to the legislative scrap-heap." In fact, declares the Bridgeton (N. J.) *News:*

"The whole silver policy is based upon unsound economic theories. It is an expensive luxury to load on the backs of the already over-burdened taxpayers. The justification for the continuance is a domestic subsidy. Certainly there is none for the continuance of foreign silver buying, particularly as it is not only driving the world off the silver standard, but also giving aid and comfort to the totalitarian nations at the expense of the democratic nations.

"Secretary Morgenthau would perform a service to his country if he would explain the Treasury's inconsistencies of silver purchases, and leave the determination of the foreign policy of our Government with the State Department, where it belongs."

Colonel Percy E. Barbour, consulting mining engineer, reminds us in a New York *Sun* article that:

"The silver bloc which perpetrated this monstrosity is comprised not only of the Senators from the so-called silver states, but also other Senators who are determined to force inflationary paper money on this country.

"For many years the price of silver has been fixed every day in London by four gentlemen representing the silver market. Their integrity has never been questioned. The price is determined by the simple process of matching the supply of bar silver available for sale against the demands for silver and for exchange from the Orient. The principle observed is that all effective offerings of silver for sale shall be absorbed. This is merely the immutable but inarticulate law of supply and demand, made articulate by this so-called price-fixing committee.

"In the world's 10,000 years of written history there is not a single instance where this law of supply and demand has ever been violated successfully or with impunity. It has been tried in all ages and in all countries, but it is unbeatable. The law of supply and demand is not a man-made law and it cannot be repealed or changed.

"In the summer of 1933, at the World Economic and Monetary Conference in London, representatives of sixty-six governments unanimously adopted a resolution, of which the principal provision was that the said governments would abandon the practice of debasing and demonetizing their silver money. Two days later a four-year silver control agreement was signed by the representatives of eight na-

214

tions: The United States, Mexico, Canada, Australia, and Peru as producers; and India, China, and Spain as holders of silver.

"When it expired by limitation at the end of 1937, not one signatory nation had asked to have it renewed. One reason was because it had ignominiously failed to accomplish its avowed objective."

It is manifestly impossible, even in a book, to quote all the newspapers which advocate repeal of the Silver Purchase Act. But the following newspapers have put themselves on record as against the Act: Paterson (N. J.) *News*, Boise *Idaho Statesman*, Hartford (Conn.) *Courant*, New York *Journal of Commerce*, Philadelphia *Inquirer*, New York *Wall Street Journal*, New York *Post*, Newport (R. I.) *News*, Providence *Journal*, Austin (Texas) *Times*, Council Bluffs (Ia.) *Nonpareil*, Washington *Post*, Indianapolis *News*, Cleveland *Plain Dealer*, Lansing (Mich.) *State Journal*, Minneapolis *Tribune*, Youngstown (O.) *Vindicator*, Jersey City *Journal*, Salt Lake City *Deseret News*, Long Beach (Calif.) *Press-Telegram*, Philadelphia *Evening Public Ledger*, Portland *Oregonian*, New Orleans *Times-Picayune*, Hoboken *Jersey Observer*, Baltimore *Sun*, Houston *Chronicle*, Louisville *Courier-Journal*, St. Louis *Globe-Democrat*, Columbus (O.) *Dispatch*, Bangor (Me.) *News*, Dayton (O.) *Herald*, Troy (N. Y.) *Record*, Boston *Christian Science Monitor*, Raleigh (N. C.) *Times*, Jackson (Mich.) *Citizen-Patriot*, and Macon (Ga.) *Times*.

Closed Doors

"The tragedy of thousands and thousands of useful men."

—*Reprinted from Ultimas Noticias of Mexico City.*

VIII

COMMUNISM IN MEXICO

Is Communism Behind Seizure of American Oil Property?—Following Russia's Example—Labor Organizes Government Employes—Mexico Spreading Communism Throughout Latin America—Mexico's Anti-American Activities—Fascism Penetrates Latin America—Japan's Influence in Latin America—The "Labor Squeeze"—Subsidizing Wheat Exports—Thousands of Strikes—Mexico's Drastic Social Reform.

"Mexico is, in form, a republic. But actually it is Communistic." Such is the conclusion of George Morris, Washington correspondent of the Memphis *Commercial Appeal*. President Cardenas of Mexico, characterized as the "problem child among statesmen of the Western Hemisphere" by the New York *Daily News*, "has been tutored, we suspect, by Leon (Stormy Petrel) Trotsky." Speaking of the expropriation of American and other oil properties, the Washington *Times* also wonders "whether Leon Trotsky hasn't had something to do with all this." Trotsky, the Topeka (Kan.) *State Journal* thinks, "is finding Mexico as fruitful as was Russia for the propaganda of Communism." The Council Bluffs (Ia.) *Nonpareil* puts it this way: "Cardenas would transform Mexico into a Communist state. Trotsky is there telling him how to do it." But the Mexico City correspondent of the Boston *Christian Science Monitor* insists that such statements are baseless:

"Mr. Trotsky was granted permission to live in Mexico with the understanding that he was not to mix in Mexican affairs. With the exception of a few verbal clashes with Vicente Lombardo Toledano, the Mexican labor leader, he has kept to his promise."

At any rate, "the United States might as well make up its mind to the fact that in Mexico it has a Communist neighbor. President Cardenas is an acknowledged collectivist." Such is the con-

217

clusion reached by the Rochester (N. Y.) *Democrat and Chronicle,* and the Helena (Mont.) *Independent* agrees that "the President of Mexico is a dictator, with Communistic leanings." *In Georgia, the Rome News-Tribune even goes so far as to declare that "Communism is behind the seizure of American oil properties in Mexico."*

President Cardenas is quoted as denying the above. "We are neither Communists nor Fascists," he maintains. "Mexico is a republic, and the acts of our Government conform to democratic principles." Despite this statement, however, *Excelsior,* published in Mexico City, asserts that "Communistic work is being carried on behind the President's back in certain government departments." Unfortunately, observes the Brooklyn *Eagle,* "there have been indications that Cardenas has been encouraged, particularly in his expropriation policy, by various radical groups in the United States."

From various sources we learn that Mexico is in the grip of a powerful Nationalist and Socialistic movement; organized labor seems to be pushing the nation toward a sweeping and complete program of confiscation of foreign capital and investments. Henry J. Allen, former Governor of Kansas and Editor of the Topeka *State Journal,* is convinced that "unless President Cardenas is stopped, he may nationalize all property in Mexico." General Hugh S. Johnson, in his syndicated column, avers that "Mexico is under a Communist dictatorship." Today, says the New York *World-Telegram,* "the Cardenas Government, apparently taking a leaf out of Soviet Russia's 1917 notebook, seems determined to go the limit in the confiscation of foreign property." Confirmation is found in Mexico City, where we find *Excelsior* saying:

"There is a relatively large group of people here who look to Russia with the greatest interest to copy its policies, with the hope of receiving aid from Moscow—moral support, at least, and in any case orientation and advice. It is said even that the Russian Communist Party has contributed money to the realization of the radical 'tactics' that we have experienced. However, in order to demonstrate the influence of the U. S. S. R. on some of our official circles, it is sufficient to mention the tendencies suggested by the Department of

Public Education in its *Review*. The contents of this publication are largely Sovietic teachings.

"Frequently official statements are made denying that Mexico favors Communist propaganda; but this is not true, and we can prove it by the example of the National Council of Higher Education, an agency of the Federal Government for necessary consultation.

"This Council has the fullest powers in matters of education and, therefore, can guide it in any channels desired.

"Let us see what is the work of the unpopular Council, according to its own report.

"The instructions for the course on political economy decisively states: ' . . . and in view of the fact that the Marxist theory is the only one that properly forsees and explains economic events that have been observed for a long time in the capitalist régime, this theory shall be followed in teaching political economy in secondary schools for workers.'

"Naturally, the bibliography includes the works of Marx, Engels, and Lenin."

Another Mexico City paper, *Ultimas Noticias*, declares that: "XEFO and XEUZ, long-wave and short-wave radio stations of the Party of the Mexican Revolution, of which President Cardenas is the leader, broadcast each week 'The Voice of the Communist Party.' Moreover, these broadcasts are announced in advance in the party's newspapers." Still another Mexico City daily, *El Hombre Libre,* has this to say:

"Not long after General Cardenas took office as President of the Republic, the Minister of Education said at the close of a labor meeting which he attended in representation of the President, that the President's ideal was that at the expiration of his term the dictatorship of the proletariat might be established in Mexico.

"Time has passed and even the blind can see that the Cardenas policy has followed a well defined trend in this regard. All efforts tend to clear the ground for the application of Communism, even if this has been denied officially in order not to awaken mistrust in certain chancelleries.

"Instead of improving the economic conditions of the workers, what is sought is the destruction of capital.

"An attempt has been made to disarm the enemy; to destroy at each step the concept of property. Thus two things have been attained: To fascinate the poor with the mirage of wealth; to acquire political force and to prepare the road for the abolition of private property."

Back in the United States, we find the Richmond (Va.) *Times-Dispatch* bluntly saying:

"The Cardenas Government of Mexico is probably the most radical Government in the world today, with the exception of that in the Soviet Union."

There is not much doubt in the mind of a California paper, the Santa Rosa *Republican,* that "the expropriation of American property in Mexico during the last two years was inspired by Leon Trotsky." (Mr. Trotsky was Minister of Foreign Affairs, following the Russian Revolution, and in recent years found a haven of refuge in Mexico City.)   As the Bristol (Va.) *Herald Courier* explains:

"When the Bolsheviks came into power they seized all foreign-owned property, but paid nothing for it. It was not possible for the United States and other nations to hold the Bolsheviks to the principle of honest dealing, but those nations have not forgotten the dishonesty of the Bolshevik régime.

"It is extremely regrettable that Mexico, adjoining the United States, seems inclined to adopt the confiscation policy of the Russian Bolsheviks."

According to the Denison (Texas) *Herald:*

"Mexico in recent months, has become the battleground of two European ideologies—Communism and Fascism.

"The Communists hold the upper hand in Mexico at present. Leon Trotsky recently informed the Communists of the world that President Cardenas was a 'better, brainier Communist than Stalin.' "

President Cardenas, it is generally agreed, is largely influenced by the armed agrarians and the Confederation of Mexican Workers. As the New Haven (Conn.) *Register* sees the labor situation in Mexico:

"Through the Confederation of Mexican Workers—a sort of American CIO—the labor movement has gradually increased its hold on the Cardenas Government, until now its demands can hardly be denied.

"Recently, by gaining the additional right to organize government employes, labor further strengthened its grip.

"As it happens, moreover, the labor movement's leadership is strongly left-wing. Thus you have a situation where the most aggressive Mexican forces of the moment are distinctly radical.

"On the other hand, conservative elements, including certain State Governors, military leaders, remaining large landholders and the like, have considerable underground strength. And between the two sides there is certain to be conflict, if the power of the central Government ever crumbles."

Of the "red" elements in Mexico, Vicente Lombardo Toledano, avers the Brooklyn *Tablet*, "is the wildest." Continues this paper:

"At present they are following the Communist line. Excite the people, confuse the issues, give the mob guns to shoot one another, then seize the power. According to reports from Mexico, the 'reds' are training their own militiamen, independently of the regular Army. As they did in Spain, they plan to arm and equip the members of the Communist unions to form a fighting force that will take over the Government and crush all opposition."

In the New York *Mirror* we find that:

"Like Russia, Italy, and Germany, Mexico is a one-party nation. Everybody who holds office, or a government job, belongs to the National Revolutionary Party.

"Every member must pay one week's wages into the Party Fund every year. The contribution is subtracted by government bookkeepers from pay envelopes. It's the "check-off."

"Cardenas summed up the purpose of his program: 'Our Six-Year Plan is to transform and replace capitalism.' "

Toledano, believes the Chicago *Tribune*, "is driving Cardenas to a smash-up. This labor leader is a Communist. He is in close touch with the Third International, and only recently returned from a conference at Moscow." To quote "The Day's News," a New York *Mirror* column:

"Vicente Lombardo Toledano is the most spectacular figure in Mexico. He is the driving force behind the seizure of foreign farm land and the confiscation of $450,000,000 worth of foreign oil properties.

"A thin, short, pale-faced, forty-two year old bundle of inexhaustible energy, he first joined labor when he was a student at the University of Mexico.

"He is Mexico's best orator, and speaks English and French.

"Four years ago, he deserted the Regional Confederation of Labor to form his own Mexican Workers Confederation. He has built it along industrial lines, organized the peasants, elected members to Congress. They now have one million members.

"Toledano insists he is not 'red' but 'Socialistic'.

"But the preamble to his Federation's Constitution reads: 'The proletariat of Mexico will fight fundamentally for the abolition of the capitalist system.' "

Following a visit of its Editor, Henry J. Allen, to Mexico, the Topeka (Kan.) *State Journal* is convinced that:

"Communism is confiscating the [Mexican] property of citizens of the United States and getting ready to build on our border a 'hell's kitchen' which will invite the 'red' element of the world and challenge us with problems that will become very real.

"Every day the United States ignores the growing challenge of the Mexican situation, the problem grows stiffer; and some day when finally we are forced to take hold of it and straighten it out, it will have become immeasurably more difficult than it would be if we moved upon it now."

Admitting, as most editorial writers do, that there is considerable Fascist penetration in Mexico, this question arises: If the Communistic régime of President Cardenas were to be unseated, would that help to establish a Fascist group in power? The Houston (Texas) *Chronicle* is authority for the statement that:

"Those twin ogres of the Old World, Communism and Fascism, are busily at work in Mexico. Each is attempting to pull Mexico its way, so as to establish a foothold in the Western Hemisphere from which to operate and expand.

"Each is willing to plunge Mexico into civil war in order to accomplish its purpose.

"Americans cannot blind themselves to the fact that unless the trend in Mexico changes, one of those systems will obtain a strong foothold—possibly after a bloody conflict with the other. From Mexico it could spread to other Latin American nations, carrying in its wake wholesale expropriation of foreign properties, destruction of American trade, and the cancellation of the 'good neighbor' policy. And in this way—by indirection—the Monroe Doctrine could be violated, with either the Soviet Union or the Fascist Powers getting a foothold in the Western Hemisphere."

In view of this country's traditional friendship for England, which has probably $5,000,000,000 invested in Latin America, and our peculiar relationship with the countries south of the Rio Grande because of the Monroe Doctrine, the delicate position in which the United States would be placed because of the incubation of radical and dangerous Communistic action just south of its border becomes immediately apparent.

"The organization of Mexico on the Soviet pattern certainly would make it more difficult to preserve a democracy in the United states," contends the South Bend (Ind.) *Tribune.* And the possibility that Mexico may become as completely Communistic as Soviet Russia is said to have caused grave concern, both in Washington and London. Already, says the Hendersonville (N. C.) *Times-News,* "Mexico is the center and hotbed of Communism in the Western Hemisphere." In fact, *La Informacion,* of Caracas, Venezuela, claims that:

"The directors of international Communism have established by means of agents located in Vera Cruz, Mexico, the contact they needed with the countries of this continent. Mexico, where Communist propaganda is carried on without restriction, thanks to protection afforded by the Government, is going to play in America the part played by Spain in Europe. At present Marxist circles in Mexico are very active, and orders and instructions are issued to the Argen-

223

tine, Brazil, Chile, Cuba, Panama, the Central American Republics, Peru and Bolivia, and especially Colombia and Venezuela.

"Complying with peremptory orders from Moscow, several active and intelligent Communists, all of them military agents of the Third International, have left Mexico to go to the above mentioned countries, carrying precise instructions. The true mission of these agents has been cleverly concealed. Some are supposed to be scientists, others are business men, and still others are tourists, and many of them conceal their mission under their true profession. Thus we see painters, sculptors, and writers who suddenly arrive at the appointed places and hold exhibits and give lectures to cloak their activities.

"The Russian Communist directors must at all costs take over the exploitation of oil in these countries by means of strikes and rebellions, obstructing by all possible means the operations of the established companies.

"The activities of these 'red' agents have already been disclosed in the Argentine, Chile, Brazil, Colombia, and Venezuela."

It is asserted by the New York *Enquirer,* after "a searching inquiry carried out in secret by competent investigators," that "the Cardenas *junta* at Mexico City, operating behind a screen bearing the hammer and sickle of Communism, has betrayed Mexico into the hands of Adolf Hitler, politically, economically, and spiritually, in defiance of the Monroe Doctrine and despite the extraordinary favors through President Roosevelt's 'good-neighbor' policy."

These investigators report Nazi influence at work in many parts of Mexico; so much so, in fact, that:

"Uncle Sam now has Adolf Hitler as a next-door neighbor, controlling Mexico economically and politically, with Japan as his eager assistant, in flagrant violation of the spirit and the letter of the Monroe Doctrine

"The charges leveled against the Cardenas *junta* by the New York *Enquirer* are not based on wild rumor or hearsay. They are fully substantiated by information gained by expert investigators, within the borders of Mexico itself.

"Mindful of the tremendous economic and political importance to the United States of what was transpiring upon the soil of our neighbor across the Rio Grande, this newspaper sent R. L. and R. P. Martin on a secret mission designed to secure the truth as to the conditions there. Its enterprise has been richly rewarded."

The significance of this situation, if substantiated, would of course be rather sinister, when taken together with Mexico's anti-American activities. *The Enquirer* reminds us:

"A vast amount of American property has been confiscated by the 'red' *junta* headed by President Cardenas. By means of excess tariffs on our goods and in other ways, it has given super-abundant evidence of being animated by a spirit of ruthless anti-Americanism.

"In spite of all this, our Government has not only refrained from taking the necessary steps to enforce American rights across the Rio Grande, but has actually been most assiduous in showing every consideration for the 'red' *junta* of Cardenas, and has gone to extreme lengths to give it moral and material support."

And if other countries in this hemisphere follow suit:

"If the Cardenas *junta* at Mexico City succeeds in consummating its designs with regard to the confiscated property, a condition of things will arise wherein our vast stake in the countries reaching from the Rio Grande to Terra del Fuego will be placed at the mercy of those governments desirous of enriching themselves by wholesale spoliation."

Some may ask what difference it makes to the American people if there is a government under European control in one or more of the Latin American republics. The answer is obvious, replies Walter Lippman, in one of his syndicated articles, for "as long as the Latin American countries are independent, no European or Asiatic Power can invade or even attack the United States except by crossing at least 3,000 miles of open ocean.

"But if such a Power had a base in this hemisphere for its fleet, its airplanes, and its submarines; if it had a colony or even a secret ally in this hemisphere, the United States would have to defend itself, not at long range, but at close range."

A hostile Power with a friendly base in a Latin American country could cut the Panama Canal, isolate our fleet in the Atlantic

or Pacific, and leave the other coast open to attack, adds Mr.
Lippman. So—

"In a matter of such vital importance to them and to ourselves, it is not the appearance, but the reality, that counts.
And the reality is this, that any revolution or any change of
party control anywhere in this hemisphere which brought
to power men allied with, encouraged by, subsidized by, or
otherwise under the influence of Russia, Japan, Germany, or
Italy, would mean that the essential principle of the Monroe
Doctrine had been violated, and that the security of the whole
hemisphere was gravely reduced. For it would mean that
the revolutionary imperialisms of the Old World had established a physical base in the New World.

"So we have to repeat today what President Monroe said
in 1823: 'We owe it, therefore, to candor and to the amicable
relations existing between the United States and these
Powers to declare that we should consider any attempt on
their part to extend their system to any portion of this hemisphere as dangerous to our peace and safety.' "

All the lands of North and South America should co-operate
for defense against imperialists from abroad, declares the Philadelphia *Inquirer*. In this paper's opinion:

"Danger to one nation in the Western Hemisphere would
imply danger to all nations. Attempts from Europe or from
Asia, either direct or indirect, to dominate a South American
nation would be a warning signal to North America. The
interests of all in this comparatively close-knit New World
are inseparately entwined.

"Brazil, Argentina, Peru and the other great nations to the
south need the defensive strength of the United States. It
is impossible to calculate the vital role played by the Monroe
Doctrine in the development of Central and South America.

"On the other hand, the value to the United States of a
strong defensive alliance among all the Americas is equally
inestimable. Canada is rich in minerals needed for defensive
armament, particularly nickel. Brazil has untold resources
in manganese, essential to modern steel-making. She has
rubber and coffee. Argentina produces vast quantities of
hides and wool. Mexico has tremendous wealth in oil. Bolivia

Service With a Smile

supplies tin. Almost every country in the Western Hemisphere has something of paramount importance to contribute to the mutual defense.

"There are recurring disputes between South American countries that should be resolved in the interests of an all-encompassing protective alliance. Furthermore, reparation by Mexico for seizure of farm lands and oil lands owned by citizens of the United States should be put on a businesslike basis. Expropriation by other Latin American nations of property owned by United States citizens should be discouraged.

"At home, it is the task of the United States Government to go straight ahead in its program for protection. The Navy should be strengthened. The air forces should be built up to a high level of efficiency and kept there. The Army nucleus should be expanded. All this is insurance for peace.

"It is possible that the rearming program will meet an unpredictable amount of more or less organized opposition.

"This opposition to sound protective measures, at a time when Europe and Asia seethe with hate and aggression, is dangerous. The New World is free of war and imperialism. But Fascism, no less than Communism, menaces some American countries. If the United States and the other Americas are to keep their hemisphere clear of war and imperialism, they must be adequately prepared.

"There is no easy road to the mutual defense goal which today is demanded of all the Americas for their own safety. It calls for effort, money, self-denial. For the United States, protection against outside aggression requires vigorous, non-political co-operation, with every dollar spent producing a dollar's worth of value. For the Western Hemisphere, protection also means non-political co-operation, with all national jealousies buried for the common good."

Mexico's agreement with Fascist Italy to barter oil from the expropriated British, Dutch, and American properties, together with her similar agreement with Nazi Germany, indicates an ever-increasing tendency toward Fascism. A Mexico City dispatch to the New York *Times* says "the Government's press department has become a typically Fascist information and propaganda agency, rather than an organization exclusively for the dissemination of information." Delbert Clark, writing in the

228

same paper, reports a relatively small, "but potentially dangerous Fascist movement in Mexico." According to the San Francisco *Wall Street Journal*, "several Mexican newspapers are already openly publishing Fascist propaganda, and there is no doubt that German and Japanese influence is steadily increasing." In fact, maintains the Charlotte (N. C.) *Observer:*

"Washington has been faced with the prospect that the Fascist combination will become the real backer of Cardenas in his fight for existence. Under such circumstances Japan, Germany, and Italy might easily entrench themselves so strongly in the economic and financial life of the country that they could dominate many of its activities. Japan, in particular, is seeking harbor facilities that might be used against us in the future.

"It is well to recall at this point that early in the World War we found Germany thoroughly entrenched in Mexico; and one of the main motives for our entry into this conflict was furnished by the discovery that she was egging on the Mexicans to harass our border and to threaten an attack on us in case we became involved."

"The time is not far distant," believes the New Haven (Conn.) *Journal-Courier*, "when the United States must face the fact of the growth of Fascism in the Western Hemisphere, and adopt a definite policy toward it." The Fascist nations are "making every effort in Latin America to break down our influence, our trade, and our financial position," asserts the Charlotte *Observer* in a second editorial, and the New York *Herald Tribune* agrees that:

"In all the South American countries, colonies of Germans and Italians are centers of revolutionary activities designed to change the existing governments of South American republics and switch new Fascist governments into line with the international aims of Italy and Germany."

Japan is the third Power that is widening its influence in Latin America, using the old familiar Bolshevik strategy of "boring from within." William LaVarre, who has traveled widely in Central and South America, says in one of his New York *Mirror* articles:

"Nazism, Fascism, and Nipponism want Latin America. Without Latin America they can't jump on the United States. "Without Latin America they can't rule the world. Moscow also wants Latin America—for if Communism could make a total or important conquest, internally, in South America, it would turn Latin Americans, when war comes to Europe, against one another, and create such strife in South America that Germany, Italy, or Japan would get little help, and few raw products for munitions or subsistence.

"An agreement has been reached between Hitler and Mussolini on how South America is to be divided up—this for Germany, and that for Italy!

"From now on, Mussolini's Fascist agents are to play a new game—with Fascism boring into Latin American politics, and Nazism concentrating on sabotaging Latin America's trade with the United States.

"Japanese agents, behind many dummies, have tried to secure large land concessions within bombing distance of the Panama Canal. Japan now hopes to sabotage United States manufacturers—working through their own distribution organizations—and to wreck both North American commerce and prestige.

"It was Japan that planned to initiate a revolution in Brazil, and engineer the birth of a new state, the 'Republic of Amazonas,' over which the Rising Sun would have absolute political and economic control. Japan actually obtained a concession for 2,000,000 acres of land on the Amazon, and sent 100,000 Japanese to take up posts in Japanese villages along the banks of South America's mighty river of future commerce and raw resources.

"In the continent south of us, made up of many nations, there is a vast storehouse of raw material. There's copper, tin, iron, manganese, nitrate, lead, quicksilver, vanadium, cotton, wool, beef, hides, sugar, wheat, corn, petroleum—all war necessities, all vitally important to men who are planning world conquest or a devastating war."

With our nearest southern neighbor in mind, the Denison (Texas) *Herald* observes:

"Mexico is torn with dissension, with these two alien ideologies fighting for control, while the United States looks on, helpless to intervene. No matter which side wins out, Mexico will remain a problem for us. Either a Communist nation or a Fascist state at our doors would be a menace to the democratic United States."

While there seems to be some question as to whether Communism or Fascism is in the saddle in Mexico, it really doesn't make any difference, declares the Tulsa (Okla.) *World:* "So far as the people of the United States are concerned, they are one and the same. The practical effect of both is to abolish personal liberty and to take over all industry and enterprise."

It is a mistaken policy, various newspapers are saying, for Mexico to alienate the United States and permit the insidious penetration of certain grasping European governments. The Augusta (Ga.) *Chronicle* prints a few items to show the "encroachment of totalitarian governments" in Latin America:

"From 1933 to 1936 Germany increased her export trade 50 per cent in Central America.

"Peru has 500 war planes, nearly all of Italian make and under Italian control, and within less than one day's flying time from the Panama Canal.

"Heavy shipments of Italian artillery and machine guns were sent to Peru last December.

"Berlin is only two days from Brazil by air.

"Germans of Brazil have productive copper mines, nickel mines, and over a million acres of presumptive oil land.

"Military and naval officers of Brazil are invited in large numbers to German training schools, expenses paid. Many return home as Nazi addicts.

"Germany has extensive air service in all South American countries except Venezuela.

"Italians are now training the Bolivian Army.

"German radio stations blanket South America with propaganda.

"One hundred thousand prosperous Germans live in Argentina.

"American trade with Brazil now takes second place to Germany."

During the year that has followed expropriation of British, Dutch, and American oil properties in Mexico, relates the Gloucester (Mass.) Times, Mexico, copying Soviet Russia in some

231

particulars, has sent a continuous stream of propaganda to all United States newspapers.

One bit of propaganda is exposed by the *Humboldt Times,* of Eureka, Calif., which says:

"In defense of Mexico's seizure of foreign-owned oil properties, a brightly printed, three-color propaganda pamphlet has been distributed to American newspapers, stressing the point that American mining and trading interests in Mexico are greater than this country's Mexican oil interests. The object of the pamphlet is to build up public sentiment against a discontinuance of silver purchase by the American Government.

"The argument begins with a statement that 60 per cent of the value of Mexican oil production in 1936 was produced by British-Dutch companies, and only 35 per cent by American companies. In effect, then, Mexico says: 'Don't feel too badly about it; we're stealing almost twice as much from others as we are from you.'"

Newspaper editors generally agree that the task of the State Department at Washington in dealing with the Mexican Government on the issue of expropriation was not made any easier by the attendance at a labor conference in Mexico City last September of John L. Lewis, Chairman of the Committee for Industrial Organization, rival of the American Federation of Labor; and Edwin S. Smith, a member of the National Labor Relations Board. According to the Portland *Oregon Journal,* "both Lewis and Smith, in their addresses, openly attacked American employers, thereby strengthening the hand of President Cardenas of Mexico at a time when he was bluntly defying Secretary of State Hull."

"No one wishes to muzzle Mr. Smith," declares the Asheville (N. C.) *Times,* "but there are some speeches which are better undelivered—such as his Mexico City address." In the opinion of *The Wall Street Journal* (New York), government officials have often shown themselves "lacking in both taste and judgment in making speeches on matters which so closely concern their official function that any public reference to them must be considered indiscreet." But, it adds, "the address of Mr. Smith was a new high in impropriety." Continues this financial daily:

232

"The speech was delivered before the so-called International Industrial Relations Institute, at an assembly of that body sponsored by the Mexican Confederation of Workers. The burden of the message was an attack on American employers.

"These utterances would have been improper even if the strained situation between the United States and Mexico did not exist. But to make a speech before a foreign labor body which is in large part responsible for the expropriation of American property, and to single out American employers for attack, would not be a patriotic gesture even by a private individual. When it comes from a government official, and a government official who is charged with a quasi-judicial function directly relating to employer-employe relationships, it would seem that impropriety can go no further."

Moreover, asserts Carter Field in one of his syndicated Washington dispatches:

"Smith praised Mexico as the only country having a capitalistic structure—presumably the only country except the Soviet Republic—which has the enlightened courage to insure the rights of all workers. Smith openly approved the oil expropriations.

"John L. Lewis, according to the reports, agreed with Smith in supporting every action the Mexican Government has taken. Four million workers in the United States, he told the delegates, had sent him to bring good wishes and encouragement to the Mexican workers. Problems of workers in all countries are similar, he said, and the tactics of big employers the same, in no matter what country they may be.

"The two great statesmen on the North American continent, he said, are also the two great humanitarians—Roosevelt in the United States, and Cardenas in Mexico.

"Most of the delegates came away with the notion, from Lewis's speech, that the aims of both Roosevelt and Cardenas on behalf of the down-trodden, and in the desire to develop national resources for the benefit of all the workers, are such that Roosevelt approved. Cardenas's action in seizing the oil properties."

Hartley W. Barclay, Editor of *Mill and Factory* (New York), "covered" the labor conference at Mexico, and on his return wrote an article for *America's Future,* also of New York.

—Reprinted from the Knoxville, Tenn., Journal.

234

The Boston *Transcript* finds this report on Mexico "amazing; almost fantastic." In fact—

"It is the story of an international conspiracy aimed at the United States, and designed, among other things, to destroy our democracy, to sabotage the policy of our Department of State, and to persuade the whole Western Hemisphere to adopt the Mexican program of expropriation of the property of foreigners.

"While there is plenty to cause Mr. Barclay concern, he is most disturbed by the aid and comfort given the Cardenas Government by the presence of John L. Lewis and Edwin S. Smith at the sessions of the Mexican Labor Congress. He accuses both of these Americans of unpatriotic activity in that they lent the impression, through their speeches, that the Roosevelt Administration approved of Mexico's crusade for social reform, and especially of its confiscation of farm lands and oil wells.

"To be sure, Mr. Smith and Mr. Lewis have denied that this was the purpose, but the quotations from their addresses show how easy it was for the Mexicans to misunderstand them. The former was bitter in his attack on reactionary capitalism, and hailed Mexico for recognizing the rights of all workers. Mr. Lewis characterized the great corporations as enemies of the workers of the whole earth.

"In ordinary times neither of these fulminations would have been taken seriously. But because of the delicate diplomatic situation which confronts the United States and Mexico it was, at the very least, a blundering performance. By endorsing the aspirations of the Cardenas Government, Messrs. Lewis and Smith not only encouraged Mexico to extend still further its expropriation plan, but may have inspired other countries to indulge in the piratical practice of seizing American property.

"Already a number of valuable mines have abandoned their properties to the workers and left the field because they could not meet the 'squeeze'. The greater properties are struggling on, trying to comply with the impossible provisions of the labor contracts, while hoping for some protection from Washington. They realize that unless it comes soon, they will have to surrender their properties to the Mexican workers without hope of restitution. They know that when they leave Mexico because they are not able to carry on under the restrictions, they will be declared bankrupt under the Mexican law, and their properties turned over to the workers."

It was the "labor squeeze" which brought about the oil land expropriation, and the end of the "squeeze" in that case is not yet, we may judge from a Mexico City *United Press* dispatch:

"The amount the Mexican Government expects to pay foreign oil companies, whose property was expropriated, was expected to be considerably reduced by a ruling of the Supreme Court upholding the severance clause of workers' contracts.

"The Supreme Court, in a unanimous decision, ruled that the companies should pay their workers three months and twenty days' wages for every year of service, amounting to approximately $30,000,000.

"The decision was based upon the refusal of the companies to accept the award of the official arbitration conciliation board whereby the companies were ordered to pay $5,200,000 in annual wage increases. This broke the contract, the Court ruled.

"The Court ruled also that the companies should pay 25 per cent of the wages for the period of the strike in 1937, or 'face embargo of their properties'."

The Cardenas régime in Mexico has brought to new perfection the technique of expelling unwelcome elements, not by direct action, but by making things so hot for them they are willing to go. This is known in Mexico today, as regards foreign capital, as the "labor squeeze."

This has already been applied to the railroads and the oil industry, and it is well advanced in the mining field, according to the St. Louis *Globe-Democrat,* the Houston (Texas) *Post,* and the Boston *News Bureau.*

Exactly how the "labor squeeze" works is explained by former Governor Allen of Kansas, in the New York *Herald Tribune:*

"The 'labor squeeze' is really not the result of any legitimate differences between operators and their workers; it is the accomplishment of a deliberate purpose to drive the mining companies, utility companies, and other properties into bankruptcy and take them over after the companies have ad-

236

mitted their inability to deal with the growing stringencies of the labor program.

"This program starts out with Lombardo Toledano, a Russian-taught follower of Trotsky, a lawyer who never marred his hands by labor. He is, however, the John L. Lewis of the Mexican situation. Under the tutelage of Trotsky, they have written new labor laws in Mexico which give to Toledano, the head of the Mexican vertical union, command of everyone who works in Mexico. He can tell employers whom they shall hire, and upon his personal edict, he can tell them when to discharge any employe from their list. He has armed 100,000 Mexican laborers who march regularly.

"Toledano has reduced the number of technical and expert employes allowed under the old Mexican immigration law for the mining industries to a point where it is practically impossible for the mines to bring in a sufficient number of technical men to safeguard their operations. The labor contracts due for signatures at this moment contain as high as 500 stipulations, and the purpose of all these regulations is to take away from the mining companies the command of their own business; in fact, to reduce the control to a point where the workers will be dominant in the conduct of the mines.

"With the growing restrictions upon the technical and administrative supervision, it isn't difficult for the labor leaders to convert a profit-making mine into a substantial loser. When these unsupportable losses begin to occur, mine owners ask the Government for permission to suspend operations, as provided in Article 116 of the labor laws, without responsibility on the part of the owners. The owner sets up that the business has become manifestly unprofitable.

"The Government delays its permission until the owner's resources are exhausted; then his only alternative is to turn the property over to the workmen."

In spite of the strain placed on it by a series of events which almost approaches the status of "international incidents," the United States has continued to maintain its "good neighbor" policy toward Mexico.

For example, when Mexican crops failed and food shortgage resulted, the republic below the Rio Grande was able to obtain foodstuffs—but particularly wheat—at bargain prices, which in

237

the last analysis placed extra costs on two classes of United States citizens and taxpayers:

1. Those living in the United States and paying taxes here.
2. Those living or doing business in Mexico and paying taxes to that nation.

The sequence of events began last October, just after the Department of Agriculture made arrangements to sell wheat to foreign nations at less than the market price—the Government first buying the wheat at the market price. The New York *Times* correspondent reported the news in a cable from Mexico City:

> "The Mexican Government has agreed to buy immediately in the United States more than 3,000,000 bushels of wheat under the new American subsidy plan. It is believed to be the first such deal since the subsidies were announced in Washington.
>
> "The contract has already been signed for 1,120,000 bushels of hard wheat at a cost of about $760,000, close to 68 cents a bushel.
>
> "The arrangement is the result of negotiations between the Mexican Export and Import Bank and the AAA of Washington, Mexico paying with money obtained from the new general export tax, of which United States mining companies bear the brunt.
>
> *"The purchase is regarded as particularly interesting, since Washington is paying a double subsidy—one on wheat and the second on the silver from which the Mexican Government obtained the money for the purchase."*

The Butte *Montana Standard* added more details:

> "Arrangements have been made for the purchase of wheat which will be sold to Mexico at a price 12 or 14 cents a bushel cheaper than it is being sold on American markets."

Near the end of 1938, W. R. Mathews, of the Tucson *Arizona Star*, summed up the international trading:

> "To December 1, 1938, Mexico had imported 50,000 metric tons of wheat (17,750,000 bushels) ; 500 tons of rice, unannounced tons of corn. Moreover, the Mexican Government is negotiating for the importation of still more corn, wheat, and beans. Growing conditions have been good, yet under the program of *ejidos* Mexico, instead of exporting

238

food as she normally does, is now importing food. If this condition should continue for two or three more years, can a government responsible for it continue in power?"

There was a time, comments the Minneapolis *Journal*, "when the Yankee trader was known around the world for shrewdness and ability to hold his own in business. That was before the New Deal in politics." Continues the Minnesota daily:

"The plan embraces buying at full market prices by the Government and resale for export at lower prices, the Government absorbing the loss.

"Mexico having seized American-owned properties valued at millions, it seems inconsistent, to put it mildly, to favor them with our cheap wheat. But we are selling Mexico wheat at prices below what our own people have to pay, and taking Mexico's silver at higher than the market price would be if our buying did not hold it up."

This, observes the Jamestown (N. Y.) *Post*, "is known as statesmanship."

At any rate, somebody along the line has lost money on this, says the Johnson (Kan.) *Pioneer Weekly*, and the somebody is identified by this paper as the American taxpayer. Summing up the wheat deal, the New York *Times* decides:

"If an individual thought he was benefiting himself by selling his own goods much below the market price and buying other people's goods that he did not need at prices higher than there was any good reason to pay, the authorities would begin to look into his sanity. The same policies, when we follow them as a nation, are hailed as masterly economic maneuvers."

The Mexican Government is adding insult to injury by shipping crude oil for refining into Texas. This creates a situation which gives serious concern to many of our oil-producing states. In Texas, as the Danbury (Conn.) *News-Times* hears, "one Houston company has contracted for from 10,000 to 15,000 barrels of Mexican crude daily, and in one month took over 375,000 barrels." This is how it is done, according to *Progressive Labor*, of Knoxville, Tenn.:

"The Eastern States Petroleum Company, of Texas, has excited interest in the State, Commerce, and Treasury Departments in Washington, since it has been reported that the company is planning to import seven and a half million barrels of oil from Mexico to the United States. This oil is produced under conditions where there is no investment at stake, and sold below prices prevailing in the United States. Naturally this undermines the American price structure. The Mexican Government is said to have invested $1,250,000 in the Eastern States Petroleum Company."

In Iowa, the Boone *News-Republican,* speaking of the arrangement, by which Americans are allowed to refine and re-export Mexican oil under bond, explains that this does not take the oil out of competition, except in the domestic market. Continues the Iowa paper:

"The refined Mexican oil does not have to be returned to Mexico, so it competes with American oil in foreign markets.
"Because Mexico has had to pay nothing for developing the oil fields, it can cut the export price, and so undersell American oil dealers."

Mexican crude oil has been shipped by hundreds of thousands of barrels to Texas, according to oil men, at a time when southwest oil companies had voluntarily curtailed production. "Bootlegging," the Lansing (Mich.) *State Journal* calls it. Governor Marland, of Oklahoma, echoed the editorial sentiments of such papers as the Denver *Post, The Wall Street Journal* (New York), and the Laredo (Texas) *Citizen* when his attitude was outlined in the Topeka (Kan.) *Capital:*

"It is a universal tenet of law that the buyer of stolen goods is an accessory to the theft, if he knew the seller had purloined the property. No buyer of crude oil is ignorant of the method by which the Mexican Government obtained the oil properties belonging to American, Dutch, and British companies."

Various details of the shipments are reported by papers, including the Houston (Texas) *Post,* the New York *Times,* the Chicago *Tribune,* and the Abilene (Texas) *Reporter-News.*

Thanks!

—*Reprinted from the Houston, Texas, Post.*

A survey of the entire situation is given in a Houston dispatch to the New York *Journal of Commerce:*

"Mexico, which seized all the vast oil properties of Americans in that country under the expropriation act of March, 1938, is now doing a good business shipping oil to Texas at cut-rate prices, in competition with companies that own expropriated properties.

"Most of the oil is being re-shipped to Italy and France, under trade agreements.

"The contract, which binds the Eastern States company to take 7,300,000 barrels of oil from the Mexican Poza Rica field over a two-year period, stipulates that none of it shall come from expropriated wells, but all must be production owned by Mexico in its own right.

"However, Texas oil operators have complained that it all amounts to the same thing, because Mexico can afford to sell its own stuff at prices below the market and make it up in domestic sales with confiscated oil, which costs the Government nothing."

The anger of the Lone Star State press is keen in the situation. "Texas won't stand for it!" exclaims the Greenville *Herald.* "What the American oil industry needs is an enlarged market, not more competition at home," adds the Beaumont *Enterprise.* And *The Texas Weekly,* of Dallas, which has been studying the problem, wants to know:

"Are the American owners of oil wells to be compelled to compete in their own local market with the output from confiscated property in Mexico which does not represent a single dollar of investment by the Mexican Government? This is a question, it seems to us, that presents an entirely new problem to the American Government."

In the nearby oil state of Kansas the Winfield *Courier* adds:

"There is a law called the anti-dumping law, but it seems inadequate to cover the case. Certainly this situation calls for a remedy.

"If there is no law to cover this case, a law should be enacted at once."

The Christian Science Monitor, one of our conservative and widely read dailies, remarked soon after the Mexican Government

242

expropriated British, Dutch, and American oil properties: "The present situation in Mexico has been precipitated by 'advanced' labor laws, and even more by the new political power of organized labor in that country."

"President Cardenas," agrees the Philadelphia *Evening Public Ledger*, "probably had little choice in the matter of taking over foreign oil properties. Pressure from the powerful labor organizations doubtless forced the Government's hand." And the New York *Times* correspondent at Mexico City reported, some weeks later, that "with the labor groups fighting for control of the Mexican Congress, political circles here are discussing the possibility of a showdown between organized labor and the Cardenas Administration." At that time, the question was whether President Cardenas could control other elements, once the vast petroleum industry had been turned over to the workers. For, as the Panama City *Star and Herald* reminds us:

"The agrarian classes and the workers of all kinds have the upper hand in Mexico today."

So far as the expropriation of oil properties is concerned, the Dallas (Texas) *News* is authority for the statement that "while the strike of the oil workers precipitated the situation that led up to the decree of expropriation, the strike and the insistence of the Mexican Government that the demands of the strikers be met was really but the means to an end." Continues *The Christian Science Monitor:*

"In fairness it should be said that President Lazaro Cardenas probably does not wish to go nearly so far as his Congress, but has been pushed to extremes by Socialistic and Communistic labor elements. He has tried to make amends in the case of the oil land expropriations by verbal assurance that payment will be made. But with all the good will in the world, the value of such assurances must depend on their being kept.

"It is not a wholesome situation if a dominant political party in any country gets the impression that it can seize property at will merely by making promises that have all the solemnity of Japanese apologies."

243

During the first three years of the Cardenas régime, say *El Mundo* (Tampico), "there have been 2,149 strikes in Mexico, in addition to the many suspensions of work and irresponsible strikes. The losses incurred run into many millions of pesos. In every case the authorities, from labor inspectors to the Supreme Court, which handles labor matters, have shown a decided partiality in favor of the workers."

Willis Thornton, writing in the Nashville *Tennessean,* gives us a picture of muddled labor and political conditions in Mexico. Says this *NEA* staff correspondent:

"Cleavage between radical and conservative is increasing in Mexico as business depression deepens and the oil expropriation controversy remains an open sore.

"New political lineups are in the making. Two deputies, expelled from the dominant *Partie de la Revolucion Mexicana* (PRM), are trying to form a 'Constitutional Democratic Front.' This, they insist, will be equally opposed to Communism and Fascism. It is bitterly attacked by the labor unions as Fascist.

"So bitter is this cleavage becoming that the unions or syndicates of the Confederation of Mexican Workers (CTM), the dominant labor organization, are trying to boycott unfavorable newspapers and to stop their distribution by strikes and refusal of transport.

"Conservative papers and magazines are fighting this move.

"Between these groups President Cardenas is caught in a tightening grip. He must have the support of the labor unions to carry on his Government at all, yet he hesitates to turn his Administration over to them entirely."

Let us see how President Cardenas himself analyzes the labor situation in his country. Anita Brenner, writing from Mexico City to the Milwaukee *Journal,* quotes him directly concerning events leading up to expropriation of the oil properties:

"It was a situation in which it had become impossible for capital and labor to work together. When such a situation exists, in a vital industry especially, it is imperative to find a solution that will guarantee the normal functioning of the industry.

"When capital and labor can no longer work together, then one or the other must remain in complete control. And the only practical thing is to let labor run it, because it is labor that has to do the work."

There we have the philosophy of the Tarascan Indian who rules Mexico today.

But the President of Mexico "is sitting on a veritable volcano," observes the Washington *Star:*

"Labor in Mexico is insisting upon greater impetus to social reforms, and oil workers particularly complain that they have not received from the Government the benefits they sought from the companies before expropriation; the agrarians are crying for greater land distributions and expansion of credits; and the Army is discontented with its subordination to labor as a directing force in Mexico's political destiny."

Now that labor has forced President Cardenas to take over the oil properties, he will be unable to retreat, argues the Dallas (Texas) *Dispatch;* "it must rather be expected that the leaders of the syndicates will bring further pressure upon the Government so as to complete the program of nationalization in all realms of industry." It is a dark prospect, as the Richmond (Va.) *Times-Dispatch* sees it:

"The trade unions, which have grown stronger during the Cardenas Administration, are arming and drilling. Peons are organizing themselves into agricultural shock troops, ready to fight for the Government that gave them back their land. The clenched fist, symbol of the united front, is making its appearance in public."

Hartley W. Barclay, Editor of *Mill and Factory* (New York), made a study of labor and industrial conditions in Mexico, following the expropriation of oil properties, and reports, in part, as follows in his magazine:

"In the majority of plants, factory discipline has been destroyed. Since employers cannot discharge an employe without encountering a legal process and paying the worker

three months' wages plus a bonus, employes often want the employer to 'fire' them because they will get more money in hand than they can obtain any other way.

"And after this payment has been made, there still remains the opportunity of getting a decision against the employer in the Labor Board, with recovery of wages for the full period during which the employe has not worked.

"In the majority of plants, union officers have more authority than the plant management, because of the power to hire and fire assured to them by 'exclusion clauses' in labor contracts.

"Under Mexican law, the labor union may force employers to discharge any employes upon the request of the union.

"If a strike occurs and is declared 'legal,' the Army and the Navy and the Government, together with the powerful political party of PRM, appears to be on the side of the strikers. Breaking a legal strike is unheard of.

"When the strike is over, if it has been declared legal by the Government, the company has to pay the expenses of the strike and wages for the whole period of the strike.

"Companies which find themselves unable to survive are liquidated, socialized or expropriated, and nationalized. Few companies can survive the combination of these powerful forces.

"The private enterprises which have survived the 'social reform' are forced to conduct their operations upon an extremely restricted scale. They are completely unionized, with few exceptions, and work under labor contracts which include a wide variety of provisions for vacations, sick benefits, free medicines, free hospitalization, allotments for burial expenses, and establishment of funds for schools. There are also many legal holidays provided. Some contracts provide for from 21 to 30 days vacation, plus 16 legal holidays with full pay."

Similar facts are noted by Henry J. Allen, former Governor of Kansas, who has been visiting Mexico and studying labor conditions there. He comes to this conclusion, writing in the Topeka *State Journal:*

"The absorption of industry by labor is the most deadly form of confiscation which fore'gn capital faces in Mexico today. It is undoubtedly the fate reserved for the mining industries, representing the largest group of foreign investors in Mexico.

"It comprises a deliberate conspiracy between the Government and the labor leadership, and works inevitably to dispossess the owners of their property without a single recourse in fact or even a legal grievance under the present laws of that country.

"The process begins with what the victim designates as the 'labor squeeze.' This procedure has been applied to several of the smaller mining industries, and is moving steadily toward the strangulation of the larger smelters and mines, as the two-year contracts expire and new labor agreements must be made.

"The United States has never encountered a challenge like this in Mexico before. An entirely new element has entered the picture. A new labor leader, Lombardo Toledano, has undertaken to organize the Mexican laborer. He is making steady progress. Toledano spent some time in Russia.

"Among the sensational things Toledano has accomplished, through his co-operation with the President, has been a program to arm labor and give it military training. Something over 100,000 of Toledano's workers have already been armed, and drill periodically.

"The whole situation, so far as it affects life and property, is stiff with uncertainty. The day I visited the Chamber of Deputies the place bristled with arms. Practically every member of the Chamber wears a pistol."

W. R. Mathews has been studying the Mexican situation for his Tucson *Arizona Star*. Economic difficulties, he finds, have been creating discontent in labor ranks, and there is a growing opposition to the leadership of Toledano. He continues:

"The Mexican railway unions openly threaten to withdraw from the CTM if Toledano continues his militant program. Workers in other unions are getting tired of the continual strikes that keep them from working. They are growing distrustful of the dictatorial power wielded by Toledano."

Radical newspapers that support the Cardenas régime in Mexico, notes the New York *Enquirer,* hail the expropriation of British, Dutch, and American oil properties because of the weakening effect upon capitalism. The idea that "it serves big business right," we are told, is being sedulously cultivated throughout the United States. Yet, observes *The Enquirer:*

"Big business has as legitimate a claim upon the sympathy and protection of the Government of these United States as has little business. Kill big business in America today, and what will remain? Take away the achievements of big business in our country in the past, and what kind of a land would we Americans have today?

"Big business has its shortcomings. But so has little business. And big business is infinitely more serviceable to mankind than big government which swallows up enterprise of all kinds—witness Russia and Germany and Italy.

"Who has given the masses of our people a pre-eminence over all other peoples by placing at their command millions of automobiles, millions of telephones, millions of radios, millions of household appliances and other things which past generations would have regarded as luxuries, but which our generation takes for granted? The answer is—big business.

"In doing all this, big business has furnished millions of jobs for millions of employes, and disbursed billions of dollars for wages, for materials, and in other ways.

"If the principle invoked by our State Department in connection with the Mexican expropriation of American property were to be applied here at home, it would mean national ruination for the American people.

"A great deal more than big business is involved in this confiscation.

"It has wiped out the income of numerous American stockholders who depended upon their Mexican investments for a livelihood, and has visited severe injury upon those American educational and other institutions which benefited either directly or indirectly from dividends on investments derived from the seized property."

IX

ANTI-AMERICAN PROPAGANDA IN LATIN AMERICA

Influence of the Totalitarian Powers in Latin America—The Old
"Boring Within" Tactics—The "Calvo Doctrine" and What It
Means—Barter of Mexican Oil for German, Italian, and Jap-
anese Goods—How Barter Displaces Sale of American Goods—
German Propaganda in Latin America—Anti-American Propa-
ganda in Latin America—Mexican Propaganda in the United
States.

Far more is involved in the expropriation policy of Mexico than
loss by United States and British citizens of hundreds of millions
of dollars worth of property. What is really alarming is the
evidence thus offered that totalitarian ideas (and Powers) of Europe are gaining an increasing foothold in this hemisphere. The
Bergen Record, of Hackensack, N. J., surveys the situation and
comes to a conclusion which cannot be reassuring to a democracy:

> "In view of the fact that Mexico's seizure of the oil prop-
> erties hinted at collectivism and that she is treating with
> Fascist nations, the conclusion is that Mexican officials favor
> totalitarian principles.
> "Thus the United States faces a problem infinitely more
> vast in its ramifications than the simple question of expropri-
> ation. To add to the difficulty, Mexico's economic status is
> not as sound as it might be; and that situation offers fertile
> ground for the seeds of dictatorship."

We have become more or less accustomed to the theory or fact
of Nazi-Fascist influence in parts of South America. But to have
it placed thus on our very doorstep brings us up sharply.

Between the "old Holy Alliance of Metternich and Alexander I"
and the "new Holy Alliance of Hitler and Mussolini," Barnet
Nover of the Washington *Post* discerns an alarming parallel.
Like the old alliance, the new one is casting "a grim shadow
across the Atlantic":

> "In the era of Bolivar and Monroe, the ghost was the
> Europe of the Holy Alliance, the totalitarian axis of its day,

whose activities threatened the newly won independence of Spain's former colonies and the security of the United States."

Today, Mr. Nover continues:

"The immediate threat of totalitarian Powers, so far as this hemisphere is concerned, may be exaggerated; but it cannot be discounted. The aggressor nations are on the march, and there is no telling in which directions they may move. Three of the six continents—Asia, Africa, Europe— have felt the impact of their expansionist ambitions. Is there any reason to believe they will stop short of this hemisphere?"

What will the United States do about all this? The Hartford (Conn.) *Courant* speaks for a host of papers and citizens when it declares:

"While the spread of totalitarianism in Europe is something that the people of the United States will not fight to prevent, its encroachment into the New World is quite another matter, a challenge that could hardly be ignored."

It is not the fear of war, but the thought of intellectual domination which concerns us, according to Dorothy Thompson, newspaper correspondent and columnist. "We are dealing," she warns in a New York *Herald Tribune* article, "with a form of imperialism which makes its way, not at first by armed conquest, but by fomenting movements inside all countries for the purpose of drawing those countries eventually into their ideological, economic, and eventually military orbits."

In fact, what James Monroe and the United States of his day never envisioned, when the fifth President formulated the famous doctrine which warned Europe to keep out of the Western Hemisphere, is coming to pass: Ideological invasion.

Since Munich particularly, the preservation of political independence inside the Americas seems to Leland Stowe, foreign newspaper correspondent, writing in *This Week* (N. Y.) "much less an idle phrase than it used to be." Continues Mr. Stowe:

"Europe's powerful dictatorships have perfected the technique of 'invasion from within.' Invasion by foreign armies has become a secondary menace, compared with the creation of ideological armies inside the frontiers of supposedly free states. The Fascist and Communist dictatorships represent ideas that are highly international and recognize no state boundaries. The Fascists, in particular and most agressively, regard the whole world as their pasture. By propaganda and internal invasion, Nazi Germany has conquered Austria and Czechoslovakia, and is now counting upon installing National Socialist government in many other states.

"It is well known that Nazi-Fascist propaganda and pressure methods are very active throughout the three Americas. *If they do not carry a serious threat today, they may tomorrow.* Until now, the Monroe Doctrine, barring the road to foreign intervention in the Western Hemisphere, has been sufficient to keep European Powers from gaining a foothold on our two continents. But how can the twenty-one American republics safely protect themselves from the Fascist device of 'invasion from within'?"

Fortunately, we are not in the dark regarding the technique of invasion from within. It is merely the "boring from within" which has become a familiar phrase in connection with other ideologies. According to Dorothy Thompson, writing in the New York *Herald Tribune:* "The Fascist and Nazi Governments use their own nationals in all countries as the basis for their first foothold, and anti-Semitism and anti-Communism as their rallying cry." Germans living in South America must contribute to the National Socialist funds, and these contributions are devoted chiefly to propaganda there. An *Associated Press* dispatch by Morgan M. Beatty tells us that German broadcasting stations "point their antennae toward South America and blast away daily with a stream of Nazi propaganda in the guise of news. Some Latin American papers pick it up because it's free, and thus spread terms and systems used by totalitarian states."

An even more detailed picture of what is being done is given by William LaVarre in the New York *Mirror:*

"To the Government of Ecuador, Italian agents have given a loan of $10,000,000—as a wedge in obtaining a concession for a strategically located naval base in Esperanza Bay; a naval or air base there would effectively blockade Pacific shipping from Peru and Chile to the Panama Canal.

"Anti-Jewish campaigns, traceable directly to Fascist headquarters, are breaking out in Colombia, Ecuador, Peru, Chile—and all up the East Coast; never before has there been any racial antipathy toward Jews or Jewish immigrants in these communities.

"A very large advertising campaign has been launched out of Rio de Janeiro to all the capitals of South America, under the innocent appearing signature of the Italian National Railway and Tourist Bureau. Large space for these scenic advertisments has been contracted for in leading Latin American papers and magazines on a month-to-month basis. Simultaneously the editor of each paper is put on the list for the complete daily 'news' and feature service of another Italian agency, Agencia Italiana. An editor who doesn't run the propaganda—primarily directed against the United States and England—does not get next month's advertising appropriation.

"Following the Nazi pattern, the Italian Government is now exhibiting in South American capitals, but in much greater magnificence, elaborate displays of school and text books, illustrated in four colors—which will be supplied, with Spanish, Portuguese, and Indian text, to South American Ministers of Education at prices far under the cost of publication.

"Money has been made available, through Italian Consulates, for the purchase by Italian or Fascist sympathizers of strategically located agricultural estates, industries, businesses.

"To all military officials the Italian Government has extended invitations to visit Italy on a military tour; cadets and children of important officials are being offered scholarships in Italian schools.

"In Peru, Italy has obtained a monopolistic contract for the manufacture of airplanes—a Caproni factory being built just outside Lima."

At the Lima Conference last December, writes John W. White in the New York *Times*, Latin American nations converged on the Peruvian city with the intention of translating the "good neighbor" policy, which is merely a declaration of policy contained in President Roosevelt's inaugural address, into principles

The Monkey Wrench Thrower

—*Reprinted from the Boston Post.*

of international law entirely favorable to themselves and entirely unfavorable to the United States.

One bloc of Latin American countries sought to change President Roosevelt's expression of good will into articles of international law by urging the adoption of certain treaty agreements and conventions. Mr. White outlines the proposals thus:

"Several of the Latin American republics sought to get the Conference to adopt treaty agreements denying any American country the right to use force or diplomatic intervention to protect the investments of its citizens.

"Argentina supported the movement by presenting a draft convention by which the American republics would pledge themselves not to use armed force or diplomatic intervention, either for collecting public or contractual debts or for supporting pecuniary claims of their nationals.

"In addition to the Argentine convention, the sub-committee also had before it a draft convention prepared by the committee of experts denying the right of countries to use force of diplomatic pressure, except in cases where justice had been denied to investors.

"*A third project before the sub-committee was a Mexican proposal by which the American countries would recognize the right of foreigners to waive diplomatic protection.* . . .

"Mexico and some other Latin American republics have often included a clause in their contracts requiring the contractors to waive the right of diplomatic protection, but the State Department, as soon as it has learned of the signature of such contracts, has made formal representations refusing to recognize the waiver clause."

It was impossible, however, for the delegates to agree on these issues—so the safe course was adopted of postponing the whole matter until the next conference, in 1943.

Mexico's maneuvers at Lima brought about considerable discussion in American newspapers of the Calvo Doctrine. It has been offered as the legal basis of Mexico's expropriation policy by the Mexican Government.

The Calvo Doctrine is described by the Oakland (Calif.) *Tribune* as "a neat little plan to aid those who owe debts to other nations." It was evolved by Carlos Calvo, an international lawyer in Argentina in the nineteenth century. Another jurist and statesman of the same land, Luis Maria Drago, worked out the related Drago Doctrine.

The history of the two doctrines is given in *The Christian Science Monitor:*

"The Calvo Clause states that the continuous claims of the great European Powers against 'the governments of the American states' is based upon the assumption 'that foreigners deserve greater consideration and more respect and privileges than the nationals of the country in which they reside'; rejects the principle that aliens may appeal to their government for protection in the event of a dispute with the nation in which they are living.

"This clause was invoked by Mexico during its controversy with Great Britain over the expropriation of American and British oil properties, and during the recent agrarian dispute with the United States. The Drago Doctrine is also involved in Mexico's position on the expropriation question.

"The Drago Doctrine declares that debts contracted by nations cannot be collected by force. It was formulated as the result of Great Britain's sending warships in 1902 to collect a debt from Venezuela. In 1907 the Doctrine was modified at The Hague when a provision was added allowing for collection of debts by force if the debtor nation refused or delayed arbitration.

"Mexico repudiated this treaty in 1927."

Neither of these principles has ever been generally accepted, says the Detroit *Free Press*. But:

"They are dear to the hearts of debtor countries the world over.

"They express the resentment and fear which many Latin American countries have felt in the past over the use of force or threats of force by creditor countries to collect the claims of their nationals, whether such claims were honest or dishonest."

Mexico's resolution declaring that when a citizen renounces the protection of his government, it cannot intervene in his behalf, drew the fire of the Boston *Transcript*, which said:

"The reason for this proposal is plain enough. It stems from a desire on the part of Mexico to have a free hand in the treatment of property owned by foreigners. Mexico's only fear today is that aggrieved nations will resort to reprisals. Moral and ethical considerations move it not at all. If, therefore, it can be assured that no force will be used, it can keep on taking what it wants in the way of resources—and either not pay for them, or pay when it gets good and ready."

What the Calvo Doctrine is, and the many things that are wrong with it, are thus summed up by the New York *Journal of Commerce:*

"The Calvo Doctrine holds that foreign-owned property should be treated on a basis of exact equality with property of the citizens of a country, even to the point of confiscation, without any diplomatic intervention.

"The Mexican Government emphasizes the personal rights of persons who immigrate into Latin American countries while retaining foreign citizenship. This puts the argument in its strongest light.

"Actually, however, it would also mean that foreign oil and mining companies, and other corporate enterprises which invest in plants and facilities abroad, would have to rely exclusively upon the courts of those countries for redress, without the benefit of diplomatic intervention where they are unjustly deprived of their property.

"In short, the Calvo Doctrine fails to recognize the concrete facts of the situation. In several countries, domestic courts have, as a matter of fact, failed to give protection to foreign investors. In that event, new capital will not flow into these countries, and their economic development will thus be seriously hampered. In the long run, therefore, the many countries of Latin America that still require foreign capital for their development would be the chief victim of the adoption of this policy."

Soon after the Cardenas expropriation decree became effective, it was officially announced that Mexico would dispose of the oil from British, Dutch, and American wells only to democratic Powers. But as the matter is working out, it is Germany, Italy, and Japan that are getting the oil. From Germany, in exchange for her product, Mexico is reported to be getting oil-refinery ma-

Shades of the Spanish Main

—*Reprinted from the Stockton, Calif., Independent.*

chinery, irrigation equipment, and electrical machinery. Italy is paying with raw silk, rayon, tankers, and cash. Japan is supplying silk and other commodities.

Naturally, the barter of Mexican oil for German, Italian, and Japanese goods is displacing the sale of American goods to Mexico, and causing increasing concern to American business firms.

Meanwhile, observes the St. Paul *Pioneer Press,* "Washington, for the first time, is getting alarmed over inroads being made, both economically and politically, into Latin America by Germany, Italy, and Japan. If it were merely a matter of commercial competition, American export industries could hold their own. But the Germans bring their political propaganda with them." In fact, says the Winfield (Kan.) *Courier,* "there is reason to believe that Hitler had some influence in causing the confiscation of British, Dutch, and American oil properties in Mexico." The three nations mentioned above need a constant supply of oil, minerals, and metals. And, as the Baltimore *Sun* points out:

"In the difficulties which it has created for itself, Mexico becomes an almost perfect and helpless objective. It is rich in the things Berlin, Rome, and Tokyo need; its Government must find an outlet for these very products or collapse, and it has cut itself off from normal trade relations with its democratic friends. No wonder Germany and Japan push the campaign, seeking to extend the 'spiritual empire' of Fascism at the same time that they gain their raw materials."

As the Sioux Falls (S. D.) *Argus-Leader* explains:

"All three nations—Germany, Italy, and Japan—are hard pressed for oil and must buy in world markets to obtain it and its by-products. Motorized army and aviation equipment must have gasoline. Such machinery also must have as lubricants oils that come from petroleum. This explains why the nations in the triangular pact have made the oil deal with Mexico, now confidently believed to have been the prime reason for the expropriation."

It will be remembered that during the early days of the World War, Germany attempted to stir up trouble between Mexico and the United States. Can it be, the Boston *Commercial Weekly* asks, that President Cardenas hopes to accept the offer made to Mexico by Germany at that time? Continues this paper:

"German diplomats reminded Mexico that Texas, New Mexico, and Arizona were regarded as lost provinces of Mexico, and it was suggested that they might be restored after a German triumph in war, as a reward for Mexico making war on the United States."

While one could go on indefinitely about war and intrigue, the fact remains that business and unemployment and foreign trade are of immediate importance. There are many economic reasons why the United States is concerned over developments in Mexico and other republics to the south. As Leland Stowe writes in the New York *Herald Tribune:*

"There is real concern among American business men over the German-Italo-Japanese trade invasion of Latin America. Recently the United States Chamber of Commerce published a report, urging that steps be taken to halt the inroads of non-American countries into this hemisphere's foreign trade. The report said, in part: 'It is significant that during the decade (1927-1936 inclusive) the share of the United States in providing the goods purchased abroad by each of the South American nations has shown a decline. While our country still does the bulk of the trade with the South American countries as a whole, this survey leaves little doubt that our leading position is being challenged constantly by other nations, particularly Germany and Japan.'

"This stresses one of the most serious problems that confront our Government in the foreign field. For, as Bernard M. Baruch warned not long ago, trade follows the flag—and political ideologies follow trade.

"The greater the commercial hold that the Fascist and military dictatorships get on Latin American countries, the more deeply they will influence the form of government among our Latin neighbors. This means that the fate of All-American government, and in many lands of democracy also, may be decided in Central and South America by the gigantic trade battle now under way.

"In 1936 the United States had direct investments in Latin America amounting to $2,847,000,000. In the same year our direct investment in Europe was $1,245,000,000, and those in Asia were only $417,000,000. On the basis of these totals, who can doubt where Uncle Sam's major trade interests are located?"

Andrue Berding, in an *Associated Press* dispatch from Washington, says the United States has at stake a total trade with Latin America, both import and export, of about $1,000,000,000. Of the three countries mentioned above, Carlos J. Videla, writing for the *North American Newspaper Alliance,* declares:

"The Germans are the most firmly entrenched in the southern continent. Through the 'blocked' or 'aski' marks, which can be used by the payee only for the purchase of German goods, the Nazis have succeeded in building a large trade. Brazilian coffee and cotton, Ecuadorean cocoa, and Argentine products are bought in great quantities by the Germans, who later often resell those staples elsewhere for cash.

"German holdings in Peru and Brazil, in the shape of mining, agricultural, and industrial enterprises, are important. The Japanese own large tracts of land in both those countries, besides operating many of the most important department and retail stores in Peru. In Brazil, they possess mining and cotton-growing holdings in the center and southeastern part of the country. They are also disputing control of rich banana zones with American and Brazilian interests.

"The Italians are operating advantageously in Peru, where one of their banks plays an important part in local finance. Italian interests in Brazil, Uruguay, and Argentina have for years held a prominent place."

In Mexico, asserts the Bluefield (W. Va.) *Telegraph*:

"German propaganda is now being disseminated, for which the Berlin Government is appropriating funds. The same thing is under way in other Latin American countries.

"The end sought, of course, is the spread of totalitarian ideology in Latin American countries.

"*Once let a Latin American country go Nazi or Fascist, and the commercial triumph is an easy step from there.*"

In the opinion of the Louisville *Courier-Journal,* "the strengthening of political-economic ties with the dictatorial nations endangers the security of the United States." And in the opinion of the Houghton (Mich.) *Mining Gazette,* "there is no doubt that European competitors of the United States are working hand in glove with Mexico." According to the Michigan paper:

"Slowly but surely a crisis in American-Mexican relations is approaching. Not only is the United States in duty bound to frustrate outright confiscation of American property, but it is faced with anti-American propaganda throughout Latin America, emanating from Mexico.

"Unless Washington takes action, Mexico will proceed with arrangements of far-reaching character with German interests at the expense of American commerce in several southern republics. Germans have originated a cunning plan for siphoning oil out of Mexico—oil belonging to American, British, and Dutch concerns—and selling to other countries such quantities as are not needed by Germany itself.

"Conceivably this plan, already materialized into a contract, would enable Mexico to stall off permanently any compensation to American owners of oil properties, agrarian lands, and mines in Mexico."

According to the Detroit *Free Press:*

"Germany's trade policy is based on an attempt to balance exactly its exports and imports to and from each foreign country. Thus Germany agrees with Brazil that it will take so much Brazilian coffee if Brazil will take so much German machinery. And it agrees with Mexico that it will buy so much Mexican oil if Mexico will buy German goods of equivalent value.

"Secretary Hull contends that this policy tends to erect barriers to general international trade."

In the opinion of the Dayton (O.) *News,* the United States yet may find itself embarrassed by "Germany, as a member of the Berlin-Rome-Tokyo triangle." "For economic and political reasons," remarks the Ann Arbor (Mich.) *News,* "Germany would like to dominate Mexico." Dr. Harry Elmer Barnes, writing in the New York *World-Telegram,* is authority for the statement that "Germany is selling war materials in Latin America, and many of the Latin American armies are being trained by German officers. All this looks forward to the next world war. At the worst, Germany hopes to sabotage aid from England from

261

that area." Furthermore, writes Morgan Beatty in the Newark (N. J.) *News:*

"Germany operates nearly 4,000 miles of commercial air lines among Latin American capitals, and runs regular air mail service between Europe and South America. *Those air lines could be converted to military use in time of need.* Aside from the United States, France, with about 3,000 miles of air lines, is the only other Power on the scene in Latin America."

The basic question, observes the Boston *Herald,* "is whether or not Mexico will be happier and more prosperous with her new-found friends than she was with her old." In this conservative paper's opinion:

"A penetration of Japanese and German propaganda may have rendered Fascism more attractive to her for the time being than democracy, but a Mexico for Mexicans, the Germans, and the Japanese can certainly hold no more charm for an oppressed nation than a Mexico for Mexicans and the Americans.

"There has been a growth of German-inspired anti-Semitism. *The Japanese have centered their espionage system for Latin America in Mexico.* The more than 6,000 Japanese who live in Mexico enjoy a freedom from molestation which has never been accorded to Americans."

In view of all this, and with South America threatened by the political and trade thrusts of Germany, Italy, and Japan, "the time has come for the Americas to discuss their common problems and the advantages of a closer union of the nations of the Western Hemisphere," maintains the San Pedro (Calif.) *News-Pilot.*

American newspapers generally condemn Mexico's attitude toward the United States during the past year, and various ways of dealing with the Cardenas régime are suggested. We present one—from the Hornell (N. Y.) *Tribune:*

"The disclosure of Mexico's barter deal with Germany, it seems to us, leaves our Government only one way of handling President Cardenas. That is to demand payment for the seized properties. If President Cardenas still refuses to talk turkey, then we must withdraw our economic support from Mexico and let that country suffer the consequences."

The most disconcerting development following expropriation of British, Dutch, and American oil properties was Mexico's plan to dispose of the product of her newly acquired oil wells by swapping it abroad for various commodities. As the San Diego (Calif.) *Union* explains: "The democratic countries, especially the United States, Great Britain, and France "were not eager to purchase oil which they regarded as having been confiscated." In the meantime, Mexican oil was literally overflowing the country's storage capacity, while the Mexican Treasury was anything but overflowing with funds. Hence the barter deals with Germany, Italy, and Japan. Moreover, as the New York *Post* reflects, "barter with Germany means payment for Mexican oil in German machinery." And—

"That means the 'No Sale' sign for American machinery. Along with the German-Italian contacts is a Mexican boycott of American goods.

"We can do several things. We can get mad as hell. We can retaliate. We can drop the 'good neighbor' policy. But these reactions, while they might soothe our feelings, won't help American business in Mexico."

Mexico's first barter deal, made last May, was a mere 1,500,000-peso proposition, as reported in the New York *Times* dispatch from Mexico City, in which petroleum and other products were to be sent to Sweden in return for newsprint. In July, announcement was made of the sale to Germany of $10,000,000 worth of oil. Of this amount 9,000,000 barrels were to go to Germany, the rest to be sold elsewhere by Germany. The oil going to Germany in this deal, according to a New York *Times* dispatch from Berlin, amounts to about 23 per cent of Germany's annual oil consumption, and approximates a third of her oil imports for a year. We note further in New York *Times* dispatches—for *The Times* has been covering the Mexican situation very thoroughly—that Mexican barter exports to Germany, through one firm, will exceed Mexico's total 1938 oil exports. During the first eleven

Under the Southern Cross

—*Reprinted from the Washington Star.*

months of 1938, the drop in United States exports to Mexico amounted to 89 per cent of the total decline in Mexico's imports from all countries, according to *The Times*.

A serious matter for the United States is the exchange of German office appliances for Mexican oil. For instance, in 1936, of the typewriters sold in Mexico, 90 per cent were American and 10 per cent German. In the first half of 1938, Germany increased her sales to 36 per cent of the total, chiefly at the expense of American manufacturers.

Unofficial figures are said to indicate that the German machines are selling at around 100 pesos, compared with the 400 to 500 pesos which the American machines are sold for—after payment of the high import duties.

It is pointed out by *The Times* that "when in competition with German products in the Mexican and other Latin American markets, before the element of barter entered into the situation, typewriter manufacturers found no difficulty in outselling the German manufacturer, despite the latter's price advantage of 10 to 20 per cent." Another important deal was the trading of Mexican oil for $3,000,000 worth of rayon and machinery from Italy. Altogether, we are told, "American trade fell off from $99,867,000 in the first eleven months of 1937 to $56,000,000 in the same period of 1938, as a result of Mexican official policies," and undoubtedly the drop has been accentuated since that period.

After the Swedish newsprint deal mentioned above, Mexico arranged to trade oil for 25,000 tons of newsprint. This deal seemed important to a Mexico correspondent of the New York *Journal of Commerce,* because this is a commodity which Mexico has bought from Americans. And the New York *Wall Street Journal* agrees that these newsprint deals hit us hard, since "prior to the expropriation of the oil properties, Mexico bought most of her newsprint from the United States."

Other deals that were, at one time, in process of negotiation, according to newspaper reports, include a trade of Italian automobiles for Mexican oil; Italian purchases of Mexican oil with new tankers; and a German offer of 50 passenger airplanes capable of being converted into bombers, in exchange for oil.

Imports of mining machinery from the United States have practically ceased, reports *The Mineral Survey*, a leading Mexican mining magazine, with the decline of the peso. It believes that eventually the industry will be forced to obtain machinery by barter, and then the chief sufferer will be the United States, which does not operate on the barter principle.

The barter of Mexican oil for German heavy machinery has been displacing the sale of American machinery for many months, and is causing increasing concern to American business firms, reports Betty Kirk from Mexico City to *The Christian Science Monitor*. "American firms cannot compete with the barter arrangements," she explains. Continues this correspondent:

"The barter arrangement is a normal trade outlet, in view of the circumstances. Mexico has raw materials to sell and needs finished goods and machinery. Germany and Italy can supply these products, but need Mexican oil. Sweden also needs oil and has machinery to sell. The exchange can therefore be made without damage to international trade of the contracting parties.

"Many adverse factors affect American trade with Mexico at the present time. We do not make barter deals and we do not need oil. The depreciated peso is a heavy drawback to imports and there is, and will probably continue to be for some time, a shortage of Mexican money with which to buy dollars.

"Considering that Mexico is one of the largest United States markets, and that 65 per cent of her imports come from the United States, it is apparent that the greatest sufferer from the oil dispute is the United States manufacturer and exporter. He is now facing a set of circumstances which are politically and economically involved, and for which no immediate relief can be seen."

An interesting complication is Mexico's campaign to sell oil to other Latin American countries. *The Christian Science Monitor* correspondent just quoted thinks it will take "months and maybe years to determine the results of this attempt, for the Latin American countries either barter or pay in fluctuating currencies. Moreover, since they also demand refined petroleum products,

Mexico must increase her refining capacities, which calls for an added investment of millions of dollars, in order to supply the new market to the south." But the Buenos Aires correspondent of the New York *Times* notes that negotiations have been successful in Uruguay, where Mexico won the contract to supply the National Petroleum Board's entire 1939 crude-oil requirements, under-bidding both United States and British companies, and clinching the deal by agreeing to take 30 per cent of the price in Uruguayan products.

The loss to American trade through these Mexican barter transactions is something that makes a deep impression upon the Dayton (O.) *Journal*, the Milwaukee *Journal*, and the Muncie (Ind.) *Press*. Furthermore, says Gardner Harding in the Toledo (O.) *News:*

"In Central America, barter trade carried on by nations of the Fascist bloc has in the last three years, it is estimated, diminished the United States proportion of exports to the six republics by more than 20 per cent."

It seems a matter for irony to the Chicago *Tribune* and the Houston (Texas) *Post* that the property taken away from American interests should be used to shut out American trade. As the Santa Rosa (Calif.) *Republican* puts it: "Mexico has delivered to Uncle Sam a double double-cross, if there is such a thing, by seizing American property and eliminating American importations at the same time."

In the absence of official figures, and on the basis of unofficial estimates that between the seizure date of March 18, 1938, and September 1st of the same year, somewhat more than 4,000,000 barrels were exported, the New York *Times* states that the export movement has been averaging only about 40 per cent of what it was during the last few years of private operation. Aside from the matter of sales volume, Mexico is warned by several American newspapers that this barter business may not be such a fine thing, after all. The exchange is not likely to prove satisfactory to Mexico in the long run, remarks the Springfield (Mass.) *Union*, which goes on to tell this little story:

267

"Turkey made a similar agreement to supply cotton, wool, and copper to Germany, but the combination of German scarcity and restrictive export embargoes left Turkey little to choose from. Germany has the cotton, wool, and copper, but Turkey has only large credit balances in Berlin."

"Mexico may learn, as have some other nations," says the Philadelphia *Inquirer*, "that when it comes to trade agreements, Germany drives a hard bargain." And the Indianapolis *Star* wonders whether the Mexican traders have read of the experience Brazil had not so long ago in finding an outlet for coffee in the German market:

"Sao Paulo hailed with delight an arrangement whereby it was to sell many millions of pounds of coffee to Germans. It was to get no money, but like Mexico, was to take German products or to establish mark balances in German banks. The deal proved to be a very one-sided affair, and Brazil lost no time in ridding itself of the compact.

"The Brazilians found that the Germans were taking shiploads of coffee, but not for home consumption. The South Americans were given credit in marks that would buy nothing except made-in-Germany products. But the worst feature was that Germany was underselling Brazil in the other coffee markets of Europe—with Brazilian coffee. Berlin got cash for the coffee—and paid the Brazilian growers in German factory products."

But the most ironical thing about this whole business, to the New York *Herald Tribune*, "is that here we have the picture of a so-called liberal republic entering into intimate dealings with the German Fascist State." In the words of the Greensboro (N. C.) *News:* "To gain its own immediate and domestic ends, Mexico would sacrifice its beneficial relations with this country and aid the sworn and rampaging champion of the Fascist cause."

In addition to the trade dangers in the new Mexican policy, it seems to the Washington *Star* that:

"The political fact cannot be ignored that the establishment of vital economic ties, such as Mexico now appears to be creating with Germany, inevitably link Mexican interests with the ultimate destiny of Nazi-Fascism in Europe, just as American loans and investments in Great Britain and France

Another Little Brother Problem!

—*Reprinted from the Jefferson, Texas, Jimplecute.*

during early years of the war tied the fate of these investments to the success or failure of the Allies.

"If such deals as Mexico is now making multiply, and Mexican oil production becomes adjusted to a German-Italian market, Mexico will have a vital economic—and therefore political—interest in the preservation of those markets, and in their expansion as the dictatorships broaden their hegemony. That connection will be difficult to break."

These Mexican barter deals with Germany, the Houston (Texas) *Post* fears, "may mean that in Mexico, as in many South American countries, Nazi ideology will flow in with German goods, which would mean a penetration of Nazism into the Americas at the very doorstep of the United States." It is realized in Washington, observes the New York *World-Telegram*, "that in a majority of cases in which Germany has entered into barter arrangements with another nation, a marked advance in totalitarian political philosophy in that country has usually resulted." It is only a step from economic to political penetration, avers the Louisville *Courier-Journal*, "and Nazi propaganda now is widespread in the neighboring republic."

Many news reports agree that a strong campaign of German propaganda is in full operation in Mexico, and in fact, in all the Latin American countries. In Mexico, says an article by Robert L. Norton in the Boston *Post:*

"The Nazis have initiated an extensive advertising campaign in the newspapers, designed not only to sell German goods, but to sell Nazi principles. This propaganda campaign is to be carried through all the Latin American countries. Display advertisments carry pictures of Hitler, Goering, Goebbels, and other leaders.

"The whole picture in Latin America today is that of a crusade being carried on in such a grand scale as to leave no doubt but that it is part and parcel of Hitler's ambition for world power."

The Germans, declares the Springfield (Mass.) *Republican:*

"Are already deeply entrenched from Mexico to Argentina, pouring out a steady smoke-screen of propaganda, entering the professions, building a powerful banking system, winning rich concessions in oil, coffee, and in the airways and

270

railroads. The Germans, more than any other nationality, have spread into the almost inaccessible interiors of the various republics, tapping a vast primitive market; have intermingled with the people and have even taken wives. In most Latin American countries—except perhaps Cuba, Mexico, and Panama—there are more Germans than Americans."

German radio propaganda in Mexico is described by Alfred Friendly in the Washington *News:*

"American radio broadcasts are rendered almost entirely inaudible in Mexico by 'blanketing' programs from Berlin or from local German-owned stations, report Mexican visitors to Washington, who ask that their names be withheld.

"They explain that German programs on the same or nearby frequencies set up interference which brings nothing but unintelligible gibberish through the loudspeakers. When American programs sign off, however, the German broadcasts come through with perfect clarity, they add.

"The German news programs themselves were characterized as 'extremely subtle and highly anti-American.'

"The visitors add that German-made receivers are sold to Mexican peons for about 10 pesos, almost less than the duty, and in some cases are actually given away. The sets are similar to those in hotels, in that they can be turned only to three or four particular stations, all of them German.

"Station W8XK, Westinghouse's 40,000-watt outlet near Pittsburgh, Pa., is cut out by German-owned stations in Mexico City itself, broadcasting in German and Spanish. Many other short-wave stations financed by German money are located in nearby republics.

"At the Federal Communication Commission, officials report that they have received many complaints of interference with American broadcasts by German programs, but have been unable to prove malicious intent by the Germans. They add that frequent checks on German stations showed they did not vary from their assigned frequencies.

"The Nazi programs they say are exceptionally interesting and so clever in their propaganda that they do not offend the Mexican listeners. They leave the impression, however, that the United States would rob the Mexican people if given the opportunity."

The United States is faced with a flood of anti-American propaganda circulating all through Latin America and emanating from Mexico, assisted by European propaganda agents, according to American newspaper reports. This propaganda is said to be inspired by the Mexican Government, which has also influenced several Mexican newspapers to take a hostile attitude. Says Betty Kirk in *The Christian Science Monitor:*

"One of the most significant creations of the Cardenas Government has been the establishment of the Autonomous Department of Publicity and Propaganda, popularly known as 'the DAPP'.

"The DAPP includes divisions of press, radio, and motion pictures, all of which are utilized to the fullest extent to arouse and mold public opinion into harmony with the Government. Its efficacy has best been demonstrated on the oil controversy, which it has played to the hilt in order to cause antagonism to the companies and gain support for the Government."

And we read in the Tulsa (Okla.) *World:*

"A press association story of the oil situation in Mexico carries the statement that the Mexican Government has instructed that nothing favorable to the oil companies and the American interests be printed in any paper in the country, and that a definite program of propaganda attacking American interests be circulated throughout the schools, colleges, and universities, as well as at labor councils, theatres, and other places of assembly."

X

MEXICO CENSORS THE PRESS

American Newspaper Men Under Pressure—Reaction of American Press—Mexico "Adopts the Tactics of a Totalitarian State" —Oil Companies Wage Legal Battle—The Dutch Government Takes a Stand—Venezuela's Policy Compared With That of Mexico—The Future of Mexico's Expropriation Program—Our Prestige in Latin America Impaired.

American newspapermen in Mexico are constantly put under pressure to send out propaganda favoring the existing Government there, instead of transmitting the news impartially, according to the Lynchburg (Va.) *Advance*. In fact, we are told that the American Press Society has urged Secretary of State Hull to use his efforts to put an end to the Mexican Government's attempt to prevent correspondents from sending their newspapers the truth about the political and economic situation in Mexico.

"The latest and stupidest action of the Mexican Government," thinks the New York *Mirror*, "was the ousting of Frank L. Kluckhohn, Mexico City correspondent of the New York *Times*." In the opinion of the *Mirror*, the reaction in the United States will be: "What is Cardenas trying to cover up? He must be hiding something!"

There were obvious reasons which led the American press to devote the extraordinary amount of space that it did, both in the news and editorial columns, to the expulsion of *The Times* correspondent.

Editors and news agencies were aroused by the manner in which the Cardenas Government acted, despite its expressed devotion to, and support of, the principle of liberty to the press.

They saw in what Cardenas here did a planned and determined effort to control them and their representatives and to discourage the distribution and printing of none but information and comment laudatory of what is being done in Mexico by striking at

273

Our "Good Neighbor"

—*Reprinted from the New York Mirror.*

the reporter of the newspaper which was foremost in its coverage of Mexican news.

It was instantly and correctly sensed that *The Times* man had been ousted not because his dispatches and articles were factually inaccurate. It seemed clear that his expulsion was due:

1. To his independence as a collector and purveyor of news.
2. To his diligence in seeking, obtaining and interpreting the "news behind the news."

His articles of this nature frequently let the "cat out of the bag" and thereby embarrassed Mexico because a great deal of this "news behind the news" by its very nature was favorable to foreigners whose property rights were being endangered by the Mexican Government's action.

As the Greensboro (N. C.) *News* tells the story of Mr. Kluckhohn's deportation, and what lies behind this drastic action:

"The New York *Times* correspondent discovered that a secret deal had been negotiated between Mexico and Germany, one of those barter arrangements we have been hearing about, an arrangement that implies a sympathetic relationship between our Leftist republican neighbor and the Nazi totalitarianism.

"It does not matter so greatly why the Mexican Government chose to cover up this transaction. But it did so choose, and Mr. Kluckhohn, who sent what he had found out to *The Times* which printed it, was expelled from Mexico. It had been years since any representative of the press of the United States had been given similar treatment. At first the correspondent was told that he must get out because he was *persona non grata*, as they say of diplomatic persons; then on second thought the explanation was given that he had, after a short trip across the border, re-entered the country illegally. Mr. Kluckhohn has published facsimilies of his papers showing that this is untrue.

"*At least ten times as much attention will be given to the transaction Mexico wished to hide from the world as would have been if the correspondent had not been pitched out of the country.*

"Any attempt to muzzle the press, as it affects our own country, at least, is reasonably certain to cause a reaction that will militate against that purpose. And that is true of

275

any suppression or falsification of the facts, by anybody, for any purpose."

To the Manchester (N. H.) *Leader*, the summary dismissal of an accredited correspondent looks like "one of the fundamental tactics of a modern dictator state, transplanted to the Western Hemisphere." Continues this New England daily:

"Had there previously been the slightest reason to doubt what kind of government exists in Mexico, this episode would remove it. Of course no such reason existed. It has been apparent for months that our southern neighbor's primary policies were being cut to the familiar pattern. The denial of the elementary rights of private property, the seizures of oil and farm lands, the constantly increased collaboration with the Fascist-Nazi bloc, pointed alike to an inescapable conclusion. South of the Rio Grande we have a totalitarian state, based upon collectivism as ruthless and all-embracing as anything that exists on the other side of the Atlantic."

Mr. Kluckhohn, observes the St. Louis *Globe-Democrat*, "seems to have run afoul of a convenient little gadget employed by the Mexican Government to rid the country of pestiferous foreigners." We read on:

"That gadget is Article 33 of the Mexican Constitution, which permits the Government to expel, without trial or other defense, any foreigner it regards as a traducer of the country's fair name. Newspaper correspondents, by the nature of their work, are its most frequent victims.

"Naturally, there were several angles of this story that the Mexican Government wished soft-pedaled. They were not omitted in *The Times* dispatches, particularly the most recent one of a $17,000,000 oil deal with Germany in which Mexico traded confiscated oil—for which it has made no compensation—for German goods.

"Unfortunately for Mr. Kluckhohn's continued residence in Mexico City, the truth hurt and he is back in the United States.

"We hold no brief for the newspaper correspondent who distorts facts and wilfully misrepresents situations. But, we do not believe *The Times* man is of that stripe. The Mexican Government is 'cracking down' — and he is the first victim.

"Well, Mussolini did it to the Chicago *Daily News* and the Chicago *Tribune;* Hitler did it to the Manchester *Guardian.* Cardenas is not acting without a precedent in countries where a free press is a myth."

Mr. Kluckhohn's expulsion from Mexico, points out the Atlanta *Constitution,* "may be taken to reflect the fact that this experienced correspondent was upholding the best traditions of a free press, in the face of both direct and indirect attempts to silence him." "His explusion," maintains the Waltham (Mass.) *News-Tribune,* "is a tribute to his honesty and independence." For, as it goes on to explain: "Facts are the last thing that any autocratic government desires to have revealed, whether it is in the Eastern or the Western Hemisphere." In his own defense, Mr. Kluckhohn is quoted by the Hobbs (N. M.) *News and Sun* as saying:

"Over a period of two full years in the Mexican republic I have sent hundreds of news stories. The Mexican Government during that period has not denied the facts in these stories.

"I think that speaks for itself."

"Mr. Kluckhohn bears an excellent reputation," notes the Lynn (Mass.) *Telegram-News,* "but that is beside the point." In this paper's opinion:

"Had he been unfair, even untruthful, there would still be no excuse for a democratic country to adopt the tactics of a totalitarian state.

"The only clue comes from the Mexican press department which said, according to *The Times,* that it had been displeased with Kluckhohn's dispatches at various times. If that were to be the standard by which our own Government judges newspapermen, nine-tenths of our foreign correspondents would be kicked out, and there wouldn't be a handful of American newspaper representatives permitted in Washington.

"We don't expect Germany, Russia, Italy, or Japan to pay any heed to the great democratic principle of a free press. But it is shocking to hear that Mexico is exerting such undemocratic pressure."

The background of the Kluckhohn incident is provided in a Washington dispatch, headed "Mexico Muzzles the Press," signed by J. E. Jones, and published in the Livingston (Texas) *Enterprise Weekly:*

"The other day a couple of American newspaper correspondents made their customary call on the official press chief in Mexico City. They inquired about Washington reports that the Mexican Government was trying to sell German equipment, obtained in exchange for confiscated oil, to other Latin American nations. The reporters were Frank L. Kluckhohn representing the New York *Times,* and William Lander, of *The United Press.*

"Instead of receiving the information they asked for, Mr. Kluckhohn was seized and brought before a Mexican government official and ordered to leave Mexico within twenty-four hours. *The United Press* was fined 5,000 pesos. Other correspondents who have been writing about the new political and economic ties between Mexico and Germany have been reprimanded."

William Lander, of *The United Press,* is said to have been told by the chief of the official press bureau in Mexico City that "there is no interest outside of Mexico in Mexican deals with Germany." But, asserts the Cumberland (Md.) *Times:* "If the Mexican Chief means that, he is 100 per cent wrong. And if his Government insists on all news for outside countries coming exclusively from the official press bureau, it is making a big mistake." As the Leominster (Mass.) *Enterprise* explains:

"The exposure of possible political connections between Germany and Mexico, as well as certain commercial relations, involving a commodity derived from land rightfully belonging to American citizens, would naturally be covered by any American correspondent in Mexico and naturally would be printed in American newspapers.

"Publication of such news stories would hardly please the Mexican Government. It would send the German Government into a tantrum. In Germany the press prints exactly what the Government permits it to print. The same has held true to a considerable extent in Mexico. Therefore, the expulsion of Mr. Kluckhohn would come in the natural order of events.

"The last thing that a totalitarian state, or a state under the totalitarian influence, wants in its midst is a group of American newspapermen who are accustomed to writing the news as they find it. Such newspapermen are likely to expose too many things."

In the opinion of the Chicago *Daily News,* "public opinion will now insist that the New Deal quit coddling the Cardenas dictatorship." Meanwhile, points out the Hornell (N. Y.) *Tribune,* "it will be difficult to determine just what is happening in Mexico, particularly under censorship." Certainly, predicts a Texas paper, the Cleburne *Times-Review,* "American newspapers will hesitate to print anything which comes from a country where the press is under strict governmental supervision, when such news has not been written by their staff correspondents." As for Mr. Kluckhohn, "he would not have been placed in charge of *The Times* Mexico City Bureau, had not his record been such as to command the confidence of the managing editor in New York City," avers the El Paso (Texas) *Times.* In this paper's judgment:

"The whole trouble in brief, seems to have been that the New York *Times* was publishing dispatches from Mexico telling of Mexico's sale to Germany of oil confiscated from American owners, taking German goods in exchange, and peddling those goods through Latin America at cut prices in order to convert them into cash."

"If the agreement had been purely commercial," observes the Cleveland *Plain Dealer,* "there would not be so much cause for concern. But there are increasing evidences of Nazi-Mexican political co-operation, as well." To the Syracuse (N. Y.) *Herald:*

"The Kluckhohn incident offers an excellent picture of the method that is being employed by dictatorial governments to regiment the press and 'crack down' on writers who dare to be something besides parrots for propaganda departments.

"Mr. Kluckhohn's dispatches dealing with such developments as the Mexican Government's expropriation of American-owned lands and the Cardenas seizure of foreign-owned oil fields were clear, concise stuff.

"But his gift for unearthing and stating facts was not appreciated in Mexico City."

279

To the Utica (N. Y.) *Observer-Dispatch,* "Kluckhohn's expulsion from Mexico is just another example of what it means for a government to control the press." "Having already applied the muzzle inside Mexico, the Cardenas régime is now apparently trying to control all 'information' dispatched to the outside world," notes the New York *World-Telegram.* To the Houston *Post,* a Texas paper located on the main highway into Mexico, the story of the correspondent's deportation "sounds more like a wireless dispatch from Berlin or Rome than from a capital in the Western Hemisphere." Moreover, this paper believes the action is short-sighted: "Chasing American newspapermen out of the republic because they insist on telling the truth will not get Mexico any new American tourist—or other—business."

"It has become only too apparent" to the Macon (Ga.) *Telegraph* "that Mexico is taking on all the semblance of a totalitarian state, with Leon Trotsky, a Russian refugee, pulling the strings. And this at the back door of the United States!" Or, to quote the Greenville (Miss.) *Delta Democrat-Times:*

"Mexico is no more a democracy than is Italy. The United States is in a delicate position. We could demand from Mexico more courteous treatment of correspondents. That would put us in the role of a domineering tyrant, in the eyes of Latin America. Or we can ignore the insult. That isn't particularly beneficial to our cause in Central and South America; for our neighbors almost universally admire strong tactics, and if they find that the United States can be pushed around in little matters they might essay bolder exploits. Yet it is imperative that we maintain a diplomatic attitude, for we are fighting a growing predilection for European ideologies."

"The Cardenas Government is just as much a dictatorship as any of the totalitarian governments of Europe," agrees the Elkhart (Ind.) *Truth.* To the Iron Mountain (Mich.) *News:*

"The expulsion of Mr. Kluckhohn indicates that Mexico intends to tolerate within her borders only those correspondents who are willing to toe the mark and become active or tacit propagandists of the régime. In view of this country's considerable stake in the republic, and the importance of

280

keeping fully informed as to what is going on there, such a stand is unlikely to succeed. The more Mexico seeks to hide unpleasant facts regarding her situation, the more important it will become to penetrate the veil of secrecy."

All of which proves to the Gloversville (N. Y.) *Herald:*

"First, we must watch Mexico. She was a hotbed of German espionage during the World War. Now she is in danger of becoming a breeding ground for the tenets of Nazism on this continent. Secondly, the 'change' in Mexico demonstrates how much alike are all totalitarian patterns, whether they be Nazi, Fascist, or Communist. Once Russia was Mexico's model. And now, without so much as a revolution, without even shifting Presidents, she is turning her eyes toward Berlin.

"As for Mr. Kluckhohn, he has been put out of Mexico for one thing—being a good reporter. He dug up the facts and presented them in news dispatches. His ouster is added proof that our neighbor below the Rio Grande is dangerously aping the dictator lands across the sea. Proof, too, that we need to keep informed on Mexican trends, lest some day we hear Hitler knocking on the nation's back door."

The Worcester (Mass.) *Telegram* also calls attention to two items:

"These may help to substantiate Mr. Kluckhohn's exposure of Mexican alliances with Germany to which the Mexican Government objected. The first is the reliability of Mr. Kluckhohn's past work, and the excellence of his professional reputation. It was he who sent the first news of Italian and German assistance to Spain, which startled the world—and prevented Kluckhohn's return to rebel territory.

"The second item in behalf of the correspondent is the absurdly lame complaint made by Mexico's chief of the Mexican press department, who said that the outside world 'is not interested in Mexico's oil deals with Germany.'

"*If that were true, what the outside world heard about the oil deals would interest no one and hurt no one. Then, there could be no harm in publishing them.*"

In expelling *The Times* correspondent, asserts the Burlington (N. C.) *Times-News,* "Mexico has joined those nations who are afraid of the truth." And—

Interrupted Communication

—Reprinted from the Baltimore Sun.

"The world is sick and weary and sadly out of joint when it fears the truth, when it must erect a false facade of hypocrisy and deceit to conceal the malodorous circumstances which its own social and economic maladjustments have created. As freedom of the press flickers and wanes and seems in danger of complete eradication, so too is civilization flickering, waning, and facing danger of imminent eradication."

Characterizing the expulsion of Mr. Kluckhohn as "a deplorable incident," the Baltimore *Sun* goes on to observe:

"There does not appear to be the slightest doubt that both Mr. Kluckhohn and the Mexican press department have told the truth in their explanations of the expulsion. The correspondent *had* learned too much; therefore, Mexican officials *were* displeased, and these things are the sole charges against an able and honest reporter. But what is suggested by Mexico City's position and by its drastic action? First and most important, it means that Mexico, having established a government censorship over its own press, means now to extend that censorship to cover the representatives of the American press. Such an assault on free reporting can only signify that Mexico is employing the methods and perhaps following the course of the totalitarian states.

"Second, the very nature of this extension of censorship stimulates the belief that Mexico is in fact engaged in, or is contemplating, relations with other dictatorial countries, which it is anxious to conceal.

"*The suspicions thus raised may well prove to be more inconvenient than exposure of the facts.*

"Mexico's highest officials might reflect that no information about any dealing with Germany or any other state could be more damaging to the American public's faith in Mexico's future than is this attempt to supress news and to punish a journalist who only told the truth. There have been many conflicting reports and opinions in recent years regarding the trend of the Mexican Government. This last foolish act will be widely interpreted as confirming the worst fears."

Finally, we come to the New York *Times*. According to this widely read daily:

"Only one inference can be drawn. Mr. Kluckhohn has been forced to leave Mexico because of the very considerations which have made him valuable as a correspondent of this

283

newspaper—namely, his independence, his enterprise, and his efficient reporting of the news.

"Mr. Kluckhohn has been a member of the staff of *The Times* since 1929, and its correspondent in Mexico City for the last two years. During these two years the news from Mexico has turned largely upon such matters as the expropriation of land owned in Mexico by American citizens, the seizure without compensation of foreign-owned oil fields, and the increasingly close co-operation in various fields between Mexico and Fascist states of Europe.

"Mr. Kluckhohn has written about these matters, all of which have been a cause of concern to our own Government, with the insight and the promptness and the objectivity of the good reporter. The accuracy of his news has been demonstrated to the satisfaction of this newspaper in two ways: First, by the corroboration which events themselves have given to trends and developments first reported in his dispatches and frequently denied in official quarters until it became necessary to admit their truth. Second, by an investigation made on the spot in Mexico City by an assistant managing editor who went there for the purpose of sifting such criticism as had been directed against these dispatches. He found that Mr. Kluckhohn's honesty was unquestioned even by his sharpest critics in the Mexican Government; that his contacts were excellent; and that criticism of him was inspired largely by his zeal in digging up facts.

"The Times is sorry to lose a good reporter in Mexico City. But it believes that its own loss is less serious than the loss of confidence and of respect which the Mexican Government incurs when, after censoring its own press into a state of helplessness, it attempts to censor the press of a good neighbor."

With the Cardenas Administration firmly entrenched in Mexico and determined to carry out the expropriation program, so far as the oil companies were concerned, the chance of winning a legal battle, observed the Indianapolis *Star* in March, 1938, "did not seem too promising." Nevertheless, the British, Dutch, and American owners of confiscated oil properties waged a court battle throughout the year in an attempt to protect their rights and the investment of their stockholders. At the same time the American companies asked the State Department to file a diplomatic claim in their behalf.

Despite an appeal to the Mexican Supreme Court embracing twenty-two charges of constitutional violation, and actions challenging the constitutionality of the expropriation law and the legality of President Cardenas's expropriation decree, the appeal against the expropriation law did not reach the Supreme Court until November, 1938, and it was unofficially announced that a ruling would not be made before March, 1939. This, however, did not surprise the litigants, for the Supreme Court had ruled against them before, and President Cardenas had put his invocation of the expropriation law on a patriotic basis. All of which induced the South Bend (Ind.) *Times* to remark: "As the Mexican courts are deeply involved in politics, and apparently must co-operate in the program of collectivism, the outcome of the oil companies' litigation can easily be predicted."

In the year that has passed since the Cardenas decree, the Dutch Government has taken an identical attitude to that of Great Britain in respect to the expropriated oil properties of her nationals. These two Governments have demanded either a prompt and adequate indemnity to the owners or a return of the properties. Several notes have been sent, and the expropriation of Dutch oil properties and the "points of view" stated by the Mexican Government remain a matter of "grave concern." The Dutch Government asserts very positively that the expropriations are in violation of the fundamental rules of fair dealing between governments, and it demands that its properties be returned to the Dutch owners.

Readers of American newspapers received somewhat of a shock last September, when the Supreme Court of Mexico handed down a ruling that the seventeen British, Dutch, and American oil companies whose Mexican properties had been expropriated by President Cardenas must pay their former employes three months' "discharge" wages—a trifling matter of 150,000,000 pesos—or $30,000,000 in American money. As a Mexico City dispatch to the *Dow Jones News Service* explains:

"This rather startling revelation followed close upon the decision of the Court, which briefly is as follows: Before the expropriation, the oil workers had been granted, by the Fed-

285

eral Board of Conciliation and Arbitration, their appeals for three months' salary for each worker, plus other accrued pensions and unsettled claims. The companies disagreed with the findings of the Board, and appealed to the Supreme Court, but the judgment was not handed down until September.

"Naturally, since there are no companies here at present, and their properties and finances all have been confiscated, the only method the Mexican Government can use to insure payment is to deduct the amount from whatever settlement it makes to the companies for their expropriated properties."

This is how things are done in Mexico, according to the Miles City (Mont.) *Star:*

"Mexican law requires payment of three months' wages plus twenty days' pay for each year of service for each worker when a contract is broken.

"In addition to this, in casting about for more 'cause of action,' the Mexican Labor Board informed the companies they must pay the remaining twenty-five per cent of wages to workers during a twelve-day strike back in May, 1937.

"All of this, of course, is only subterfuge. Mexico is under obligation to pay to the companies whose properties were expropriated what is considered to be their reasonable value. This may run into something like $450,000,000.

"A liberal Government and a liberal Supreme Court now appear to be in 'cahoots' to shave off as much as possible of this reasonable value in order to reduce the total amount."

If the Supreme Court of Mexico were to consider the expropriation question objectively and in the light of established precedents, believes the New York *Journal of Commerce,* "it would rule, in all probability, that the decree by which expropriation was carried out was unconstitutional. However, grave doubts are entertained that the Court will act upon the matter dispassionately."

To the Baltimore *Evening Sun,* "the Supreme Court of Mexico is a body which closely approximates, in personnel and philosophy, the United States Supreme Court visualized by President Roosevelt's court-packing scheme." J. H. Carmical, writing in the New York *Times,* gives us an example of what the Baltimore paper apparently means. Says this authority on conditions in the Mexican oil industry:

"In the trial in the Supreme Court of Mexico of the appeal of the oil companies from the Labor Board's award, one of the Justices, whose right to sit in the case had been challenged because of his radical activities, called the controversy with the oil companies not economic, but political. He declared that Mexico was determined to impose its domination on foreign capital as an example to other countries, such as Venezuela and Colombia, adding that it was his conviction that the duties of a Supreme Court Justice were to pass on issues from a revolutionary political aspect, and not from a basis of law."

A sharp contrast appears when we turn from Mexico's oil policy to that of Venezuela. Production in Venezuela has mounted rapidly under its fair and equitable treatment of foreign oil companies in the past two decades, while Mexico's production has been dwindling. Venezuela now ranks third among the oil-producing nations of the world, while Mexico has fallen from second place to ninth. The situation is thus outlined by the New York *Journal of Commerce:*

"The large revenues derived by the Government of Venezuela from the oil industry have enabled it to liquidate both its internal and external obligations and to engage in an extensive public works program. The policy of fair treatment of foreign property has greatly strengthened Venezuela's sovereignty and economic strength.

"The foreign oil companies, in turn, have co-operated with the Government in raising the standard of living of the population. They employ Venezuelan labor as far as possible, and promote workmen to positions of greater responsibility as opportunity offers. Through the erection of homes and the establishment of free medical services and sanitary facilities, significant contributions have been made to the improvement of the health, not only of the people employed in the oil fields, but also of others in their communities. The development of new oil fields also leads invariably to the construction of new roads and the opening up of new stretches of territory to economic development.

"The history of the oil industry in Venezuela furnishes an impressive example of the contributions foreign capital can make to the economic development of a country. Where effective co-operation between foreign capital and the government exists, important benefits result for the country which thus receives the capital and managerial skill from abroad. On the other hand, a program of confiscation of foreign properties drives capital and managerial ability out of a country, and thus undermines its economic equilibrium and greatly handicaps the development of its natural resources."

A remarkable financial situation is seen in Venezuela, where the treasury owes no internal or external debt, according to Henry E. Linam, President of the Standard Oil Company of Venezuela. Red ink is apparently unknown in government bookkeeping there. Mr. Linam's company uses 93 per cent native labor, although the law requires only 75 per cent. He is quoted as saying:

"When I went down there in 1925, all the drillers were Americans. Today a lot of the Venezuelan boys are drillers. We send about ten of the boys every year to colleges in America. It's good for us, and it's good for their country.

"Standard Oil controls about half of the Venezuelan production; the rest is divided among five other companies. Because of the tariff here, very little of the oil comes to America. It's refined in the Standard plant, biggest in the world. Then it goes to Europe.

"Venezuela is just the opposite of Mexico. Venezuela knows that when we profit, they profit. Venezuela papers criticize Mexico's expropriation program very severely."

But we must not forget, some editorial observers remind us, that the Mexican people have been oppressed and exploited for centuries, and it is not surprising that their resentment should carry them to extremes. The people, says the Manchester (Conn.) *Herald:*

"Have been bullied and exploited most of the time during four hundred years—for three hundred years by the Spaniards, during the last century sometimes by dictators of her own, sometimes by the United States, and oftener by a combination of the dictators and American and European business adventurers."

The Dallas (Texas) *News* also writes sympathetically:

"Consider the actual plight of Mexico. It is a new nation, groping its way forward from centuries of ignorance and exploitation, in which some of these claims undoubtedly had their origin. Mexico is resentful of its former leadership, distrustful of those who dealt with the former leaders. Mexico has made mistakes, and expropriation may be in part both mistake and injustice. But Mexico merits a good deal of sympathy."

Conjecture over the future of the expropriation program in Mexico naturally hinges largely on the policy or personality of the next President, for the term of President Cardenas expires in 1940. A Mexican President cannot constitutionally succeed himself. But Mexico's Chief Executive, remarks the Greenville (S. C.) *News*, "is in a somewhat similar position to that of Mr. Roosevelt in that he is anxious to have his policies continued, and the allotted time appears to be too short in which to bring his program to full fruition."

President Cardenas has denied that he seeks a second term, but, the New York *Times* suggests, modification of the Constitution is possible between now and the expiration of the Cardenas term in 1940. And the New York paper recalls that four Central American chief executives have recently taken action to disregard or modify constitutional provisions against second successive terms.

But there are those who believe that a change is inevitable, and may perhaps be welcomed in Mexico. The Los Angeles *News* quotes a leader in the large Mexican colony in its city, Juan Ruiz, who has just returned from Mexico to report that "while the Mexican people are convinced Cardenas is sincere, they distrust his advisers, who are mostly Leftists untrained in practical government."

"It cannot be a matter of indifference to us," said Theodore Roosevelt in 1916, "what kind of government arises in Mexico. Mexico in its geographical and physical aspects, with the Panama Canal adjoining, represents to the United States what the Balkans and Asia Minor represent to Europe." In studying Mexico's Government, we find that the Army has considerable influence. It played a large part in the series of revolutions that followed the Diaz régime. The higher officers in the present Army favor a moderate policy, says Frank L. Kluckhohn in a dispatch from Mexico City to the New York *Times*. President Cardenas, we are told:

"Has developed further the system of moving Generals and commanders about. Few are left in any district long enough to get a local following such as they once had. Some spend as little as six months in one district.

"Most suspicious of the Generals' power is the new breed of politico-labor leaders who have lately come to the front in Mexico. That explains the recent formation of a workers' militia, uniformed and drilled, which outnumbers the Army. In addition, President Cardenas has armed vast numbers of peasants to act as 'Army reserves' in a move to offset the more reactionary Generals. Some see danger in the formation of these subsidiary organizations, which is resented in some Army quarters. Followers of President Cardenas, however believe they offer a safeguard to the régime."

It is a bit difficult to figure the exact size of Cardenas's Army, including as it does not only the regulars, but various kinds of police and the irregulars noted above. Upton Close, well known writer on foreign affairs, says in the Buffalo (N. Y.) *News:*

"Cardenas's Army is the largest and best that Mexico has ever had. It is centralized and purged of excess Generals. Its size is not made public, but counting Federal police and State troops under officers cleverly placed by the Federal staff, it numbers somewhere between 200,000 and 300,000— *certainly larger than the standing Army of the United States.* Though the equipment does not compare with ours, it is by far the best ever enjoyed by a Latin American army.

"A goodly portion of the army appropriation goes to aviation. The Mexican Army has procured crack aviators by compelling Pan American Airways and small native companies to carry a Mexican co-pilot on each plane."

Can't Blame Him for Being Nervous

—*Reprinted from the Chicago Tribune.*

Canned!

—*Reprinted from the Philadelphia Evening Public Ledger.*

XI

SHALL WE DEAL WITH MEXICO WITH A FIRM HAND?

Ambassador Daniels Criticized—House and Senate Resolutions Call for Investigation—Mexico a "Danger Spot" in Western Hemisphere—"Mexico Long on Promises and Short on Fulfillment"—Danger That Other Latin American Republics Will Imitate Mexico's Expropriation Experiment—Suggestions for Solution of Mexican Problem—Principle at Stake More Important Than Money—Mexico Needs U.S. Market and Good-will.

The most important diplomatic post in the world, in the opinion of the New York *Daily News*, is that at Mexico City. At least, so far as the United States is concerned. Our Ambassador there is Josephus Daniels, who is characterized by *The Daily News* as "a lovable old character." Ambassador Daniels was Secretary of the Navy during our participation in the World War. His chief assistant was Franklin D. Roosevelt, now President.

While *The Daily News* believes that Mr. Daniels "doubtless has his place in the scheme of things," it does not think that place is Mexico City. "This country is keenly conscious of the need for an Ambassador like the late Dwight Morrow, who was unusually successful in working out a reasonable compromise of international problems," agrees the Indianapolis *Star*. The public utterances of our Ambassador to Mexico "have approved the general course of President Cardenas," is the complaint of General Hugh S. Johnson in his *United Feature Syndicate* column, while the Chicago *Daily News* believes that "if we had had a competent Ambassador in Mexico, he might have warned President Cardenas that the latter was taking too much for granted." In California, the Santa Rosa *Republican* is convinced that "it is time for Secretary of State Hull to bring Daniels home from Mexico, and turn on whatever economic pressure is necessary to convince our Mexican friends that we do not intend to be robbed of our shirts."

While we have seen no editorial comment that endorses Ambassador Josephus Daniels unqualifiedly, in Wisconsin the Apple-

293

ton *Post-Crescent* says: "Incompetent as Mr. Daniels is, there can be no side-stepping the fact that full responsibility for his appointment belongs to just one man—the President of the United States." As the Seattle *Argus* explains:

"Our diplomatic relations with Mexico have long been strained, often to the breaking point; wherefore, it is plain that we should employ the services of a wide-awake, skilled, and tactful person to represent this country in its constant efforts to remain at peace with our turbulent neighbor. Mr. Daniels, we think, should give way to a younger man more capable of exertion and more competent to meet the exactions of his position. He should resign or be replaced, for his own good as well as that of the country he represents."

H. V. Kaltenborn, radio commentator and writer, agrees in his Brooklyn *Eagle* column that:

"The United States Government must take some blame for the complete failure of its 'good neighbor' policy in Mexico. The Roosevelt Administration sent to Mexico City as Ambassador a man totally unfit for this difficult diplomatic post. Josephus Daniels is a genial, high-class southern politician of the Woodrow Wilson school, who is altogether alien to the hard-boiled, radical-minded politicos of the Cardenas régime. He does not speak their language literally or figuratively. They pulled the wool over his eyes from the beginning of his term. He did not know what was coming or what it meant when it came. If he had been able to mediate between the American oil companies and the Mexican Government, confiscation might have been avoided."

Resolutions calling for an investigation of conditions in Mexico were introduced in both the House and Senate at Washington in January, 1938. The Senate resolution was sponsored by Senator Robert R. Reynolds, of North Carolina, and the House resolution by Representative Martin J. Kennedy, of New York. Late in February, Representative Kennedy demanded in another resolution the recall of Ambassador Daniels from Mexico City, to report directly to Congress concerning repeated violations of American rights in Mexico, and to explain the futility of the Ambassador's representations there.

Representative Kennedy made a statement, accompanying his resolution. It read, in part, as follows:

"Today we see the richest and most powerful nation in the world surrendering the rights of its citizens to an irresponsible Mexican dictator.

"There has been so much confusion created by the inept manner in which the State Department has handled our Mexican relations that I believe it is time for Congress to have a direct report from Ambassador Daniels as to the exact happenings in Mexico.

"There surely must be something wrong in our representation. The inconsistency between the Mexican promises that are fed to Congress through the State Department and the published reports of outrages more than justifies Congress in taking a real hand in this situation. *The Mexican muddle must be cleaned up.*"

His resolution read as follows:

"Resolved, by the House of Representatives; that it is the sense of the House of Representatives that the President of the United States immediately recall the Ambassador to Mexico, Honorable Josephus Daniels, for the purpose of having him report directly to the proper committee of the House of Representatives concerning the repeated violations of American rights in Mexico, as well as the reasons for the futility of his representations and protests to the Mexican Government in respect of these violations, which are constantly recurring despite the fact that the State Department has led the American people to believe that negotiations with Mexico are pending which will satisfactorily result in adjustments caused by the earlier outrages against American citizens since the inception of the Cardenas dictatorship."

Most observers will agree, thinks the Springfield *Illinois State Register*, "that in the last two or three years, Mexico has become one of the real danger spots in the Western Hemisphere, so far as checking the influence of the totalitarian nations is concerned. She has been flirting rather openly with both Germany and Italy, and the extent of her dealings and understanding with these Powers has become a matter of real concern to the United States." The Elkhart (Ind.) *Truth* feels that "President Roosevelt and Secretary of State Hull are responsible for neglect to uphold

295

American rights in Mexico, but Ambassador Daniels should share a part of the blame." Continues this outspoken paper:

"Although Mr. Daniels personally is a pleasing gentleman to meet, we think he is a misfit as our Ambassador in Mexico and should promptly be replaced with a strong man who will know how best to represent our very great interests in that country and to deal firmly with a dictator government which is almost Communistic in character.

"Mr. Daniels will be seventy-seven years old next May. His work as our Ambassador during the Roosevelt Administration has been undistinguished. Indeed, we would have been just as well off if we had never had him representing us in Mexico City.

"It was the New York *Times* correspondent in Mexico, and not Daniels, who gave the information to the American people that Cardenas was selling the stolen American oil to the Germans. Daniels was not able, or willing, to protect that correspondent when the Mexican Government expelled him."

"President Roosevelt," believes the Philadelphia *Evening Public Ledger*, "should recognize that there is a growing feeling in this country that Mr. Daniels has not measured up to his job." And the New York *Herald Tribune* agrees that:

"In addition to the difficult negotiations which will have to be carried out in connection with the seizure of the oil properties, the State Department has to face the fact that the assurances given last autumn, that there would be no further expropriations, are as valueless as so many other similar promises that have been made by Mexican officials. Under the circumstances two things would seem to be elemental: First, that the Administration follow consistently a policy based on demanding respect for American rights; second, that it pick—preferably from among the career diplomats—a man of experience, force, and tact to serve as American Ambassador to Mexico in place of the futile— even though amiable—Mr. Daniels. There can be no doubt that Mexico is one of the most important diplomatic posts.

"On what is done in Mexico in the next eighteen months will depend the future of the 'good neighbor' policy."

Says the Indianapolis *Star* in another editorial:

"It is unfortunate that the State Department has ignored the need of strengthening a weak spot in the diplomatic line. The grave problems which have been created by the régime of President Cardenas in Mexico require the presence in our Embassy of the best material available. An envoy grounded in financial and industrial affairs, as well as an able and forceful bargainer, is badly needed in the City of Mexico if relations between the two countries do not go from bad to worse.

"Josephus Daniels is a genial gentleman who has remained in public life as a product of the old political school. Daniels never was regarded as a forceful figure at the head of the Navy Department, and now will be deemed little more than a pensioner in party service. In spite of fine personal character, he is not the man for a post that demands an Ambassador of the Morrow type or one of our outstanding career men.

"An effort has been made in the House to effect the recall of Ambassador Daniels, that he may be questioned regarding the repeated violation of American rights by the radical Mexican Government. The State Department might take advantage of that maneuver to suggest to the envoy the desirability of retiring to the serene North Carolina environment."

Of Representative Kennedy's resolution in the House, the Manchester (N. H.) *Leader* observes:

"This may serve a useful purpose by bringing the Mexican mess to a head and requiring a showdown.

"Ambassador Daniels may or may not share in the responsibility for the Mexican situation. It is probable that he has been over-ruled by the State Department, and that he has been little more than a go-between in the transaction. In any case, he has not added to his reputation, but has rather given a marked example of ambassadorial incompetence.

"Moreover, the Mexican situation has reached a point where justice demands that a showdown shall be made in defense of American rights.

"There is no longer any doubt regarding the attitude of the Mexican Government. First, it seized American-owned farm lands and American-owned oil properties, and refused to make any compensation.

"Then an agreement was reached last November between the Mexican Government and the State Department, whereby negotiations were to be undertaken toward a settlement of the land claims, with the understanding that there would be no further expropriations of American-owned property until a basis of settlement was reached.

"But since then several important new seizures have taken place, the latest of which is an American-owned sugar property valued at several million dollars. No one questions the right of the Mexican Government to seize property within its domains so long as it makes a fair compensation.

"But this continued expropriation of American-owned property without any evidence of compensation is a flagrant violation of international requirements. Justice and national self-respect demand the adoption of a policy by the United States Government that will rectify the situation."

When President Lazaro Cardenas of Mexico said in October, 1938, "I will settle the [expropriation] question in justice and equity," a number of American newspapers were moved to remark that the Cardenas statement was admirable in principle, but depended largely on what constituted "justice and equity." In the past, we are reminded by the St. Louis *Globe-Democrat*, "Mexico has been long on promises and short on fulfillment."

A few days later, some light was cast on this point by a statement issued by Eduardo Hay, Mexican Foreign Minister, agreeing to make payments of $1,000,000 a year on claims for agricultural lands expropriated by the Mexican Government since 1927. A victory for the chief American claim—that expropriated property must be paid for—is seen here by the Rochester (N. Y.) *Democrat and Chronicle:* "The main thing is that an important principle of international law has been recognized by Mexico."

This principle of international law has not yet been applied to the seizure of the oil properties. And, declares the Houston (Texas) *Post*, "as long as that controversy remains unsettled, there will be strong resentment in this country, regardless of what attitude the American Government may adopt."

Senator Key Pittman, who heads the Senate Committee on Foreign Relations, believes the United States has not been firm

298

enough in dealing with Mexico in the matter of expropriation of American-owned oil properties. In Senator Pittman's opinion: "It would be very injurious to the United States if various governments of the world were led to understand that our Government does not stand firmly upon the international doctrine set forth in Secretary Hull's note. Without the maintenance of such doctrines throughout the world, commercial intercourse would be so unsafe that it would be impractical, if not impossible." In California, the San Bernardino *Sun* agrees that "if this nation had made vigorous representation to Mexico when that country first seized properties of American citizens, we might have avoided the serious implications of the present situation." "Instead of taking a firm stand, however," notes the New York *Herald Tribune*, "the Administration began to coddle Mexico, to be 'neighborly' by shutting its eyes to attacks on American rights, while at the same time it lauded the Communistic Mexican Government and continued to pour money into the country."

Newspapers have various explanations for the lenient attitude of our State Department towards Mexico. Some say the State Department has hesitated to exert pressure upon the Mexican Government for fear such action might have an ill-effect upon its "good neighbor" policy toward all Latin America. The Pittsburgh *Post-Gazette* objects to this attitude on the ground that "our neighbors to the south should not be encouraged to mistake good-will for softness. To give ground on basic principles does not win friendship; it merely forfeits respect."

"Unless the United States deals with the Mexican situation with a firm hand," asserts the Dayton (O.) Journal, "other Latin American countries may be tempted to imitate this experiment in expropriation."

"It is high time our Government challenged the Socialistic trend which threatens the security of American investments in foreign countries," declares the Galveston (Texas) *News*. It has been proved to the satisfaction of the Philadelphia *Inquirer* that "soothing words and 'good neighbor' preachments get us nowhere in our dealings with Mexico." To quote the Houston *Post*, which is published near the Mexican border:

Is He Going to Get Away With It?

—Reprinted from the Marshfield, Wis., Journal.

"Just how much the Cardenas Government appreciates the Roosevelt 'good neighbor' policy may be surmised by reading the report that within twenty-four hours after Secretary Hull's second note, warning Mexico that the 'good neighbor' policy was being jeopardized by Mexico's refusal to arbitrate, was received in Mexico, the Mexican Government seized nearly 23,000 more acres of land belonging to American citizens, and parceled it out among native peasants.

"Rarely has the American Government been as sharply slapped in the face. Not since the days of Huerta has our Government been quite so openly insulted in Mexico City.

"This new seizure of American-owned land leaves no other alternative for the American Government than to insert some steel knippers into the kid gloves with which it has been handling American-Mexican relations lately, and make it unmistakably plain that it means business in demanding a settlement for the American-owned oil properties that have been confiscated.

"This stand will have to be taken by the American Government with the suspicion, if not the actual knowledge, that one or more foreign Powers is putting Cardenas up to this truculent attitude. Japan, Germany, and Italy each would like to keep the United States busily engaged on this continent, to avoid any likelihood that this country might aid in checking their ambitious programs in Asia and in Europe. Each of these countries is deliberately attempting to make trouble for the democracies of the world.

"It must be apparent to all that if this country is to command any respect abroad, it must protect its nationals by seeing that they are properly recompensed when their property is taken by foreign governments.

"It was a mistaken policy on the part of the American Government from the beginning to be lenient with the Mexican Government in the latter's derelictions in paying for the property of American citizens. It would have been better for Mexico, better for American investors there, and better for the relations between Mexico and the United States if Washington, in the beginning of these expropriations by the Socialist Government in Mexico, had enforced its demand that fair compensation be provided immediately for the property taken."

It requires no great stretch of imagination for the New Haven *Journal-Courier* to conclude that "the mild attitude of the United

States toward the land controversy helped to bring on the oil expropriation. The Mexican Government apparently had concluded that it could proceed with complete impunity to disregard the rights of the United States citizens in Mexico." Continues this Connecticut paper:

"Under Theodore Roosevelt, the United States used to talk softly but carry a big stick. Nowadays we talk softly. Yet we are faced with the probable fact that if Mexico can get away with confiscation, the same tactics will doubtless be adopted by other nations.

"The problem keys in to the world-wide decline of respect for what little international law this poor old earth has managed to achieve. There is something almost pathetic about Secretary Hull's insistence: 'When aliens are admitted into a country, the country is obliged to accord them that degree of protection of life and property consistent with the standards of justice recognized by the law of nations.' *What nations?*"

Of the soundness of Mr. Hull's philosophy, there can be no question—if one refers to old-fashioned doctrine. "But," points out the Charleston (S. C.) *Post*, "Mexico has a New Deal now, and new political and economic concepts. It must be a little difficult for an Administration that is so tolerant of radicals in its own capital to be harsh towards the Mexicans seeking the more abundant life in their own way." The Moline (Ill.) *Dispatch* suggests that we take a page from the diplomatic book of both Great Britain and The Netherlands. Says *The Dispatch:* "Both the British and the Dutch have refused to temporize with Mexico in regard to these oil properties. Both Governments have made unqualified demands for restoration of property to their nationals." In this paper's opinion, the United States should view with great concern "the theft of Old World property by our neigboring republic, lest we be accused of compounding an international felony by giving protection to the villain." "A firm stand by the Administration," believes the Topeka (Kan.) *Capital*, "will do much to straighten out the difficulties in Mexico." In the opinion of the Freehold (N. J.) *Transcript*, "we must take a firm stand with the Government of Mexico, and if it will not act honorably, we should confiscate enough Mexican Government money and property in the United States to pay our nationals for property stolen from them." "The job of our Government," believes the Newark (N. J.) *News*, "is to back Mexico down from its present stand." This is also the attitude of the Topeka (Kan.) *State Journal*, although it would "expropriate the property of Mexicans in the United States, and hold it as a balance against the American property that Mexico has expropriated."

Certainly, observes the Tulsa (Okla.) *World*, "something will have to be done about the expropriated property." In the opinion of the Cincinnati *Enquirer*, "the United States is partly to blame for Mexico's present plight. At the very beginning of these expropriations, when the intent of the Mexican Government became apparent, Washington should have taken a firm stand by demanding that the owners be given full and immediate compensation, or that their property be restored to them." Instead, we are reminded by the Chicago *Tribune:*

"While all this has been going on our Treasury has continued to buy silver from Mexico for more than it is worth. Thanks to our so-called 'good neighbor' policy, we have permitted our oil properties to be stolen, we have permitted the sale of the swag to the dictator countries to their great benefit, and we have lost the market for our products in Mexico. But we have continued to subsidize the despoilers with cash."

This, believes the Boston *Globe*, has "given the impression abroad that other nations may tread on our toes without fear of retaliation."

It is only a matter of time, believes the Denver Post, "until the United States is going to have to 'crack down' on Mexico. For diplomacy makes no impression whatever upon the Cardenas Administration."

The suggestion is made that the United States withdraw diplomatic representation from Mexico, as it did from Germany; and that Mexico be placed on the most-favored-nation black-list, just as we have refused to enter into a trade agreement with the Reich, partly because of its penchant for barter arrangements with other nations. A Texas paper, the Plainview *Herald*, believes that "if

Secretary Hull would say to President Cardenas: 'Unless you return or pay for all confiscated American property, the United States will apply an economic boycott', the whole problem would be solved. Mexico could not survive without American trade."

In the opinion of the New York *Journal of Commerce*, the restoration of the oil fields to the American owners would really pay Mexico, for "such action would restore the millions of dollars of taxes the oil companies formerly paid annually to the Mexican Government. It would improve Mexico's balance of international payments, and would restore jobs to employes." Others are for a strong policy. The Lexington (Ky.) *Herald* urges:

"This Government should join with the British and Dutch in bringing pressure to bear upon President Cardenas, demanding an immediate settlement of a satisfactory nature. Delay only complicates matters and encourages the Mexican Government to believe that it can escape the consequences of its unjustified policies."

In a letter to the Editor of the New York *World-Telegram*, a subscriber would have the United States do some expropriating:

"I suggest we retaliate by expropriating all properties and and business and bank accounts belonging to Mexicans living in the United States. Perhaps this would check Mr. Cardenas."

This country should "clamp down" on Mexico "like a trip hammer landing on a nickel," is the picturesque advice of the Leominster (Mass.) *Enterprise*, and other papers say we should follow Great Britain's example and call our Ambassador home. The Anaheim (Calif.) *Bulletin* has other suggestions:

"We do not want to go to war over this affair, and there is no thought of doing so. However, there are certain economic measures which might be helpful.

"We could cease accepting Mexican silver. This country does not need that metal and we purchase it at a loss to the United States.

"We could tighten up on our border restrictions, stopping the influx of Mexicans. There are many thousands of Mexicans in this country illegally. They could be deported, with full justice to our own people. Mexican people hold, in the aggregate, large properties in the United States. These properties might be given to those who have lost their holdings in Mexico.

"Other ingenious ways might be suggested to supplant the notes we have been sending. It became evident that it will take something more than words to impress our neighbor on the south."

"The only policy that Mexico understands is that of firmness," agrees the Chicago *Daily News,* and in New York we find *The Daily News* agreeing:

"For the sake of American prestige and dignity all over the Western Hemisphere, and incidentally for the sake of the Mexicans now tightening their belts as the peso's bread-buying power evaporates, we believe the State Department would do well to stiffen its attitude toward Neighbor Cardenas.

"Our State Department has just been a bit weak-kneed in this affair. It told Mexico at the start that any government has the right to take property within its borders from foreigners, provided it pays them for it. But it hasn't hammered that point home hard enough, so far as we can make out.

"This is no debate over national philosophies or economic ideologies; this is a fight, and the stake is the kind of power a modern nation must have to stay modern—oil."

The United States, explains the Boston *Transcript,* "cannot and will not go to war to enforce its own rights and the rights of its nationals in Mexico. But, 'good neighbor' or no 'good neighbor,' it must act forcefully and effectively or lose the esteem of the world generally, and specifically of the countries of the Western Hemisphere. In Latin and South America, a cult of weakness inspires no respect." A less patient nation than ours, the Grand Rapids (Mich.) *Press* is convinced, "would have taken steps toward retaliation or toward active coercion long ago." One reason for our exceptionally patient stand, as set forth by the Joplin (Mo.) *News-Herald,* is that "if the United States were to declare war against Mexico, it would hurt us internationally, since we are much bigger and stronger and richer than Mexico." Just the

Japan Is Not Without Precedent Over Here

—*Reprinted from the Chicago Tribune.*

same, it goes on, "something will have to be done. We cannot sit idly back and let our citizens suffer for the failure of the Mexican Government to reimburse them for expropriated property." We find these suggestions in the Hartford (Conn.) *Courant:*

"A realistic and well-informed view of the situation in Mexico is necessary if the United States wishes to guard its prestige and the property of its nationals in other Latin American countries, and to avoid the necessity of using force against Mexico to do it.

"Mexico presumably knows that the public of the United States is not likely at this time to support any attempt to recover the value of the expropriated properties by force. But while it is hard to conceive of the United States sending an expeditionary force into Mexico, there are other effective means of bringing pressure on the neighboring republic."

"If Mexico cannot pay," suggests the Manchester *Union,* the only other alternative, as Secretary Hull has pointed out, is for the Mexican Government to turn back the properties to their owners." Moreover, maintains this New Hampshire daily:

"On this issue there should be no compromise or vacillation. We have tried to be friends to Mexico, and we have received in return insult and injustice. The time has come when the Mexican Government should be made to understand that a continuance of these tactics will no longer be tolerated."

"The money to be had out of Mexico," points out the Eugene (Ore.) *Register-Guard,* "is not nearly so important as the principle which is at stake." "If we are to submit to Mexico's seizure of American property without making some effort to obtain justice for the owners," remarks the Fullerton (Calif.) *News-Tribune,* "we may as well admit our impotency and advise our nationals hereafter that they cannot expect the protection of the American flag in other lands." We have been frank to demand our rights of Japan, recalls this California paper, "and we should be no less frank with Mexico. To tolerate open theft of property belonging to our citizens is to invite still further aggression." As the New York *Herald Tribune* explains:

307

"The State Department has reason for caution. But it has equal reason for firmness, and it will not help matters unless all parties appreciate this fact. The United States cannot simply allow the properties to go by default without jeopardizing all other American property in Mexico, and thereby shattering the 'good neighbor' policy just as effectively as it would be shattered by aggressive ultimata.

"The United States must insist on payment for the confiscated property in real money; and since the only way in which that sort of money can be provided would seem to be through the more or less normal operation of the properties themselves, a return to the operative *status quo ante* is the easiest and simplest way out."

"If a forceful word is not spoken now," asserts David Lawrence in one of his Washington dispatches, "the way is open to a dislocation of the whole economic system in Latin American countries."

On the theory that we may have lost track of the story in quoting numerous newspaper editorials, the Columbus *Dispatch* suggests that we refresh our memory on this matter of expropriation. Says the Ohio paper:

"American capital, representing the investments of thousands of citizens of this country, built up in Mexico over a period of years a flourishing and prosperous oil-producing business. It was a development unquestionably far beyond anything that Mexican resource, initiative, or industry could have achieved. It benefited both countries by furnishing a good investment for American dollars and by giving employment to thousands of Mexican citizens.

"A radical, revolutionary party came into power in Mexico, and embarked at once on an ambitious program of social reform. With true Communistic rationalizing of the ethics of such an action, it has arbitarily made use of the legitimate principle of expropriation of foreign properties in an unfair manner by seizing British and American oil properties and attempting to run them in the name of—and as the property of—the Mexican Government.

"What makes this amount to a plain steal is that *the Cardenas régime had—and still has—no intention of paying for the properties*, as is always done in such cases by reputable governments when expropriation takes place. The Mexican

Government has no money for proper indemnities, and it knew this when the properties were taken over."

Down in Texas, the Wichita Falls *Record-News* quotes an expert on Mexican character and temperament:

"If Dr. John L. Meacham, Professor of Latin American Government at the University of Texas, is correct, it would be better if Uncle Sam did get a little rough with Mexico. The university professor, one of the outstanding experts on Latin American affairs, declares bluntly that neighborliness and friendliness have nothing to do with trade, and cites the figures to show that trade was better with Latin America when the United States Marines were keeping order with machine guns in some of the southern republics. He also points out that our trade was proportionately as good last year with the three nations with which we have no trade agreements as it was with the three with which agreements have been made."

Other newspapers throughout the United States, which agree that sterner measures toward Mexico should be taken by our State Department include the Peoria (Ill.) *Journal-Transcript,* Astoria (Ore.) *Astorian-Budget,* Norfolk *Virginian-Pilot,* Coffeyville (Kan.) *Journal,* Worcester (Mass.) *Post,* Columbus *Ohio State Journal,* and Boston *Transcript.* As the Boston paper puts it:

"Obviously the time has come for this country to speak a different language. We cannot allow the issue to go by default and expect to retain the respect of the world. We must not sit by while any nation establishes the vicious principle that the rights of foreigners—in this case our own nationals—may be disregarded with impunity.

"Of course, we will not go to war; but we may have to use the one other weapon which will force an adjustment. Large-scale economic reprisals, brutally employed, remain a possibility. They would soon prove effective."

Other newspapers are still more specific. The Philadelphia *Inquirer* recalls that "since the Latins are sticklers for effusive courtesy, a blunt note, demanding that they pay—and pay quickly—might shock them into action." The Mobile (Ala.) *Register,* however, is of the opinion that "it will take political and economic pressure of a singularly forceful kind to bring about a settlement

of the expropriation question." Henry J. Allen, former Governor
of Kansas and Editor of the Topeka *State Journal,* believes that
"all that would be necessary to persuade President Cardenas to
restore the property which has been confiscated would be to
threaten a trade boycott unless the demands are met. Our demands would be met, because the Cardenas Government could not
stand a boycott a month." Another suggestion is that we urge
American tourists not to visit Mexico until American citizens
whose property has been confiscated have been indemnified. Still
another is that we pass the word to American bankers that any
private financing of Mexico would be objectionable. In the opinion of *The State Journal:*

> "The United States should deliver just one more note to
> President Cardenas, notifying him that the orgy of confiscat-
> ing American property is over, that we shall require at once,
> under the treaties between us as well as under international
> law, restitution; that this restitution shall take either the
> form of payment for the confiscated properties or a return
> of them to their rightful owners.
>
> *"If he doesn't respond with a satisfactory program, we
> should recall our Ambassador to Mexico, hand the Mexican
> Ambassador in Washington his passports, and establish a
> peaceful boycott on Mexico.*
>
> "The situation in Mexico will not wait. The Administra-
> tion in Washington will save Mexico's future if it moves
> determinately now to crush the Communistic program."

There is still another ace in the deck, but it probably never
will be played, writes John Clayton, in the Los Angeles *Times:*

> "President Cardenas knows he would face a revolution
> should the United States lift the embargo on arms shipments
> to Mexico and permit a ready flow of guns and cash into the
> country.
>
> "Cardenas could hardly survive a serious, well-financed,
> well-armed revolt. But the consequences of such warfare
> would be so serious, the loss of human life and destruction of
> physical property so great, that it is not thought of.
>
> "What have we left?
>
> "Granting the premise that the United States will not act
> as collector for Europe by force, nor permit Europe to collect

310

On the Wrong Side of the Atlantic Ocean

—*Reprinted from the New York Herald Tribune.*

by force, we come back to diplomatic persuasion—which never has been successful unless backed by a show of force."

Still another suggestion for bringing pressure to bear on Mexico is provided by the Philadelphia *Evening Public Ledger,* which says:

"Pegging of the world silver price and the standing offer to buy Mexican silver in any amount have been a boon to the Mexican worker and to the Mexican Government. The United States is under no compulsion, except that of friendship, to continue this scheme.

"We want Mexico's friendship—and ours is Mexico's for the asking. But Mexicans need be under no illusions that they can get along without the market and good will of the United States—or that any other nation or nations can fill the gap."

APPENDICES

A. NEWSPAPERS FROM WHICH EXCERPTS ARE QUOTED

318

WISCONSIN
APPLETON Post-Crescent, 294
MADISON Wisconsin State
Journal, 90

MILWAUKEE Journal, 19, 52,
64, 73, 143, 163, 175, 176,
244, 267

B. SPECIAL WRITERS AND PUBLICISTS

Aikman, Duncan, 73
Allen, Henry J., 64, 93, 110,
174, 180, 218, 222, 236,
246, 310
Barbour, Percy E., 214
Barclay, Hartley W., 77, 233,
245
Barnes, Harry Elmer, 261
Barth, Alan, 116
Beatty, Morgan M., 251, 262
Berding, Andrue, 260
Bratter, Herbert M., 212
Brenner, Anita, 244
Carmical, J. H., 9, 22, 55, 72,
83, 101, 286
Carothers, Neil, 188
Clark, Delbert, 228
Clayton, John, 310
Close, Upton, 290
Crane, George, 182
Creel, George, 52, 176
Culler, Arthur J., 36
Duncan, C. William, 90
Eccles, Marriner S., 212
Field, Carter, 233
Fish, Representative Hamil-
ton, Jr., 120
Forbes, B. C., 65
Friendly, Alfred, 271
Gaither, Roscoe B., 59, 60
Gould, Margaret, 49
Harding, Gardner, 164, 200,
267
Hooper, Clifton E., 37
Hulen, Bertram D., 83, 147
Hull, Secretary of State Cor-
dell, 13, 68, 82, 111, 113,
161, 167

Johnson, Hugh S., 4, 87, 218,
293
Jones, J. E., 278
Kaltenborn, H. V., 15, 16, 123,
294
Kennedy, Representative Mar-
tin J., 295
Kirk, Betty, 36, 41, 75, 110,
202, 266, 272
Kluckhohn, Frank L., 24, 50,
61, 67, 108, 110, 120, 203,
277, 290
Krauss, E. C., 5, 57, 58
Lander, William H., 38, 278
Lawrence, David, 2, 12, 14,
25, 130, 308
La Varre, William, 229, 251
Linam, Henry E., 288
Lindley, Ernest K., 84
Lippman, Walter, 225, 226
Lyon, W. A., 212
Marland, Governor E. W., 240
Marshall, S. L. A., 157
Mathews, W. R., 238, 247
Moley, Raymond, 44
Moore, Fred, 28
Morris, George, 217
Norton, Robert L., 270
Nover, Barnet, 249, 250
O'Brien, John C., 169
Perrin, Frank L., 11, 84
Pittman, Senator Key, 299
Pound, Roscoe, 147
Roosevelt, President Franklin
D., 113
Roosevelt, Theodore, 289
Rovensky, J. C., 6
Rowell, Chester, 144
Ruiz, Juan, 289
Starr-Hunt, Jack, 108
Stewart, Charles P., 114